Objective Description of the Self

When I open a book, whether it is a narrative or not, I do so to have the author *speak to me*. And since I am not yet either deaf or dumb, sometimes I even happen to answer him.

Gérard Genette

The artist represents the object as it is and not as it appears to him.

Boris Uspensky

Subjektiviteten er sandheden, subjektiviteten er virkelighed. (Subjectivity is truth, subjectivity is reality.)

Søren Kierkegaard

Yōichi Nagashima

Objective Description of the Self

A Study of Iwano Hōmei's
Literary Theory

AARHUS UNIVERSITY PRESS

Published with the financial support of the
Danish Research Council for the Humanities

AARHUS UNIVERSITY PRESS
University of Aarhus
DK-8000 Aarhus C
Fax (+ 45) 8619 8433

73 Lime Walk
Headington, Oxford OX3 7AD
Fax (+ 44) 1865 750 079

Box 511
Oakville, Connecticut 06779
Fax (+ 1) 860 945 9468

∞
ANSI/NISO
Z39.48-1992

Preface

The writer Iwano Hōmei (1873-1920) was a phenomenon. One moment he could be illogical, odious and irritating, the next rational, charming and amiable. Both as a man and as a writer.

There were three things that he loved immensely all through his life: himself, Japan, and women. His writings, which consist of fiction and journalism, actually functioned as symbols of his relationship to his own 'I', to what is specifically Japanese and to the female sex. His writings are indeed manifold, but they are also 'coherent' in the sense that a common thread runs through them. They are centred around his egocentricity, his fanatical nationalism and his belief in monogamy.

The centripetal tendency that we find in Iwano Hōmei's writings of fiction came to be expressed in the theory of 'monistic narration', which is the subject of this book. As we will show, Iwano's term *ichigen byōsha* is untranslatable, because to Iwano *ichigen*, the monistic relationship, is paradoxically manifold and at times even equivocal. By some *ichigen byōsha* is translated as 'one-dimensional' or 'simple-dimensional', but I prefer the term 'monistic' which is associated with Iwano's 'mono'-oriented philosophy of life.

Please note that in accordance with Japanese custom, all Japanese names have been written with the surname first.

This book is a revised edition of my dissertation which was written in Danish in 1982. On the occasion of this publication, I wish to thank the two Iwano Hōmei experts, Prof. Ōkubo Tsuneo who has given my research a clear perspective, and Prof. Ban Etsu whose profound knowledge of literature on and by Iwano Hōmei has been of great importance to my retrieval of literature and information. I also owe many thanks to my wife Mette Toft for her patient perusal of my original manuscript. Likewise I am most grateful to Line Henriksen and Christina Lemonius who have rendered this book accessible in English.

Helsingør, 1996   *Yōichi Nagashima*

Contents

Abbreviations   9

Introduction   11

I. An Overview of Iwano Hōmei's Work   18

    1.   The Island of Awaji, Iwano's Birthplace   19
    2.   The Early Years   21
    3.   The Creation of a Poet   25
    4.   The First Marriage   27
    5.   The Book *The Mystic Semi-Animalism*   30
    6.   The Novel *Tandeki*   33
    7.   The Journey to Sakhalin   35
    8.   Iwano's Novel-Series and Monistic Narration   38
    9.   'The Conqueror and the Conquered'   42
   10.   The Productive Author and His Death   46

II. The Background For Iwano Hōmei's Literary Theory   50

    1.   Iwano Hōmei the Man   50
    2.   The Anti-social Male   53
    3.   *The Mystic Semi-Animalism*   57
    4.   'Momentariness' and Iwano Hōmei's Views on Love and Sex   64
    5.   Iwano Hōmei's View on Literature/Art and 'the New
        Naturalism'   68
    6.   Iwano Hōmei's Theory of Narration   74

III. The Creation of The Theory   77

    1.   The Point of Departure   77
    2.   The Creation   78
  2.1. The Prerequisites   78
  2.2. The First Phase   85
  2.3. The Second Phase   91
  2.4. The Third Phase   94
  2.5. The Fourth Phase   97
  2.6. The Fifth Phase   100

IV. The Theory in Translation with a Commentary   105

V. Criticism and Practice   124

    1.   Criticism of the Theory   124
    2.   The Theory and Iwano Hōmei's Writings   136
    2.1. Short Stories in Monistic Narration   137
    2.2. Concrete Examples   142
    2.3. A Few Grammatical Problems   161
    2.4. Revisions   166

VI. The Theory in a Broader Perspective   171

    1.   Iwano's Theory in Relation to that of *watakushi shōsetsu* -
       Japanese Confessional Writing   171
    2.   The Theory in Relation to Point of View Theories in General   179
    2.1. Henry James and Iwano Hōmei   179
    2.2. Point of View Theories through Time and
       Iwano Hōmei's Theory   187
    2.2.1.   Norman Friedman   187
    2.2.2.   Wayne C. Booth   189
    2.2.3.   Bertil Romberg   191
    2.2.4.   Scholes and Kellogg   192
    2.2.5.   Mikhail Bakhtin   194
    2.2.6.   Franz Stanzel   195
    2.2.7.   Tzvetan Todorov   196
    2.2.8.   Lubomír Dolezel   198
    2.2.9.   Jurij Lotman   200
    2.2.10.   Boris Uspensky   201
    2.2.11.   Gérard Genette   208

VII. Conclusion   216

Appendix: Iwano Hōmei's Major Works   222

Bibliography   225

Index to the Writings of Iwano Hōmei   234
Index of Persons   237

Abbreviations

GBT	*Gendai Bungaku Taikei*
GNBT	*Gendai Nihon Bungaku Taikei*
GNBZ	*Gendai Nihon Bungaku Zenshū*
HJAS	*Harvard Journal of Asian Studies*
HZ	*Hōmei Zenshu*
JJS	*Journal of Japanese Studies*
KBHT	*Kindai Bungaku Hyōron Taikei*
KKK	*Kokubungaku Kaishaku to Kenkyū*
KKKK	*Kokubungaku Kaishaku to Kyōzai no Kenkyū*
MBZ	*Meiji Bungaku Zenshū*
MN	*Monumenta Nipponica*
NB	*Nihon no Bungaku*
NBZ	*Nihon Bungaku Zenshū*

Introduction

Les écrits sont un réside de la pensée.
Pierre Teilhard de Chardin

Iwano Hōmei is not well known in the West. According to the findings of Sugimoto Kuniko, the poet Noguchi Yonejirō (1875-1947, known also as Yone Noguchi) wrote an article in English on Iwano for the journal 'Shinshisō' in 1907, but it remains doubtful whether this had any influence on the understanding of Iwano's poetry in the West.[1] In Noguchi Yonejirō's article, Iwano was furthermore presented merely as a different kind of poet. Iwano did not make his début as a novelist until 1909 when his *Tandeki* (Dissolute Living) was published.

In 1939 the cultural institution *Kokusai bunka shinkōkai* which was charged with the task of disseminating the knowledge and understanding of Japanese culture abroad, published a voluminous and ambitious work with the title *Introduction to Contemporary Japanese Literature*. In the first part of the work which comprises the period 1902-35, the reader is introduced to Iwano through microcosmic pieces of information on his life and on 'demi-animalism' as well as through the synopsis of the novel *Tandeki*.[2]

It was probably on the foundation of this work that the French scholar George Bonneau composed his version of *Histoire de la littérature japonaise contemporaine 1868-1938* in 1940. Also here Iwano and his *oeuvre* are discussed only sparingly.[3]

With the article 'Naturalism in Japanese Literature' (1953), Oscar Benl, a German expert on Japan, was the first in the West to give an outline of the development of Japanese naturalism. The importance of the article is not in the least lessened by the fact that it is mainly based on the work of Japanese literary scholars. Iwano's *oeuvre* is discussed briefly but coherently in the section 'Japanese Naturalism'.[4]

1. Published also with the Japanese title 'Iwano Hōmei ron' (On Iwano Homei). Cf. Sugimoto Kuniko, 'Sankō bunken' in MBZ, vol. 71, 1965, 438.
2. Cf. 32-35 and 'Introduction', xv.
3. Cf. especially 136-38.
4. Cf. *Monumenta Nipponica* vol. 9, 1953, 24-26.

Two years later in 1955, 'Japanese Literature in the Meiji Era', a volume on literature in the series *Japanese Culture in the Meiji Era*, was published in Tokyo. The book was originally edited by Okazaki Yoshie and all contributions to the book were written in Japanese. As is usually the case with such voluminous works on Japanese literary history, the book is packed with names and titles, while a proper presentation of the problems as well as in-depth discussions are lacking. Iwano is thus mentioned here and there in the book, as one of the less known writers of the Japanese naturalistic school.[5]

In the article 'Naturalism in Japanese Literature' (1968), William F. Sibley discusses the peculiarities of Japanese naturalism. On the basis of his thesis that 'The most salient trait of *shizenshugi* (Japanese naturalism), and its most striking point of divergence from Western naturalism is its thoroughgoing egocentricity',[6] he considers such typical aspects as the romantic background and impressionistic traits in the style, and concludes as follows:

But under the partial misnomer of naturalism, for the first time a whole group of writers succeeded in creating works free of undigested influences. Neither imitations of Western literature nor throwbacks to an eclipsed Japanese tradition, these works stand on their own.[7]

This claim is highly interesting, even if we disregard Sibley's lacking knowledge of among others (1) the literary tradition of Japan in general, and (2) Iwano's writings and literary theory.

With regard to point (1) we may mention that William Sibley has overlooked the fact that the literary tradition of Japan is characterised by the very process of Japanisation that he himself points out in connection with *shizenshugi*. As far as (2) is concerned, the fact that without any comment Sibley has translated the term, *ichigen byōsha*, which is a keyword in Iwano's literary theory, as 'one-dimensional description' and considered it 'a rallying cry', is highly revealing of his lack of understanding of Iwano's theory.[8] Furthermore William Sibley has failed to see that Iwano played a leading part in the formation of the specifically Japanese naturalism.

The following year, in 1969, Iwano's novel *Dokuyaku o nomu onna* (The woman who takes poison, 1914) was translated into Czech by Miroslav Novák under the title *Zena, ktera si vzala jed*.[9] This is so far the only of

---

5. Cf. among others 259-61, 352, 528-29 and 580-81.
6. Cf. *Harvard Journal of Asian Studies* vol. 28, 1968, 160.
7. Ibid., 169.
8. Ibid., 164.

Iwano's works that has been translated in its entirety into a Western language.

In his impressionistic essay in the Japanese 'Iwano Hōmei', Prof. Donald Keene gives a dense description of Iwano's *oeuvre* in a few pages.[10] He characterises it as being *masculine* and therefore not traditionally Japanese as far as the style is concerned, as being *philosophical* in its attitude to literature and life in general, and as *contemporary*, i.e. still of current interest, as far as Iwano's central topic, the relationship between man and woman, is concerned. Donald Keene has furthermore written a section on Iwano Hōmei in his voluminous and encyclopaedic work on modern Japanese literature, *Dawn to the West* (1984).[11] This is really an elaboration of what Keene has already written, but this time all the major aspects of Iwano's writings have been included. The section is an excellent introduction; his presentation of Iwano's literary universe is concise and informative, but it does not introduce any new elements to the scholarly studies of Iwano.

Irmela Hijiya-Kirschnereit's epoch-making book *Selbstentblössungsrituale, Zur Theorie und Geschichte der autobiographischen Gattung 'Shisoshōsetsu' in der modernen japanischen Literatur* on *watakushi shōsetsu* (the Japanese version of confessional literature) was published in 1982.[12] The book is thorough and

9. In the book *5 Japonských Novel*, Prague, Odeon 1969, 37-147.

10. In the book *Nihon bungaku o yomu* (I read Japanese literature, 1977), 68-71. Originally published in the journal *Nami*.

11. Donald Keene, *Dawn to the West*, 288-295.

12. The English version is entitled *Rituals of Self-Revelation: Shishōsetsu as Literary Genre and Socio-Cultural Phenomenon*, 1996.

    The discussion on the use of the sign 'I' in the term *watakushi shōsetsu*, and on whether it should be read as *watakushi* or as *shi* (cf. *shisōsetsu*), has been going on for as long as the term has existed. This is partly due to the fact that the term has never been defined clearly and unequivocally, and partly because the sign is always written in *kanji*, which usually cannot indicate how the sign 'I' should be read or *is* read. Unfortunately there are far too many theories about the 'right' reading of the term, but none of them are convincing. Even the dictionaries provide ambiguous explanations. But there is one common characteristic. Firstly, *watakushi shōsetsu* always refers to *shisōsetsu* and *vice versa*. Secondly, *watakushi shōsetsu* is normally referred to as the translation for 'Ich-Roman'. Irmela Hijiya-Kirschnereit, on rather questionable grounds, has chosen the reading *shisōsetsu* in her book. She refers to what is apparently a standard dictionary, *Kōjien*. It uses *shisōsetsu* as its headword (cf. the original German version of her book, 1-2). She must have used either the 'second' or the 'second revised' edition of *Kōjien*, from 1969 or 1976 respectively. The fourth edition from 1991 has *watakushi shōsetsu* as the headword. Under the entry for *shisōsetsu*, we find the reference 'Cf. *watakushi shōsetsu*'. This is simply to illustrate how confusing the *watakushi shōsetsu* debate has generally been and how pointless it is to motivate the choice of one or comprehensive. It covers the background for the development of *watakushi shōsetsu*, previous studies of *watakushi shōsetsu*, definitions of *watakushi shōsetsu* as a genre, changes in and the development of *watakushi shōsetsu* through time illustrated by an analysis of eight representative works, and finally the function of *watakushi shōsetsu* in the literary 'communication system'. The book testifies to the author's ability to deal with the phenomenon of *watakushi shōsetsu* theoretically and to her comprehensive overview of modern Japanese literary history.

However, the chapter on Iwano Hōmei, whose work *Tandeki* (Dissolute Living, 1909) is analysed as the first example of *watakushi shōsetsu*, is somewhat superficial and mediocre. The explanation for this can un-doubtedly be found in the author's lacking knowledge of or access to the fundamental literature on and about Iwano Hōmei's *ouevre* as a whole. In the above mentioned chapter, the author only refers to the introductory essays (*kaisetsu*) in the anthologies GNB, vol. 13 and GNBT, vol. 21; relevant sections in the three key works on modern Japanese literary history; two en-cyclopedias of literature; and a single monograph by Ōkubo Tsuneo. It is probably understandable that Noguchi Takehiko's book from 1980 *Shōsetsu no Nihongo* has not been included in the bibliography, but it is unfortunate that the author did not have the oppportunity to use Wada Kingo's book *Byōsha no Jidai* (1975).

Tandeki is cited from GNBT, vol. 21, and besides this work the author only refers to two other novels and an essay by Iwano Hōmei in the whole book. The choice of *Tandeki* is both suitable and sufficient in the attempt to throw light on the role that Iwano played in the early stages of the development of *watakushi shōsetsu*. However, Irmela Hijiya-Kirschnereit's analysis of the work seems somewhat stereotypical and at one point even misleading, when it is seen in relation to the research that exists on Iwano's writing as a whole, and which was accessible to her. Hijiya-Kirschnereit writes in section IV.2.2.1: 'In *Tandeki*, we see for the first time the implementation of narrative technique, which was developed by Hōmei, 'one-dimensional description' (*ichigen byōsha*).'[13] I simply want to add to this that Iwano's theory of monistic narration (*ichigen byōsha*) was *not* completed until 1918, nine years after the publication of *Tandeki* in 1909. Iwano first

another reading. Therefore I choose to employ the term *watakushi shōsetsu* in my book *without* further explanation.

13. Irmela Hijiya-Kirschnereit, *Selbstentblössungsrituale*, 147. 'In Tandeki sieht man erstmals das von Hōmei selbst entwickelte erzähltechnische Konzept der 'eindimensionalen Beschreibung' (ichigen byōsha) verwirklicht ...'

coined the term *ichigen byōsha* in 1918 after a developing *process* which took many years and which can also be traced in the period's characteristic striving for 'objectivity' in fictional narration — a search that we find particularly in naturalistic writers.

It is precisely this process that will be described in the present book. Incidentally, a prototype of the discussion on *watakushi shōsetsu* took place already during the process of the genesis of *ichigen byōsha* up till 1918. In retrospect one might say that the debate on *watakushi shōsetsu* was simply a parodic repetition of the process which had led to Iwano's theory on monistic narration.

While Irmela Hijiya-Kirschnereit's book distinguishes itself by its exposition of the historical prerequisites for *watakushi shōsetsu*, Edward Fowler's book *The Rhetoric of Confession: Shishōsetsu in Early Twentieth-Century Japanese Fiction* from 1988 focuses its analysis on the *form* of *watakushi shōsetsu* — on the narrative structure.[14] Fowler writes partly under the strong influence of Miyoshi Masao's theory about *watakushi shōsetsu* as the key to modern Japanese *shōsetsu* in general, and partly in the wake of the growth of 'discourse analysis' and narratology in literary research overall. Fowler bases his description and analysis of *watakushi shōsetsu* on two main factors: 1) the peculiarity of the Japanese language which results in an unclear distinction between the narrating subject and the narrated object; and 2) traditional Japanese epistemology which despises all that is artificial and invented, including fiction.[15] Fowler's book is intellectually stimulating to read. It attempts to show how the canon of the Western realist novel inevitably became 'Japanised' in a society which was undergoing modernisation at the beginning of this century, and how *watakushi shōsetsu* developed as a consequence of this. His argument is both refreshing and convincing when he concentrates his analysis on the *form* of *watakushi shōsetsu*, by first and foremost calling it 'single-consciousness narration'. However, the reader misses a more precise and comprehensive description of the process of Japanisation.

To this purpose, Iwano's theory of narration would have served as an

---

14. Fowler chooses the reading *shishōsetsu* in his book and he motivates his choice in the following: 'The Sinified reading of the first character, because of its brevity, is more common. Semantic distinctions that have occasionally been made between the two readings seem unsatisfactory and will be ignored here.' (*The Rhetoric of Confession*, xv). His last comment is sensible, but I would like to challenge the validity of his claim that the reading *shishōsetsu* 'because of its brevity, is more common'.

15. Ibid., 297 and 11, respectively.

appropriate example. It not only crosses, but at times cuts through both of
Fowler's two principal points. Iwano's interest in creating a 'consistent voice'
in his works falls into the category of 1). With regard to 2), Iwano's theory
or rather his tendency to deny dualism and his insistence upon unification
may even add a new dimension to Fowler's analysis. Unfortunately Fowler,
like most other researchers, has not taken Iwano's theories and work into
serious consideration in his research.[16] Fowler's description of Iwano barely
fills three and a half pages including footnotes.[17] Certainly he has used *Hōmei
Zenshū* (The collected works of Iwano Hōmei), but only peripherally and
Iwano's essays, three of them altogether, are all cited exclusively from KBHT.
In fact, Fowler's main sources are Yoshida Seiichi's *Shizenshugi no Kenkyū*
(vol. 2), Wada Kingo's *Byōsha no jidai* and Noguchi Takehiko's *Shōsetsu no
Nihongo* — all excellent but insufficient choices. Of Iwano's literary texts,
Fowler briefly names 'Osei no shippai' (O-sei's mistake) in a footnote; *Hōmei
gobusaku* (Hōmei's pentalogy) is also mentioned in a footnote in the form of
a resumé of seven lines; and there are superficial references to *Tandeki*
throughout the book.[18] On the one hand, this is an altogther too flimsy
foundation on which to base the positioning of Iwano in the larger debate on
watakushi shōsetsu. On the other hand, Fowler is both dependent upon and
limited by his sources, both in type and range. It should also be noted that
although Fowler mentions Irmela Hijiya-Kirschnereit's book from 1982 in his
preface, he does not draw it into the main discussion of his book. It has not
even been included in the bibliography. It is to be expected that in the near
future a work will appear which will unite these two fine, comprehensive
books and thus provide us with a more nuanced description of *watakushi
shōsetsu*.[19]

   This is the situation with regard to knowledge of Iwano's *ouevre* in the
West today.

In the following we will give an account of Iwano's distinctive body of work
with special reference to his literary theory. Iwano was the first writer in
Japan to concern himself theoretically with the problem of point of view.

16. Among other things Fowler writes 'Hōmei is an anomaly in Japanese letters. Although
    usually grouped with the naturalists, he was something of an outsider who relished his
    role as gadfly to the *bundan*,' ibid. 124. (*Bundan* is the world of coterie-like literati.)
17. Ibid., 124-27.
18. Ibid., 124-26.
19. I have heard word of the publication of Tomi Suzuki's *Narrating the Self: Fictions of
    Japanese Modernity*, 1996, but I have not yet had the opportunity to see it.

In this context one ought to mention the translator Morita Shiken (1861-97) who, in his article *'Shōsetsu no jijotai kijutsutai'* ('I'narration in novel-writing, 1887), brought up the problem of 'narrative form' long before Iwano.[20] But Morita Shiken's article was actually a review of the novel *Kyōbijin* (A real man, 1887) by Yoda Gakkai (1883-1909). As Morita Shiken noticed, it was unusual that the author had chosen to narrate the book in the first person. This was actually the discovery of a narrative, which had been constructed as an autobiography, but Morita did not submit the problem to debate. He treated the topic superficially, not theoretically.

First we will become acquainted with Iwano's life and his body of work (Part I). Then we will throw light on Iwano's theory of literature (Part II). In the central part of the book, we will deal with the actual theory through an analysis of its process of development and its content, as well as through a consideration of reactions to the theory. This main part of the text will end with a chapter in which we will look closer at the way in which the theory was put into practice (Part III, IV and V). Finally the theory will be placed within a larger context. We will compare the theory with *watakushi shōsetsu* and with Western theories of point of view, among these the work of Henry James (Part VI). The significance of the theory in Japanese literary history will be briefly commented in the conclusion.

Aside from minor revisions throughout the text, two sections have been added to the original manuscript from 1982. These are 2.2.10 Boris Uspensky and 2.2.11 Gérard Genette in Part VI. It should be noted that neither Irmela Hijiya-Kirschnereit nor Edward Fowler have used Boris Uspensky's *A Poetic Composition* (1970, English translation 1980). Fowler has only employed Gérard Genette's *Narrative Discourse* (1972, English translation 1980), but not *Narrative Discourse Revisited* (1983, English translation 1988). Genette's book is not to be found in Irmela Hijiya-Kirschnereit's bibliography. However, she does refer to Genette's work in the preface to the Japanese version of her book from 1992. At present I have not yet seen the English version of her book from 1996.

20. Cf. the journal *Kokumin no tomo*, no. 8, 1887, 38-40. Kamei Hideo has analysed this article in *'Kindaibungaku ni okeru "katari" no mondai'* (The question of 'narration' in modern literature). Cf. *Nihonbungaku*, vol. 27, no. 305, November 1978, 1-8.

I. An Overview of Iwano Hōmei's Work

> A large part of his (Strindberg's) work is thought to be
> autobiographical, often unjustly. His gift for making us believe
> what he wants us to believe is exceptionally great.
>
> Olof Lagercrantz

Iwano Hōmei was a contemporary of both Natsume Sōseki (1867-1916) and
Mori Ōgai (1862-1922), the two greatest authors in modern Japanese literary
history. He is also considered one of the five greatest naturalistic authors in
Japan, equal to Tayama Katai (1871-1930), Shimazaki Tōson (1872-1943),
Tokuda Shūsei (1871-1943) and Masamune Hakuchō (1879-1962). Iwano's
distinguishing trait, when compared with the other four, is the vitality which
seemed to flow from him throughout his life. He was not an author who
dealt with *l'art pour l'art*. He was a man of action. To him 'action' was 'art'
(literature). This was precisely what was at the core of his originality.

Deeply impressed by Futabatei Shimei (1864-1909)'s decision to abandon
literature in order to travel to Russia to work as a journalist in 1908, Iwano
in 1909 likewise launched his project: a crab-cannery in Sakhalin. However,
unlike Futabatei Shimei who chose 'action' instead of 'literature', Iwano
sought 'literature' in the actual 'action'. That is not to say that Iwano
immersed himself in action in order to find material for his writing.[1] First
and foremost he lived. He lived every second of his life with his whole heart.
Therefore he could not write about eternal love. The only thing that existed
for him was instant passion. The present moment was everything. In the
flash of the moment, 'literature' and 'action' were of equal value to him. It
was from this that his distinctive 'monism' originated. His ingeniousness lay
in his ability to implement his philosophy of life, that of momentariness,
right through to his death.

To speak of his life is synonymous to looking at how his philosophy of
life was created and afterwards developed.

---

1. In the prologue to his novel *Hōrō* (Wandering, 1919) Iwano writes the following: 'My
novel *Hōrō*, ... is based on material which I had never dreamt of putting to use in this
way when I was in Hokkaido.' Cf. *MBZ* vol. 71, 63.

1. The Island of Awaji, Iwano's Birthplace

Iwano's pen name Hōmei is a combination of two signs: *hō* (foam) and *mei* (roar). The first sign can also be read as *awa* and this is homonymous with *Awa* which is the district where the Naruto strait, which incorporates the sign *naru/mei*, is found (Awa is today part of the Tokushima prefecture). Iwano's pen name tells us a great deal about his close ties to the Island of Awaji, his first home.

Iwano was born in Sumoto on the island Awaji on January 20, 1873. His real name was Yoshie. He was the first-born son of his father Tadao and mother Sato, which according to Japanese custom meant that he was the hope of the family, its future provider. He was therefore well-cared for by all of the family, including his grandparents. But his childhood was not a very happy one. Later in life when he would long for his first home, it was not because of childhood memories, but because of the sea and the sea foam (*awa*) that he had seen roaring in the strait of Naruto. He had been so lonely and unhappy as a child that to reflect upon the sea had been his only comfort. In the essay 'Kioku jussō' (Ten different memories) he writes about his relationship to his birthplace: 'My hatred [towards it] has nourished my loneliness and my pride, and my thirst for vindictiveness caused me to avoid friendships ...'[2]

Iwano's 'hatred' and 'vindictiveness' were the results of the discrimination and mistreatment that he experienced on the island as a child. This had roots in the so-called Inada episode which occurred in May 1870.

Two rival samurai groups ruled the Island of Awaji. The one group consisted of vassals to the Hachisuka family, the feudal overlords in the province of Awa to which the Awaji island belonged. The other group were of the Inada family which had been sent to the island for strategic reasons by the Tokugawa Shogunate in Edo (today's Tokyo) in order to keep an eye on the Hachisuka family. As a result of the reforms which were initiated after the Meiji Restoration, the head of the Hachisuka family was appointed Governor of the Tokushima prefecture. Meanwhile the Inada family was put on the street, their fortune was confiscated and they were given a very low pension. The Inada family complained to the Governor, but with no results. With time, their dissatisfaction grew and finally they demanded that the Governor at least appoint their young heir Kunitane as Commander-in-Chief of the island's army. This, too, was rejected by the Governor. The explanation

2. Printed in *Taiyō*, June 1909. Cf. *HZ* vol. 11, 50.

given was that Kunitane was too young for the position. Meanwhile, the
Meiji government in Tokyo became involved in the case and ordered the
Inada family to move to Hokkaidō. This simply made the situation worse.
The Inada family put their complaint directly to the government and at the
same time suggested that the Tokushima prefecture be divided into two. As
a result, the government ordered the striving parties to come to Tokyo. This
decision irritated the Hachisuka group on the island to such an extent that
they stormed the Inada family property in May 1870. During his childhood
Iwano was bullied by children whose parents were supporters of the Inada
family. Iwano's ancestors were samurais for the Hachisuka family.

Memories of harassment imprinted themselves deeply and indelibly in
Iwano's consciousness. Moreover, his experiences on the island provided the
origins for his scorn and at times contempt for all those who were weaker,
among those also the Ainu-people on Hokkaidō and Sakhalin whom he
encountered during his stay there in 1909.[3] This was actually the other side
of his fanatical Nipponism which was a hymn of praise to those who were
strongest. But it remained a hymn because here, as in the case of his hatred
and contempt for those who were weak, Iwano lacked insight into social and
historical conditions. It was simply an irrational, emotional reaction.

Although Iwano's childhood in Sumoto was far from happy, at home he
was spoiled by his family — especially by his grandfather Sakubei and his
grandmother Nami, and also by his sister Hatsu who was six years older
than him.

In the period 1876-88, Iwano's father was a police officer. Iwano writes
about him in the following passage from his memoirs:

My father was firm and unswerving; everybody trusted him because he was
exceptionally honest. He was adopted into the Iwano family. His stepfather had a
very large debt because of drunkenness, but my father assumed the entire debt and
without in the least having to mortgage his property or sell any of his bonds, he
paid back the entire amount over a period of about ten years during which he
worked, first as a regular police officer, later as a police inspector and finally as a
police commissioner, for miserable wages. This very day I still remember that he
expressed a desire to return to Tokyo where our ancestors had lived. He accepted
everything and simply perservered ... In my memories from that time, my father
is like a tree-stump or a stone: boring, taciturn and a total abstainer.[4]

3. Iwano's numerous essays on the Ainu are collected in *HZ* vol. 11.
4. '*Kioku jussō*' in *HZ* vol. 11, 31-32.

But his father was nonetheless an ordinary man of flesh and blood. When he had almost finished paying off his stepfather's debt, he suddenly became interested in a young lady who was about 25 years old. He was so taken by her that he neglected his work. Reasonably enough, this resulted twice in his degradation, and he was moved to a less important department in Kariyaura. One of the natural consequences of his affair was financial problems for the family. In May 1888, the family was practically forced to leave Sumoto and move to Tokyo.

While Iwano was still in Sumoto, from 1885 to 1887, he studied *kanbun* (Chinese texts) and English at various private schools.

2. The Early Years

According to Iwanaga Yutaka's short article '*Iwano Hōmei no rirekisho*' (Iwano Hōmei's curriculum vitae, 1956), Iwano studied English at Taisei-gakkan in Osaka from July 1887 to August 1888. Before he moved to Osaka, he had been living alone in Sumoto for about a year. This was the case because when the family was moved to Kariyaura, he had been allowed to stay in Sumoto in order to continue the English course which he had begun.[5] But he was not able to learn very much on the island. In the passage entitled '*Kyōshi no ie*' (At home in my teacher's house) in the autobiographical essay '*Kioku jussō*', Iwano writes about the jealousy that filled him every time he saw his older fellow students come home from either Osaka or Kobe where they had spent a couple of years studying English.[6] He longed to go to Osaka. It made no difference to his family whether he was in Sumoto or in Osaka since he was on his own either way. Iwano was only fourteen years old when he travelled to Osaka to study at Taisei-gakkan which the Christian priest Miyagawa Nobuteru had founded. But Iwano was only there for about a year.[7]

After Taisei-gakkan, which was his first school, Iwano moved from one school to another: Meiji-gakuin, Senshū-gakkō in Tokyo and Tōhoku-gakuin in Sendai. However, he did not complete his courses at any of them. This tells us a great deal about the restlessness that characterised his youth, but also about his immense curiousity both with regard to knowledge and

---

5. At this point his grandparents had already died, his older sister had married and left home. Aside from himself, the family consisted of his parents and his two younger sisters.

6. Cf. *HZ* vol. 11, 57.

7. '*Shūkyō yori bungei ni*' (From religion to literature, undated) in *HZ* vol. 11, 109-13.

life/love. In order to discuss Iwano's body of writing, it is necessary to throw light on this period of his youth which shaped him as a writer.

At the age of nine Iwano fell in love with his older sister's friend and at the age of thirteen he came to know a girl from his school class more closely. Later when he left the island he became engaged to her.[8] But when he became a Christian in Osaka and began dreaming about becoming a missionary, the relationship between the studious Iwano and the girl chilled and eventually ended.

Iwano writes about his baptism in Osaka:

When I was baptized it was almost a sensational event at my school and in the Church. They said that it was a miracle that such a lazy, nonchalant and proud student as myself suddenly converted, confessed in tears and decided to follow the missionary calling. Because my school and Church had a certain connection with the Dōshisha School,[9] Mr Niijima was also present the day I was baptised and he preached with great sincerity. He cried out aloud. I was convinced that I was as pious and sincere as him, but I nonetheless thought that it was too weepy and womanly for a grown man to cry aloud, and therefore I had certain misgivings about his attitude. Personal experience caused me to consider women loathsome already at this point in time.[10]

Iwano was baptised in Osaka Church where Miyagawa Nobuteru, the above mentioned founder of Taisei-gakkan, was the priest. Miyagawa Nobuteru was a member of the *Kumamoto-bando* (the Kumamoto band), a group of young Christians who were baptised collectively in Kumamoto on the island Kyushu in 1876.[11] The group was renowned for their passion. They endured every kind of oppression; mainly as a result of their common samurai background, they were all male. When Iwano decided to be baptised, it is

---

8. Iwano describes his meeting with her some years later in two of his short stories 'Shin yori Tamae e' (From Shin to Tamae, December 1914) and 'Hata no saikun' (Hata's wife, September 1916). Cf. *HZ* vol. 4, 106-53 and 432-61, respectively.

9. Founded in 1875 by Niijima Jō (1843-90), missionary J.D. Davis and others in Kyoto as a private school where teaching was primarily conducted in English. After returning home from a study-trip in the United States, Niijima founded the Dōshisha School. He was one of the most important figures for Christianity in modern Japan.

10. Cf. '*Boku no jūdai no me ni eijita shojinbutsu*' (About the different characters, seen with my teenage eyes, printed in *Chūgaku sekai*, November 1910) in *HZ* vol. 11, 3.

11. There were 36 all together and they were under strong influence from a certain missionary Jones. *Kumamoto-bando* made up one of the three gatherings of Japanese Christians. The two other bands were *Yokohama-* and *Sapporo-bando*.

very likely that he was just as attracted to Miyagawa Nobuteru's masculine personality as he was to Christianity.

In Osaka Iwano read the newly started journal *Kokumin no tomo* with great enthusiasm.[12] An article by Tokutomi Sohō (1863-1957) which was carried by the journal under the title '*Fukuzawa Yukichi to Niijima Jō kun'* (Mr Fukuzawa Yukichi and Mr Niijima Jō, no. 16, March 1888), made a deep impression on Iwano.[13] In this way he became interested in politics. Among the politicians of the time, Nakae Chōmin (1847-1909) and Baba Tatsui (1850-88) were the ones he admired the most.[14]

As was mentioned earlier, the Iwano family moved to Tokyo in May 1888. They first lived in Azabu and the father obtained a position with the palace police force. But before long he resigned because the pay was far too low. The family moved at least five times before the father finally built a boarding house in Shiba where they settled.

Iwano temporarily broke off his studies at Taisei-gakkan and moved to Tokyo in August 1888. He started his studies anew at Meiji-gakuin. In an essay he explains his reason for once more choosing a private school: 'I didn't like police officers or other public employees nor public schools.'[15] In his words one can trace the influence of that time's advocates for the civil-rights' movement which placed itself in uncompromising opposition to the government.

Iwano's desire to become a missionary was actually closely tied to his dream of becoming an orator. But things changed. He writes about it in the following passage:

[In Tokyo] neither the people at Church nor my friends were as devout as I had expected. That was when it occured to me that Christianity did not have any real influence on ordinary people. I lost interest in becoming a missionary and instead

12. *Kokumin no tomo* (The people's friend) was published by a literary organisation, *Min'yūsha*, and edited by Tokutomi Sohō from February 1887 to August 1889.

13. Tokutomi Sohō (1863-1957) was a critic, a member of *Kumamoto-bando* and founder of *Min'yūsha*. In the 90s he was one of the most influential people in Japanese cultural life. With his nationalistic ideas he played an active part in Japanese militarism.

14. Cf. '*Boku no jūdai no me ni eijita shojinbutsu'*, in *HZ* vol. 11, 5-7. Nakae Chōmin was one of the leading advocates for democracy and civil rights in Japan and was called the Jean-Jacques Rousseau of the Orient. Baba Tatsui was one of that time's most energetic politicians. Baba Tatsui is remembered for his numerous articles about Japan and the Japanese. The articles were written in English for Western readers.

15. Ibid., 4.

developed the desire to become a politician, which had in any case been my original wish.[16]

As a result of this change of attitudes, Iwano gave up his studies at Meiji-gakuin and moved to Senshū-gakkō in Kanda in September 1889 in order to study economics, which was 'the most discussed subject within the academic world of the time'.[17] But he found the lectures boring and inane. He spent his days frustrated and full of longings for the opposite sex. His interest in women was obsessively strong during this period. Day and night, he was obsessed by his compulsive ideas. As his longing for all things female grew, so did his interest in literature. He was groping for an identity. He developed himself through a reading of various types of literature. It was also during this period that he mistook Ralph W. Emerson's book *Repre-sentative Men* (1846), believing it to be about members of parliament.[18] But he read the book nonetheless and in this way became aware of Emerson's philosophical point of view. Emerson's ideas were to be of great importance to Iwano's life and work as a writer. It was indeed a very fruitful meeting.

The strangest incident from Iwano's time as a student was, however, when he tried to use Sir Thomas Gresham's famous law 'Bad money drives out good' to explain why he had chosen to become a writer:

When I read Gresham's law, about the bad coins always driving out the good coins from the market, I realised that the same was true for human society: Those that survive cannot be the important people. It's going to flourish with slovenly people. The idea of a perfect golden period, no matter whether it concerns the material or the spiritual, is only a dream. It is nonsense to think of saving other people or society. Even if one succeeds in saving some people for a short time, they soon degenerate again. That which many religious leaders and politicians have been doing since the beginning of time, is nothing more than child's play: building castles in the sand. One must keep at a distance, at a higher level in order to develop oneself. To think in any way different from this is only possible for a hypocrite or a vain person. In order to develop my thoughts there was no other way but to immerse myself in literature, with the whole of my heart.[19]

16. Ibid.
17. Cf. 'Ware wa ikanishite shijin to narishika' (How I became a poet, printed in *Shinkobunrin*, March 1907). In *HZ* vol. 11, 85.
18. The book is about six 'great men' in world history: Plato, Swedenborg, Montaigne, Shakespeare, Napoleon and Goethe.
19. Cf. 'Ware wa ikanishite shijin to narishika' in *HZ* vol. 11, 86.

3. The Creation of a Poet

While Iwano was a student at Meiji-gakuin from 1888-89, he spent most of his time at home where he was writing a historical novel about the Persian king 'Sailas'. He got the idea for the novel from *Nansō satomi hakkenden* (A story about the eight samurais in the Satomi family in the Shimōsa District, 1814-41) by Takizawa Bakin (1767-1848). Iwano was also inspired by Yano Ryūkei (1850-1931)'s success with the political novel *Keikoku bidan* (Noble episodes about the art of statesmanship, 1883-84), the story of which takes place in ancient Greece. Iwano took his manuscript to the publisher Shun'yōdō, but to no avail. The manuscript was later destroyed in a fire.[20]

In 1890 Iwano became a member of a literary group that was publishing the journal *Bundan* (The literary world). His article about Emerson 'Dai-shijin to bundan' (The great poet and the literary world) was published in the third issue in December 1890. He had his début as a poet in the same journal, with 'Shinri no jinbutsu' (People of truth). The poem was published under the pseudonym Iwano Hakutekishi. However his literary career at *Bundan* was brief.

Already in January 1891, he travelled to Sendai with the hope of getting a job as a teacher with Oshikawa Masayoshi (1849-1928) who was the headmaster of a Christian private school, Sendai-shingakkō. Iwano hoped to become financially independent so that he could engross himself in literature, but he was mistaken. To his great surprise he was interwieved by an American missionary. Consequently, he became enrolled as a student once more. Sendai-shingakkō was reorganised to become Tōhoku-gakuin and Iwano remained there until June 1894.

This was a chaotic period for Iwano. He was groping in the dark, flowing with and against the stream, between life and death. He characterised his days in Sendai in a letter addressed to the critic Yoshino Gajō (1876-1926):

It was a time when I suffered from unhappy love affairs and agony of the soul; it was a time when I had freed myself of the Christian understanding of God which I had had since childhood, but I had not yet found out what course to take on the great sea of literature.[21]

In Sendai he read Emerson, Man'yōshū, Shih-ching, Shakespeare and Milton.

---

20. Ibid., 86-87.
21. Cited in Funabashi Seiichi's *Iwano Hōmei den*, 18-19.

He studied Greek, German and Sanskrit. He studied zen in a temple at Mat-sushima. He even attempted suicide in Tatsunokuchi.

Among the countless episodes from Iwano's youth, the greatest event was his writing of a tragedy in *kabuki* style, *'Tama wa mayou getchū no yaiba'* (The soul wanders and the dagger flashes in the moonlight, published in 1894).

The publication of the journal *Bungakukai* in January 1893, affected Iwano. He was impressed and influenced by one of the contributors to the journal, Kitamura Tōkoku (1868-1894). He also became aware of the literary work which his rival Shimazaki Tōson had done both in and outside of the journal.[22] Iwano and Shimazaki Tōson were both students at Meiji-gakuin. They were not in the same class because Shimazaki Tōson was a year older, but they knew one another. When Shimazaki published his play *'Shumon no urei'* (Shumon's worry, August-October 1893) which was written in imitation of Shakespeare, Iwano was busy writing his tragedy. He could not tolerate the thought of Shimazaki Tōson publishing before him. He spent all his energy on the play, finished it and hurried back to Tokyo with his manuscript in 1894. In the Japanese literary world it was fashionable to write plays at this particular time. The interest in theatre was large. This provided the basis for Iwano's decision to become a playwright.[23] In Tokyo he met the learned diplomat and theatre-lover Tanabe Renshū (1831-1915) and with his recommendation in hand, he visited the playwright Fukuchi Ōchi (1841-1906) in order to show him his manuscript. Iwano wanted to become a *kabuki* playwright, but Fukuchi Ōchi advised him against this, explaining that it was not the proper thing for a well-educated man to do.[24] Instead he got a job at Kabuki-shinpō-sha, a publishing firm that put out various publications about *kabuki*. But the job did not suit him. Disappointed and dissatisfied, he left the firm after about a year.

In Tokyo he was spending time with the members of the Bungakukai group. Through this group Iwano met Kitamura Tōkoku, just before Tōkoku committed suicide in May 1893. He also met Shimazaki Tōson, who was working as a teacher at Meiji-jogakkō (Meiji girl's school) at this time, as well as the critic and translator Togawa Shūkotsu (1870-1939). Most of these meetings took place at the home of Iwamoto Yoshiharu (1863-1943).

22. *Bungakukai* was one of that time's most important literary journals. All together 58 issues were published during the period from January 1893 -98.
23. Cf. *'Boku no kaisō'* (My memoirs) in *HZ* vol. 11, 118.
24. All theatre people, no matter whether they were involved in *kabuki* theatre or in modern theatre, were considered outsiders. They were isolated and scorned.

Iwamoto Yoshiharu was the principal of Meiji-jogakkō and editor-in-chief for the journal *Jogakuzasshi* (Feminine Education).[25] Iwamoto Yoshiharu was willing to print Iwano's tragedy in *Jogakuzasshi*. It was thus published in three parts (August-October 1893) in the journal and later in book-form under the title *Katsura Gorō* in December 1893. It was also Iwamoto who recommended printing the poetry, which Iwano had written in Sendai, under the collective title *Kodama-shū* in the journal *Hyōron* in July 1893.[26] For the tragedy Iwano used the pseudonym Awaji Narutozaemon, while for the poetry he used Hōmeishi. Later he always used his pen-name Hōmei.

Iwano's first tragedy was reviewed by, among others, the critic Kaneko Chikusui (1870-1937) in the essay '"*Katsura Gorō*" *o yomite*' (After having read 'Katsura Gorō'.) which was carried by the journal *Waseda bungaku* in February 1895. He wrote: 'The idea is quite interesting, but the technique is still infantile.'[27]

After having resigned from the publishing firm Kabuki-shinpō-sha, Iwano regularly visited the American methodist missionary J.C. Davison in order to help him with the revision of *Kirisutokyō seikashū* (Hymn book, published in July 1895). Iwano provided the new Japanese translations. For Iwano who, following the failure with his tragedy, chose to become a poet rather than a playwright, it must have been good practice to work on the hymns.

4. The First Marriage

Iwano returned home from Sendai partly because his parents were caught in conflict over the issue of his father's lover Kumagai Matsu. In October 1893, his mother gave birth to another child. This indirectly caused her early death in March 1894. The child also died shortly thereafter, in May of the same year.

It was in the same year, 1894, that Iwano married Takekoshi Kō who was three years older than him and the eldest daughter in a high-ranking samurai family. Takekoshi's family were against the marriage because Iwano was descended from a samurai family which had a very low standing in the samurai hierarchy. In his novel *Dokuyaku o nomu onna* (The woman who

---

25. *Jogakuzasshi* was one of the time's cultural idealistic Christian journals for women. Altogether 526 issues were published in the period from July 1885 - February 1900.
26. The same poems were published again in the journal *Jogakuzasshi* in October 1894 - December 1895 and most of them were collected once more in Iwano's first collection of poetry *Tsuyujimo* (Dew and frost, 1901) which he published at his own expense.
27. Cited in Ōkubo Tsuneo, 'Iwano Hōmei no jidai', 24.

takes poison, 1914) he describes Takekoshi Kō who is depicted as the
character Chiyoko:

She lived in a rented room on the first floor out in Koishikawa. There she made her
own food; she worked as a school teacher during the day, but in the evenings she
was a student, she went to music classes. Different from now, she then had an
elegant, oval face with fresh skin and she shone with the mildness of an older
sister. She dressed so well that she could not be compared with the other women
students from the provincial areas. Yoshio [read: Iwano] was attracted to her
pleasant figure. Even though he was three years younger, it did not matter; he
could finally free himself from the despair he had been drowning in until then;
madly in love with another girl, who had rejected him and ... The very same night
that close to panic, she (Chiyoko) had told him that 'her uncle in Fukagawa was
going to come and get her the following day', he acted fast, as if in an emergency;
he placed her in a car and drove her to his father's house. The father was certainly
surprised, but he received them generously.[28]

Takekoshi Kō is described in Iwano's novel series as the hysterical Chiyoko
and in four of his last short stories, she appears as the witch-like O-sei.
However, at the beginning of their marriage, Iwano was a good husband and
father to his family, at least until 1900-01.

In January 1896 his father's lover Kumagai Matsu became Iwano's stepmother; in November of the same year Takekoshi Kō officially became
Iwano's wife and in the same month he became father to a daughter who
unfortunately died of diphtheria in 1899.

From 1897-98, Iwano worked hard at evening school where, among other
things, he taught English. But his hard work had dire consequences. He
contracted tuberculosis. When his wife showed the symptoms too, they left
together for a sanatorium in Chigasaki. In April 1899 they both moved to
Ōtsu, near the Lake of Biwa, to live a quite life of recuperation. In the town
of Ōtsu, he worked as an interpreter for the police and also taught English
at the Police School. It was during this period that he decided to publish his
collection of poetry at his own expense. To make some money he wrote an
English phrase book for police officers and published it in August 1899. In
May of the same year, his second daughter Fumi was born.

From April 1901 he taught English at Shiga dai-ni chūgakkō. Iwano

28. *HZ* vol. 3, 510-11.

recounts in detail about his life in Ōtsu in, for example, his essay *'Kohan no ichinen'* (A year by the lake, August 1902).[29]

The most interesting thing about this period is undoubtedly Iwano's intense interest in Buddhism. First he studied *Rinzai*, the zen practised at the Eigenji Temple, and then *Tendai*-theories at the Enryakuji Temple, which is located on the mountain Hieizan.

Iwano's third child, a son named Yuzuru, was born in May 1901, but died of pneumonia eight months later. In September 1902, Iwano returned to Tokyo where he obtained a position at Ōkura shōgyō gakkō, a business school. He maintained the position until 1908 when he left for Sakhalin.

Tsuyujimo (Dew and frost), Iwano's first collection of poetry was finally published in 1901. A characteristic trait of Iwano's poetry from this period is his use of a strict form which is his own invention. This distinct form means that every line has ten syllables, distributed in groups of three, four and five. In addition, the last two syllables of every line rhyme. Let us look at an example:

> *Miyako tōku tachiide*
> *kaeri kiteshi furusato*
> *furuki kotono omoide*
> *kokoni shinobu hashiato.*

> Far away from the capital
> Having returned to the homestead,
> Longing for a lost time
> Standing here by the ruin of the bridge.[30]

Iwano's experiment did not really succeed because of the altogether too restrictive form which almost became a strait-jacket for his poetic fulfillment and development. But his emphasis on poetic form was continued in the lecture *'Shiku kakuchō kanken'* (My view of the style and tone in poetry, 1902, later published in the book *Shinpiteki hanjū-shugi*) which later resulted in the book *Shintaishi no sakuhō* (The method of the new style of poetry, December 1907). Iwano was a poet/novelist who never neglected the aspects and methods of form.

29. Iwano finished this essay in August 1902, but it was published posthumously in 1921. Cf. *HZ* vol. 11, 316-428.
30. Cited in Ōkubo Tsuneo, *'Iwano Hōmei no jidai'*, 28.

5. The Book *The Mystic Semi-Animalism*

In his essay '*Shūkyō yori bungei ni*' (From religion to literature, undated) Iwano writes:

During the ten years or so that I lived in the provinces, I studied eagerly and read about a wide variety of topics, but without any results. I returned to Tokyo for the third time and for the first time in my life, I read the new literature from France and Germany with the result that my 'philosophy' gradually developed in a positive direction. And finally the foundations for my present 'philosophy' were laid.[31]

This short quote tells us quite well, although briefly, what the stay in Ōtsu meant for Iwano's writing and how, when he returned to Tokyo he had constructed the 'philosophy' which eventually took shape in the book *Shinpiteki hanjū-shugi* (The mystic semi-animalism) in 1906.

As was mentioned above, it was only when Iwano had returned to Tokyo in September 1902 that he seriously began to develop as a writer. In Tokyo he first stayed at his father's boarding house, but before long he moved to Shiba and in 1903 he moved on to Ueno. During this period he frequently published his poetry in the journal *Myōjō* and he participated actively in the Myōjō-group's poetry readings.[32] But Iwano could not satisfy his literary needs through the Myōjō group. He therefore created a new literary group together with the poet Maeda Ringai (1864-1946) and the critic and poet Sōma Gyofū (1883-1950). They put out the journal *Shirayuri* in November 1903. Here Iwano published his long dream-like poem '*Narutohime*' (Princess Naruto, November 1903 - October 1904).

Aside from his fictional work, he wrote poetry for a children's journal *Shōnen* and published two poems in each issue beginning in October 1902. To write poetry exclusively for children was a completely new notion in Japan, and Iwano's poetry greatly fascinated the young readers.[33]

31. *HZ* vol. 11, 112.
32. *Myōjō* was published by the poet Yosano Hiroshi (1873-1935). It was in circulation from April 1900 to November 1908 with a total of 100 issues. *Myōjō* was at the core of the Japanese romanticist movement during the Meiji period. Symbolism was, in part, also introduced through *Myōjō*. A group of Japanese poets, considered very influential by modern literary history, was connected with the journal, the most important of these being without a doubt Yosano Akiko (1878-1942). Iwano's abovementioned lecture '*Shiku kakuchō kanken*' was read at one of these readings in Kanda in October 1902.

Iwano moved back to his father's house in Shiba in January 1904. At this point he was publishing one poem after the other in *Shirayuri*, for example *'Hiren no uta'* (A poem about unrequited love, May 1904), *'Aa yo no kanraku'* (Oh this world's amusements, June 1904) and *'Segai no dokuhaku'* (A monologue outside of this world, November 1904). These poems made up the main body of Iwano's second collection of poetry *Yūjio* (The wash of waves at night) in December 1904. The book was much discussed by the poets of the time.

But the best poems Iwano published in *Shirayuri* were probably *'Shoku no yuragi'* (The flickering flame, April 1905) and *'Yami no yokogi'* (The boom in the dark, May 1905). Together with the poem *'Tokiwa no izumi'* (The fountain of eternity), the threesome made up *'Sangai dokuhaku'* (Monologue in three worlds) which in turn became the core of his third collection of poetry *Hiren Hika* (Unhappy love, unhappy poem, June 1905). Iwano withdrew from the Shirayuri group just before the book was issued, partly because he was dissatisfied with the romantic turning *Shirayuri* had taken and partly because he could not accept Sōma Gyofū's leading position in the daily work on the journal. At this point Iwano had already established himself as a poet and had no trouble in finding another journal that wanted to publish his poems and essays.

The book *Hiren Hika* received good reviews. His love poem *'Sangai dokuhaku'* was praised for its moving and at times heart-wrenching tone. The content of the poem was in accordance with the mode of the so-called *kumon-shi* (a poem on suffering), but its form was, according to Iwano's own description, a monodrama. The monodrama is one of the first expressions of what he later develops as his theory of monistic narration.

Iwano's monistic relation to literature first manifested itself explicitly in the book *Shinpiteki hanjū-shugi* (June 1906) which actually became the key to his development as a novelist. The book was a major turning point for his art.

The book can actually be seen as a summary of all Iwano's previous literary interests. First and foremost, he introduces Ralph W. Emerson's philosophy which was also at the core of his own 'philosophy'. He also introduces Swedenborg, Maeterlinck and Schopenhauer. In brief, most of the new philosophical movements which at the time were being imported from the West, were represented in the book.

33. The critic and novelist Ishikawa Jun (1899-1988) writes about his first meeting with Iwano's poetry, which he read as a child, in the journal *Shōnen*. Cf. Ishikawa, *Bungaku Taigai*, 230.

The style and method that Iwano employs in the book are neither very metaphysical nor very analytical, but rather metaphorical and intuitive, something which is also true of Emerson's writing. The book abounds in dogmatism and shifts in logic. But despite all this, one also finds Iwano's own 'philosophical' thoughts in the book. There are definitely many misleading and confusing passages and too many disjointed quotations. He mentions many names, both Japanese and foreign, for which there are no references. But behind all this we find his own thoughts; his own idea is what holds the work together.

The word 'semi-animalism' is very misleading. He explains the basis for it in Chapter 18 of his book:

My theory 'semi-anima/semi-animalism' (*hanrei/hanjū-shugi*) is abbreviated to 'semi-animalism', but when I speak only of 'semi-animalism', it is a contradiction to my own theory because I never deal with the body and soul dualistically. On the contrary I actually claim that the body and the soul have been united from the outset. But every philosophy becomes dogmatic as soon as it becomes systematised. That is precisely why one must return to the stage at which a theory was given its name in order to grasp the original idea behind the name.[34]

We can describe semi-animalism, in the manner of Iwano, as a theory which is based on a belief in the union of body and soul; it is a sort of philosophy of life which glorifies the sudden and momentary outburst of life.

The origins of Iwano's 'philosophy' can be traced to his poetic experiments and experience. He pursued his 'philosophy' — semi-animalism — further in his literary theory on monistic narration and in his theory of action *hitsū no tetsuri* (the metaphysics of sufferance).

In 1908 when the book's sequel *Shin-shizenshugi* (The new naturalism) was published, the word *shinpiteki* (mysterious) had been removed and from then on his 'philosophical' term was *hanjū-shugi*. This signalled that his 'philosophy' and literature had freed themselves of the influences of mystic symbolism, and that Iwano was moving towards naturalistic symbolism or rather symbolic naturalism. But this change was also an expression of the changes that were taking place in his own life. The protagonist in Iwano's novel-series, Tamura Yoshio, who functions as Iwano's alter ego, is described in the novel *Hatten* (Development, 1911-12):

---

34. HZ vol. 15, 75. This unity which is described in Iwano's theory of semi-animalism can possibly be compared with the Ying-Yang philosophy.

During the last two or three years, he had been confronted with life's brutal realities. All that which before had seemed to him to be deep and very valuable, all those illusions have now disappeared.[35]

This was the period immediately following the death of Iwano/Tamura's father and the beginning of his relationship with his young lover Masuda Shimoe (Shimizu O-tori in the novel) in 1908, and it was just prior to Iwano/Tamura's departure for Sakhalin in 1909. It was a tumultuous time in his life and as such it provided a turning point in his writing.

6. The Novel *Tandeki*

Iwano's novel *Tandeki* (Dissolute living) redirected the poet Iwano to become the novelist Iwano. It was printed in the journal *Shinshōsetsu* (New novels) in February of 1909. The material for the novel was taken from events in Nikkō, a health resort in the mountains north of Tokyo, where Iwano had gone immediately after the publication of *Shinpiteki hanjū-shugi* in 1906. In the novel the setting has been changed to Kōzu, a town on the coast of the Pacific Ocean, the sea which fascinated Iwano throughout his life.

Iwano inherited the family fortune after his father's death in May 1908. As a result he became the owner of the boarding house Hinodekan. He let his wife run the place and continued his unanchored life as a writer.

Iwano's life immediately after his father's death is described in his autobiographical novel *Hatten*. Tamura Yoshio becomes acquainted with Shimizu O-tori during her stay at Tamura's boarding house, where she lives because she has recently arrived in Tokyo to look for work. He tempts her to Kamakura, a holiday town by the Pacific Ocean, and they spend the night together at an inn. When they return to Tokyo, she has become his lover. During the summer of the same year, they travel together to the health resort Enzan in the Yamanashi prefecture where he writes the novel *Tandeki* with her help. An entire paragraph from the beginning of *Tandeki* is quoted in *Hatten* without any changes, in order to emphasise the realist aspects of the narrative.[36] But in *Tandeki* the character of Masuda Shimoe (Shimizu O-tori) is clearly present even though the novel is based on experiences Iwano had had two years earlier with another woman in another place.

About the method employed in *Tandeki*, Iwano writes the following in *Hatten*:

---

35. *HZ* vol. 2, 370.
36. *HZ* vol. 2, 397.

But he is sure that he can now look objectively at the things he has done. He writes resolutely about all the things he has experienced, precisely as they have happened. Naturally there are a few modifications: a change in disposition is represented as an action or the other way around — a feeling which has taken an exterior form is treated as an invisible change of emotions.[37]

Tandeki is an 'I'-novel narrated by a 'philosopher' who has lived in Kōzu (Nikkō in reality) and who has had a love affair with the village *geisha* Kichiya who is called 'Crow' because of her dark skin. The 'philosopher' comes to the health resort to write a play, but instead of working he spends all his time, both day and night, with Kichiya. He promises to help her get the necessary training to become an actress.

During 1906 Iwano was still best known as a poet. His second collection of poetry *Yūjio* and his third *Hiren Hika* were collected in one book under the title *Hōmei shishū* (The collected poems of Hōmei) in November 1906. But he had not yet given up the hope of becoming a playwright. In 1905 he published his 'contemplative play in verse' *Kaiho-gishi* (The dike technician) and this was followed by the tragedy *Honoo no shita* (The flame's tongue) from October 1906.[38] He joined the Ibsen-society in February 1907, and in March of the same year he published his social tragedy *Ono no Fukumatsu* (Fukumatsu with the axe) in the journal *Bungei Kurabu*.[39] But after this he seems to have taken a break from writing plays, at least until May 1909 when he published the comedy *Kagurazaka-shita* (At Kagurazaka-shita) in the journal *Gendai*. But during the intermediate time he wrote one short story after the other. His first short story was 'Geisha Kotake' (The *geisha* Kotake, in *Shinkobunrin*, March 1906). This was followed by 'Koi-inja' (The love hermit, in *Shinkobunrin*, January 1907)[40], then 'Hinode mae' (Before dawn, in *Taiyō*, April 1908), 'Rōba' (The old woman, in *Shumi*, May 1908), 'Senwa' (An episode from the war, in *Shinshōsetsu*, June 1908) and 'Kekkon' (The marriage, in *Chūgaku Sekai*, November 1908). These were all of poor quality, however, and should be regarded as literary études. Until the publication of *Tandeki* in 1909, Iwano was first and foremost known as a poet with four poetry

37. Ibid., 398.
38. *Kaiho gishi* is regarded as a poem and is therefore placed in volume 9 of Iwano's collected work with the other poetry. Iwano's plays are collected in volume 13.
39. The Ibsen Society was established in February 1907. Among the original members were the theatre producer Osanai Kaoru (1881-1928), the poet Kanbara Ariake (1876-1952), the ethnographer Yanagita Kunio (1875-1962) and the writers Shimazaki Tōson, Tayama Katai and Masamune Hakuchō.
40. This short story does not appear in Iwano's collected works. The reason is unknown.

collections to his name (his fourth *Yami no haiban*, The cup of darkness, was published in 1908) and as a critic with the book *Shinpiteki hanjū-shugi*.

Iwano's breakthrough as a novelist came with *Tandeki*. It was immediately compared to Oguri Fūyō (1875-1926)'s novel of the same name which had been published a year earlier, in 1908. Critics noted that Iwano described the *tandeki* of modern time.[41] But *Tandeki* could not have been written if Tayama Katai's short story 'Futon' (printed in *Shinshōsetsu*, September 1907) had not already been published.[42] 'Futon' had caused quite a stir when it came out. In the preface to *Tandeki* which was published in May 1910, Iwano admitted to the connection. In the same text he dedicates his book to Tayama Katai and thanks him for his pioneering work.[43]

Like 'Futon', *Tandeki* is about a middle-aged writer's love affair with a young lady. Whereas Tayama Katai tries to depict the episode through the objective third-person of Takenaka Tokio, Iwano describes his own experiences in a direct and straightforward manner through the confessing 'I'. The difference in character and artistic temperament between Tayama Katai and Iwano is apparent already in the formal aspects of their respective works. In contrast with Iwano's 'monistic narration', Tayama Katai was the creator of 'flat narration' (*heimen byōsha*). Tayama Katai's character depictions are supposed to be more objective than Iwano's. But a closer look at the effects of his 'flat narration' reveals that description in the short story 'Futon' paradoxically seems to be very emotional and subjective. The reader is constantly aware of the narrator's (author's) voice. But Iwano's description in *Tandeki* seems to be more objective, or rather, the reader senses an almost ironic distance between the narrator and the protagonist's 'I' even though it is the 'I's account that is presented.

7. The Journey to Sakhalin

Even though Iwano received recognition as a novel writer with *Tandeki* in 1909, he soon put all his energy into the Sakhalin project. His cousin Kobayashi Saisaku (1878-?) suggested that he start a crab-cannery in Sakhalin and Iwano was immediately taken with the idea. In April, Iwano began by mortgaging the boarding house in order to get the neccessary capital and then he sent his brother Iwano Iwao (1887-?) to Sakhalin. Kobayashi Saisaku

---

41. Oguri Fūyō's writing straddled the period between the Ken'yūsha group's rhetorical romanticism and Japanense naturalism.

42. Cf. Masamune Hakuchō, 'Shizenshugi seisui-shi' in *NKBT* vol. 22, 420-21.

43. Ibid., 414. Tayama Katai was Iwano's rival and opposite in many matters.

received him on the island and they immediately set about building the factory. It was very poorly constructed, but production was nonetheless initiated. Things went splendidly for a while, but then the brother fell ill. Iwano was forced to travel to Sakhalin to help and to make an attempt to save his company where production had almost come to a complete stand still. He left in June, but by the time he reached the factory, the financial situation was so hopeless that there was no other solution than to simply give up the whole project. What he experienced in Sakhalin during the two months that he was there, is described in 'Karafuto tsūshin' (News from Sakhalin).[44]

Iwano was calm even though his project ended in ruin. His primary interest was neither the result of the project nor the profit. His goal was to act. Whether he had success or not was of secondary importance.

While on Sakhalin, Iwano came to know the head of the office of the Sakhalin Bureau, Nakagawa Kojūrō (1866-1944). Iwano joined him on his inspection routes and had the oppportunity to visit Ainu villages, fishing harbours, forest, coal mines and the like, and finally he also visited Russian territory. He left Sakhalin in the middle of August and sailed back to Hokkaidō where he sought out old friends. This was a hellish period for Iwano, physically and mentally and also financially. In his despair, he fell in love with a *geisha*, but this relationship had no positive effects for any of those involved. His only comfort while on Hokkaidō was the trip he made to the Hidaka and Tokachi areas together with a member of the country council. During this trip he had the opportunity to be alone in a piece of virgin forest. In his imagination he became one with nature. This precious experience gave him new energy.

He stayed on the island until the beginning of November and his time there was later depicted in the novels *Hōrō* (Wandering, 1910), *Dankyō* (The broken bridge, 1911) and *Tsukimono* (The possessed one, 1912-1918).

At this point one might ask: Why did Iwano involve himself in this high risk venture just when he had established himself as a promising author?

About a year before Iwano went to Sakhalin, Futabatei Shimei, the first realist author in Japan, had left for Russia after having abandoned his literary vocation. But he fell ill in St. Petersburg and died on the way home aboard a ship in 1909. Futabatei Shimei's struggle to separate literature and action from one another and his choice of action and consequent rejection of

---

44. Published in the newspaper *Tokyo niroku shinbun* from June 29 to September 7, 54 episodes all together. Cf. *HZ* vol. 11, 558-643.

literature deeply impressed Iwano. Just before his departure for Sakahlin, Iwano wrote a sort of obituary for Futabatei Shimei:

Last year at his farewell party he (Futabatei Shimei) spoke at length of how he despised literature. I found his point of view interesting because it might make our literary world reconsider its *l'art pour l'art* tendency. I was happy to find that I almost agreed with him even though he apparently hadn't thought of the possibility of a 'literature of action' (*jikkō bungei*) ... Had he thought of it, he could have appreciated literature in exactly the same way that he emphasised the importance of his becoming an economist. I have already written of this in an essay in the journal *Shumi* ... With this I have made the additional point, that it might have been better for him to have remained a writer rather than dreaming of becoming an economist which really did not suit his personality.[45]

Both Futabatei Shimei and Iwano chose 'action' rather than 'literature', but there was a significant difference between the two. For Futabatei Shimei, his 'action' — going to Russia to work as a journalist with the additional intention of becoming an economist — meant a direct and immediate rejection of literature. Whereas Iwano chose his 'action' as a writer. In other words, Iwano, the man of action, who put money into his venture and went to Sakhalin, was not separate from the writer. His project was actually a literary one. To him art (literature) and life (action) were indivisibly united; if only the 'I' would flare up every moment, the two would achieve exactly the same value.

Certainly Iwano's poor economy just after the publishing of *Tandeki* was a direct result of his foolhardy investment on Sakhalin. But by carrying through his risky plan, he wanted to try out his 'philosophy of action' and prove that his literature was his life, and likewise that his life was his literature.[46]

---

45. Cf. '*Futabatei to Doppo*' (Futabatei and [Kunikida] Doppo) in *HZ* vol. 17, 558-643. The article is dated May 1908, but the date probably only pertains to the part about Doppo. The part about Futabatei Shimei is thought to have been written just after May 10, 1909, when Futabatei Shimei died. See also Ōkubo Tsuneo's article '*Hōmei to Futabatei Shimei*' in the book *Iwano Hōmei no jidai*, 214.

46. The poet and critic Ishikawa Takuboku (1886-1912) was deeply moved by Iwano's understanding of literature. Like Iwano he was dissatisfied with Japanese naturalism which had become more and more contemplative and aesthetic in its orientation. Cf. Ban Etsu, '*Iwano Hōmei to Ishikawa Takuboku*' in *Takuboku kenkyū* no. 4, 1978, 107-16.

8. Iwano's Novel-Series and Monistic Narration

Iwano's novel-series first took its present shape in July 1919 when the first part — the novel *Hōrō* — was published. Iwano had originally planned a series of autobiographical novels which was to be started off by *Tandeki*. According to the preface to the first edition of *Hōrō* (1910), he had had no intention of writing a novel based on his experiences on Hokkaidō, but he had planned to write a novel about the time before, that is before he had gone to Sakhalin, under the title *Doryoku* (Exertion). Already during his stay on Sakhalin and later also on Hokkaidō, he tried to contact two newspapers to inquire whether they would be interested in printing his new novel as a serial story. But his proposition was rejected. Meanwhile he changed his mind and began to write *Hōrō* instead.[47]

Iwano's novel-series has a very complicated history of creation and development. It was revised numerous times as Iwano's theory of monistic narration took shape. Here we will sort out the threads of this complicated, but exciting, creative process.

The earliest piece which was to become a part of this work had already been written in January 1910 under the title 'Kōmoto-shi' (Mr Kōmoto) and the last piece — the short story 'Tsukimono' (The possessed one) — was completed in May 1918. But the novel *Tandeki* which was supposed to be a part of the work, had already been published in February 1909. The novel-series was kept under revision by Iwano right up to his death in May 1920. He worked on it for over eleven years. It would be fair to say that this novel-series was his life achievement.

According to Iwano's original plan from July 1912, his novel-series was to evolve as follows:[48]

1. *Tandeki* (Dissolute living).
2. *Hatten* (Development).
3. [*Dokuyaku o nomu onna* (The woman who takes poison).]
4. *Hōrō* (Wandering).
5. *Dankyō* (The broken bridge).

---

47. *MBZ* vol. 71, 63.

48. Ibid., 167. Note that at this point, in July 1912, Iwano had not yet published the novel *Dokuyaku o nomu onna*. Therefore he wrote 'not yet published' next to number 3. It is included here for the sake of clarity. A resumé of the novel-series can be found page 163-64.

But the actual order of publication of his work was:

1. *Hōrō* (July 1910, in book-form).
2. *Dankyō* (the first part in the newspaper *Mainichi denpō*, from January to February 1911; the second part in the newspaper *Tokyo nichinichi shinbun* in March 1911).
3. *Hatten* (in the newspaper *Ōsaka shinpō* from December 1911 to March 1912; later as a book in July 1912, but prohibited by the authorities in August 1912 because of certain 'indecent' passages).
4. *Dokuyaku o nomu onna* (in the journal *Chūōkōron* in June 1914; later as a book in two parts, printed in December 1914 and February 1915 respectively).
5. *Tsukimono* (consisting of the short stories 'Neyuki' (Unmelted snow), 'Zokuhen Neyuki' (A continuation of 'Neyuki') and 'Shūhen Neyuki' (The end of 'Neyuki'); they were all printed in the journal *Shinshōsetsu* from May to June 1912; the collection also included the short story 'Kōmoto-shi' which had been printed in the journal *Shumi* in January 1910 and the short story 'Tsukimono' which had been printed in the journal *Shinchō* in May 1918).

When the publishing firm Shinchō-sha put out Iwano's novel-in-five-volumes, a thorough revision took place and they were published in the following order:

1. *Hōrō* (July 1919, with a number of omissions and corrections).
2. *Dankyō* (September 1919, the last eight chapters of the first edition of *Hōrō* were incorporated in the new edition of *Dankyō*. One part from the original version was left out. This part became a short story in its own right with the title 'O-tori no kurushimi' (O-tori's suffering). The last five chapters were omitted and incorporated into *Tsukimono*. In addition, there were minor omissions and corrections.)
3. *Tsukimono* (May 1920, opens with the five chapters carried over from the first edition of *Dankyō*. Otherwise unchanged from the first edition except for minor omissions and corrections.)
4. *Hatten* (July 1920, published post-humously. The last three chapters of the first edition are omitted. They were supposed to have been moved to the next volume. Otherwise minor corrections and omissions were made, among those omitted were 'indecent' passages which the authorities had subjected to censorship in 1912.)

5. *Dokuyaku o nomu onna* (Not published, the title should have been changed to *Dokuyaku onna*.)[49]

The course of action in the novels proceeds in the following order:

1. *Hatten*
2. *Dokuyaku o nomu onna*
3. *Hōrō*
4. *Dankyō*
5. *Tsukimono*

Iwano's restructuring of his work was successful. He succeeded in tightening the loose composition of the original version of the work and as a whole it came to reflect his theory of monistic narration with the single exception of *Dokuyaku o nomu onna* which Iwano did not finish revising.

Removing *Tandeki* from the novel-series was an ingenious solution. It stands isolated from the other novels both with regard to time and content. About two years elapse between the episodes recounted in *Tandeki* and the father's death which is described at the beginning of *Hatten*. But the events in the novel-series are connected, from *Hatten* to *Tsukimono*, and cover a period of one and a half years. Most importantly, however, *Tandeki* only describes a single episode, that involving the *geisha* Kichiya. The novel-series as a whole, however, is concerned with the minor theme of the protagonist's relationship with his lover Shimizu O-tori and with the more central theme of the protagonist's attempts to put into practice the 'philosophy of momentariness'. Iwano wrote about the theme of his novel-series in his preface to the first edition of *Hōrō*:

The background that is depicted in the novel *Hōrō*; the living nature, local customs and business life, [were all things] I had observed on Sakhalin and Hokkaidō. But in the foreground is the description of a wanderer — a man of action of the philosophy of momentariness — his undertakings and his real life.[50]

Iwano categorically denied considering the protagonist in his novel-series as identical with himself. He said:

49. When the novel was included in Iwano's collected works, vol. 3, the title was changed to *Dokuyaku onna*. The three chapters from the first edition of *Hatten* are included, but the text is otherwise unchanged. Iwano was unable to finish his revisions of it. Cf. Ban Etsu, 'Iwano Hōmei ron', 194-96.
50. *MBZ* vol. 71, 64.

... in speaking of a work of fiction, it is arrogant for a critic to imagine the author in the figure of his mediator in the work, or to even entertain such a notion.[51]

Iwano's point of view is understandable, but nonetheless it is possible, with certain reservations, to regard the novel-series as reliable documentation of his life on Sakhalin and Hokkaidō. In the abovementioned preface to *Hōrō*, Iwano describes the relationship between the novel-series and 'reality' as follows:

... most of the people in the novel are accquaintances of mine. Some of them are well-known people. In addition, I have described not only their positive sides, but also their negative sides. It may be that the novel will result in a so-called 'model' scandal. But even though the protagonist is actually the author himself, he has been depicted in his *natural* size. The reader will have to assume that all the other people have been likewise described. But just as the episodes involving the protagonist have been selected, likewise the other people's conditions have not necessarily been described fully. Changes have taken place; two people have been melted into one or one person's conditions have been given to someone else. In short, I have strived to give a completeness to the true picture of Hokkaidō which provides the setting.[52]

As was mentioned before, Iwano went through his five-volume novel and revised it according to the criteria of 'monistic narration'.

Iwano's theory of 'monistic narration' was formulated in opposition to 'flat narration', the 'objective' narrative technique in which an omniscient narrator may enter all the characters in the work. According to Iwano's 'subjective' method of narration, the author has a single 'mediator' in his work. The author looks through and relates to the other characters through the mediator's point of view. In his article *'Gendai shōsetsu no byōsha'* (Narrative techniques in the modern novel, printed in *Bunshō sekai* in February 1911), Iwano tries to justify his technique as it is used in both *Tandeki* and *Hōrō*. He writes about his basic concept *hakai-teki shukan* (the destructively subjective point of view):

It is unthinkable for a serious author who does not employ the subjective point of view to undertake a serious description of life. The more serious and the greater the author's subjective point of view actually is, the more efficient his destruction of superficial narrative techniques and of unimportant inner experiences becomes.

51. In the article *'Ichigen-byōsha no jissai shōmei'* (Monistic narration in practice, June 1919) in *HZ* vol. 10, 582-83.
52. *MBZ* vol. 71, 64-65.

The resulting work is a proportionally more serious and greater literary work. Such a subjective point of view — which is, by the way, much more important than the question of the author's objective attitude — is what I call the destructively subjective point of view.[53]

Iwano's theory of narration was strengthened and adjusted through numerous polemical discussions that he had through time with his rival writers. It finally took shape in an article with a very long and ambitious title '*Gendai shōrai no shōsetsuteki hassō o isshinsubeki boku no byōsharon*' (My theory of narration which will renew the idea of the novel today and in the future, in the journal *Shinchō*, October 1918).

Iwano abandons 'flat narration' — a method of narration with a simple bird's-eye perspective, in which the author sees through the minds of and observes the lives of each of the characters in the work, equally and directly. He chooses 'monistic narration' (*ichigen byōsha*) instead. Its main principles are the following: The author feels his way into one particular person A in the work. He observes the other characters through A and all that which A does not see, hear or feel remains an unexplored world to A, and as such it cannot be described, even though the author is well aware of these different things.

Iwano thought that with this method he would be able to establish a metaphorical relation to his protagonist, in other words, the protagonist would be a metaphor for the author, his life and philosophy.

In accordance with this principle, all the passages and paragraphs in the novel-series that did not conform to the theory, were either omitted or reformulated during the revisions.

9. 'The Conqueror and the Conquered'

A unique aspect of Iwano's writing was his ability to unite his art (literature) with his life in a 'monistic' way. He was a man of action in accordance with momentariness, not only in his literary universe, but also in his real life. The immediate moment during which his whole being might flare up, was the single most important thing to Iwano.

When he came back to Tokyo in November 1909, he immediately cut the ties with his lover Masuda Shimoe. But he did not want to continue his icy marriage to his first wife Takekoshi Kō either. Before long he was separated

53. *HZ* vol. 10, 499.

from her, and he soon moved in with Endō Kiyoko (1882-1920) whom he had recently met.

In the essay 'Sando tsuma o kaeta hanashi' (The story of a man who has had three different wives, undated) Iwano recounts that the first thing that needed his attention upon his return was the article 'Hitsū no tetsuri' which he had begun writing while he was on Hokkaidō.[54] Relieved when it had been printed in the journal Bunshōsekai, Iwano sought out his old friend, the author Masamune Hakuchō.

Masamune Hakuchō writes that 'He looked miserable and depressed ... but he had enough energy to try to find himself a new woman. He had two candidates; one was a waitress at a restaurant and the other an intelligent woman'.[55] After much consideration, he chose 'the intelligent woman' Endō Kiyoko, who was one of the best-known spokespersons for the Japanese women's movement of the period. They moved in together in December of the same year.[56] Their slightly strange relationship with one another is carefully described in the short story Seifuku hiseifuku (The conqueror and the conquered, printed in Chūōkōron in February 1919). At first Iwano sought her out in her house in order to suggest and try to convince her that they move in together. He 'unconditionally wanted a woman he could talk with and who could help him with the daily household tasks'.[57] Because she respected Iwano's person, especially his honesty, openness and passion, she finally agreed to try living with him as two independent people in a platonic relationship — the latter being her essential condition. From the start she was aware that Iwano intended to marry her, but she did not want to initiate a sexual relationship until they were married. She wanted to live with him, but she wanted to wait a while before marrying him. Iwano did not really agree with her, but he respected her desire to postpone a marital relationship.[58] Thus they began their new life as 'friends'. It was not long before Iwano initiated his attempts at 'conquest'. He tried to convince Kiyoko to 'capitulate' on the basis of his belief in 'momentariness'. The newspapers got word of their 'war' and began writing one article after another about them and their struggles. For example, Yorozuchōhō carried the title 'Rei ga

54. 'Sando tsuma o kaeta hanashi' in HZ vol. 17, 329-41.
55. Cf. Masamune Hakuchō, 'Hōmei o tsuiokusuru' (Remembering Hōmei, 1947) in Masamune Hakuchō zenshu vol. 12, 1965, 254-55.
56. Cf. Hiratsuka Raichō, 'Seitō-jidai no hitotachi' (1949) in Tō vol. 24, issues 6-7.
57. Cf. 'Sando tsuma o kaeta hanashi' in HZ vol. 17, 336.
58. Cf. Iwano Kiyoko's preface to the book Ai no sōtō in Iwano Hōmei shomoku, 1979, 151-52.

katsu ka, niku ga katsu ka' (Will the spirit win or will the body?), mocking Iwano's ideas about the unified body and soul (*rei-niku-gatchi*).[59]

Endō Kiyoko had marriage in mind from the beginning, but Iwano did not care about the formalities of the relationship. Meanwhile the 'war' ended with his 'victory' and they continued living together. In September 1912 Iwano finally managed to get a divorce from his first wife. Endō Kiyoko had to wait until March 1913 before legally becoming Iwano's wife.

Meanwhile the couple moved to Osaka in April 1911, where he worked as a journalist for the newspaper *Ōsaka shinpō*. It was in this paper that he was able to publish his novel *Hatten* in one hundred parts. The novel was published in book form in July 1912, but it had been, as has already been mentioned, prohibited by the authorities in August. Iwano reacted sharply by writing open letters to the Premier Saionji Kinmochi (1849-1940) and to the Minister of Interior Affairs Hara Takashi (1856-1921), but to no avail.

When he moved to Ikeda in Osaka he began to keep a diary which he maintained right up to his death in 1920.[60]

Iwano returned to Tokyo once more in September 1912. This time he settled in Meguro. Where he experienced the most peaceful period in his otherwise eventful life, despite the fact that his first wife Takekoshi Kō was suing him for damages. His economy was stable and his family life good. Even though he was busy writing, he also spent time keeping bees, something he had learnt in Ikeda, Ōsaka. He even wrote a number of essays on the topic.

The newly married couple Iwano and Endō Kiyoko moved to Sugamo in the northern part of Tokyo in April 1913. He was quite productive in his writing. One of his most noteworthy works at this point was probably his translation of Arthur Symons' *The Symbolist Movement in Literature* (1899). This translation is known for its errors and misunderstandings, but because of Iwano's modern language and clear style, the book became quite popular with young poets and the critics of the 20s and 30s — such as Nakahara Chūya (1907-37), Kobayashi Hideo (1902-83), Kawakami Tetsutarō (1902-80).[61]

Iwano also published two collections of short stories in 1913: *Bonchi* (The young master, June) and *Sumiya no fune* (The coal-dealer's boat, December).[62]

---

59. Cf. '*Seifuku hiseifuku*' in HZ vol. 6, 472.

60. There are six diaries altogether and they are collected in volume 12 of his collected works.

61. Cf. for example Kawakami Tetsutarō, '*Iwano Hōmei*' in *Nihon no autosaidā*, 1965, 86-103.

62. The book *Bonchi* also includes a comedy with the title '*Enma no medama*' (The devil's eyes) from 1911.

After the divorce, Takekoshi Kō lived with her three children, her daughter Fumi and her sons Kaoru and Masao, in Shiba in Tokyo. But the boarding house that she had received from Iwano as a sort of compensation landed in the hands of a carpenter because of her naivety and stupidity. She was burdened by such a bad economy that she could not manage without Iwano's financial help. In May 1914 their daughter Fumi died and in December of the same year Kaoru moved into his father's house.

Iwano and Kiyoko had a son, Tamio, who was born in February 1914. In 1915, however, they ceased to live together.

In 1915 when Iwano was translating Plutarch's *Bioi paralleloi* (Parallel Lives), he hired the schoolteacher Kanbara Fusae (1890-?) to make the fair copy. Their team work developed into an intimate relationship. Iwano confessed the affair to his wife in August and they agreed upon a separation. Iwano immediately moved in with Kanbara Fusae. But she had not yet been divorced from her husband and their moving in together caused a major scandal. The press wrote of 'double infidelity'. Conservative powers within Japanese intellectual circles attacked Iwano and his way of life — a way of life that was based on his philosophy of momentariness.[63]

Iwano responded to the criticism, bravely and thoroughly. He collected his essays about this topic and published them in a book with the title *Danjo to teisō-mondai* (Man and woman and the question of fidelity, October 1915). In answer to this, Iwano (Endō) Kiyoko published her book *Ai no sōtō* (The fight for love, November 1915).

At this point Iwano was involved in three lawsuits at the same time. Kiyoko took him to court, demanding that he live with her. Iwano sued Kiyoko for a divorce. At the same time Iwano sued the historian Ukita Kazutami (1859-1946) who had insulted him in public and who had described Iwano as sexually unstable. In the end Iwano lost all three cases. In the beginning of 1916 he appealed to a higher court, but without success. Throughout 1916 there was one court case after another. On December 31, Iwano noted with strong, thick strokes of his brush in his diary that 'it had been a deadly dull year'.[64]

Iwano's son Kaoru, who had been living with Kiyoko until September 1915, moved into his house. Likewise, in March 1916, his son Masao, who

---

63. Cf. for example Kamitsukasa Shōken, et. al. '*Iwano Hōmei-shi fusai no bekkyo ni taisuru bundan shoka no konponteki hihan*' in *Shinchō*, October 1915, 41-56; Kitagoe Tarō, et. al. '*Iwano Hōmei-shi no teisō-kan ni taisuru wakaki hitobito no hanbaku*' in *Shinchō*, December 1915, 102-8.

64. *HZ* vol. 12, 411.

had been living with Takekoshi Kō, also came to live with him. Iwano finally managed to obtain a divorce from Kiyoko in February 1917. Iwano let Kiyoko adopt the new-born Tamio in April 1917. With his new wife Fusae he had a girl, Miki, in December 1916. Since Fusae already had a son, Masahide, by 1917 Iwano's household consisted of two adults and four children.

Iwano published the journal *Shin-nihonshugi* (The new Nipponism) from January 1916, with the help of his friend, the poet Yamamoto Roteki (1884-1916). The name of the journal was changed to *Nipponshugi* in October of the same year. Iwano's Nipponism was a natural result of his momentariness. Momentariness had its roots in *Kojiki*, a book about Japan set in a time when the gods reigned and the Japanese empire was just dawning.

In *Nipponshugi* he published many articles and essays about a variety of topics right until his death in 1920. But Iwano had earlier been engaged in writing journalistic and socially critical work. This work was collected in *Kindai shisō to jisseikatsu* (Modern thinking and real life, December 1913) and *Kindai seikatsu no kaibō* (An analysis of modern life, January 1915). He also wrote about philosophy and intellectual history in, for example, *Kakei hakushi no Ko-shintō taigi* (On Dr Kakei's 'The essence of old Shintoism', January 1915); and about the newest currents in Western literature which resulted in *Akumashugi no Shisō to bungei* (Ideas and literature of 'diabolism', February 1915)[65]

The most important event in Iwano's writing in 1916 was without doubt his conclusion in the translation of Plutarch's *Parallel Lives*. It had taken him three years.[66]

10. The Productive Author and His Death

Iwano's work as a fiction writer was put on hold in the period from 1914-17, partly because of the many lawsuits and problems within his family, but in the latter half of 1917 he became active again. The background for this change was a monthly get-together that took place at Iwano's house. About a dozen young people who all shared an interest in literature, met to discuss news in the literary world, both Japanese and Western. Among the participants were Ōtsuki Takayori (1883-?), Nakazawa Shizuo (1885-1927)

---

65. Wilde, Poe and Baudelaire are representative poets and writers of the diabolic mode.
66. He finished it on July 20 1916. It was a huge work, 4,744 pages of manuscript. Cf. *HZ* vol. 12, 390.

and Ishimaru Gohei (1886-1969). Accounts of the meetings were published in the journal *Nipponshugi*.

As was mentioned earlier, Iwano completed his theory of monistic narration in 1918. Besides his work on the theory and the vehement debate that followed with critics and authors about the theory, Iwano also published his tragi-comic stories. He called them humorous (*ujō-kokkei*) stories. By 'humorous', Iwano meant 'not the artificially created, but warm human humour which flows like poetry from life when the author has observed and studied life thoroughly'.[67] Representative of this work are *Nekohachi* (Nekohachi, September-October 1918), *Ietsuki nyōbō* (The woman with a house, November 1918), *O-take bāsan* (O-take, the old woman, March 1919), *Yama no Sōbei* (Sōbei on the mountain, June 1919), *Tetsuko* (Tetsuko, September-October 1919) and *Gisei* (The victim, November 1919). In these stories a special event in the life of perfectly ordinary people is depicted from *within*. That is to say from the protagonist's viewpoint in a real and living manner in accordance with the monistic method of narration. A (so-called) ironic distance is established between the narrator and the protagonist, which is what provokes the distinctive humorous response from the reader.

The year 1919 was probably the best in Iwano's life, certainly with regard to his literary production and his economy. On December 31 1919 he wrote in his diary:

I have written about twenty short stories. My income was 4,500 yen, including the royalties for my books.[68]

When compared with other writers in 1919, Iwano had one of the highest incomes.

On the occasion of the publication of *Seifuku hiseifuku* in June 1919, Masamune Hakuchō and others arranged a reception on July 5.[69] Iwano's friends and accquaintances were gathered to celebrate the day with him. Among the guests were the writers Tokuda Shūsei, Kamitsukasa Shōken

---

67. Cf. the preface to the collection of short stories *Nekohachi* (Nekohachi, May 1919) in *Iwano Hōmei shomoku*, 109.

68. HZ vol. 12, 564.

69. The book consists of four short stories which are all based on Iwano's relationship with Endō Kiyoko. They are the title story *'Seifuku hiseifuku'*, *'Mitsubachi no ie'* (The house with the beehive, April 1919), *'Kūkijū'* (The air gun, October 1918) and *'Rikon made'* (Until the divorce, March 1917).

(1874-1947), Toyoshima Yoshio (1890-1955) and Okamoto Kanoko (1889-1939), the poets Noguchi Yonejirō (1875-1947) and Saijō Yaso (1892-1970) and the critics Nakamura Seiko (1884-1974) and Maeda Akira (1879-1961).

Most noteworthy in Iwano's body of work from this last part of his life is probably the short story series with the female protagonist O-sei. The character of O-sei was based on his first wife Takekoshi Kō. Four of the short stories were collected and published posthumously in the book *Onna no shūchaku* (A woman's stubbornness) in September 1920. The book included 'O-sei no heizei' (The daily life of O-sei, the original title was 'O-sei', February 1920), 'O-sei no shippai' (O-sei's mistake, March 1920), 'Kanojo no junrei' (Her pilgrimage, the original title was 'O-sei no junrei', June 1920) and 'Junrei-go no O-sei' (O-sei after the pilgrimage, unfinished). They were all instances of monistic narration. The plots were told exclusively from the viewpoint of the protagonist O-sei.

The last story 'Junreigo no O-sei' was supposed to have been about 300 pages long, according to Iwano (Kanbara) Fusae's preface to the book. Iwano finished only about a third of the story before his death. The preface also recounts that as he lay dying, Iwano expressed his regret at being unable to finish the last story and another work about monistic narration which he had begun in December 1919.[70]

The other two short stories in the series are 'Jisshi no hōchiku' (Expelling children from home, December 1919), and 'Konashi no Tsutsumi' (Tsutsumi, the childless, December 1919). They are both about O-sei's children. O-sei is not the protagonist of the two stories. The protagonists are Taguchi Gosuke and his friend Tsutsumi, respectively. The two short stories are based on events that occurred in 1918 when Iwano's sons were chased from Iwano's house as a result of the family conflict.

Iwano married Kanbara Fusae in May 1918 and had a child with her in December of the same year. It was a boy and he was called Yuzuru, the same name that had been given to Iwano's first son who had been born in 1901 and died in 1902.[71] The conflict in the family was partly due to the usual complications in the relationship between stepmother and stepchild, and partly to Takekoshi Kō's continued interference in the family's affairs. Iwano's first wife had no legal rights over her sons at this time, but she

---

70. Cf. *Iwano Hōmei shomoku*, 115.

71. It sounds as if everything was going well, but in his account Ebe Ōson claims that Iwano had confessed to him that his marriage to Fusae was a failure. Cf. Ōkubo Tsuneo, 'Iwano Hōmei no jidai', 49. Fusae was very jealous of the woman writer Araki Ikuko (1888-1943) whom Iwano had recently become acccuainted with.

frequently visited them in secret and made them steal from the house for her. The children were forced to do this 'favour' for their mother. Iwano wanted to talk about the problem with his children, but they would not admit to what they had done. This was too much for Iwano and after many attempts to talk with them, he finally decided to arrange apprenticeships for them — they were at an age when they would otherwise have been in school — in order to get them out of the house.

These events are described in the short story '*Jisshi no hōchiku*'. The story is told by the protagonist Taguchi Gosuke — Iwano's alter ego. But the exact same event is recounted by his friend Tsutsumi in the other short story '*Konashi no Tsutsumi*', however, only that part of the story which he himself experienced — saw, heard and felt.

The two stories were experiments and the natural and inevitable result of Iwano's theory of monistic narration. On their own, they are not very different from Iwano's other short stories, but they become interesting and captivating when they are read as a whole. It is certainly justifiable to consider his experiment as a successful and pioneering work in the field of novel-writing in modern Japan.

Iwano worked on the short story series about O-sei right up to his death in May 1920. On April 25 he caught a cold when he walked home in the rain from the Kenkyūza theatre in the centre of Tokyo. On May 6 he contracted terrible diarrhea. He was admitted to the hospital at Tokyo's National University on May 8 because there was concern that he might have typhus. He was operated on the very next morning, but it was already too late. He died of peritonitis.

Just before the operation Iwano told his friend, the critic Ebe Ōson (1884-1969):

I have always wanted to experience something like having my stomach cut open. When I get well again, I'm sure I'll be able to write an exciting story about it.[72]

Following this he dictated his will and signed it. He died at the age of 47.

72. In Ebe Ōson's '*Hōmei-shi no rinjū*' (Mr Hōmei's death, May 20 1920) cf. *Iwano Hōmei shomoku*, 139.

II. The Background for Iwano Hōmei's Literary Theory

> To lend himself, to project himself and steep himself, to feel and
> feel till he understands and to understand so well that he can say,
> to have perception at the pitch of passion and expression
> as embracing as the air, to be infinitely curious and incorrigibly patient,
> and yet plastic and inflammable and determinable, stopping to conquer and
> serving to direct — these are fine characters for an active mind, chances
> to add the idea of independent beauty to the conception of success.
> Henry James

1. Iwano Hōmei the Man

Much has been said and written about Iwano Hōmei's strange qualities and
ideas. His contemporaries were busy calling attention to one episode after
another in which the eccentric writer had let himself get involved.

But also the reader who comes across Iwano's five volume novel with no
preceding knowledge of the author's sensational behaviour, will be confused;
either by Iwano's style or by his line of thought. For instance, the protagonist
of the work, Tamura Yoshio — Iwano's alter ego — is introduced as 'an
active metaphysical philosopher of momentariness' (*setsunashugi no jikkō
tetsurika*), without any further explanations. Furthermore, Tamura preaches
his own original philosophy throughout the work, and that no matter who
is the interlocutor. This alone should suffice to make the reader question
Tamura's common sense. But even the curious reader who makes an effort
to understand the philosophy of Tamura (or of the author), will immediately
find himself lost. For 'the active metaphysical philosophy of momentariness'
is based upon the concatenation of various obscure concepts which are
comprehended only with difficulty and which do not as a whole seem to give
any clear meaning, at least not at a first glance.

To this we may add the fact that in his novels as well as in his essays,
Iwano repeatedly presented his ideas as a synthesis of the Western
philosophies and literary theories of the age. Thus, he considered his theory
the most progressive and original in the world. This was no joke on Iwano's
part; he was completely serious. For this reason, he was often laughed at and
misunderstood by his contemporaries, and at times considered insane.

Even the anarchist Ōsugi Sakae (1885-1923), who was original in his own way and one of the most eccentric 'outsiders' of the time, called Iwano a 'fabulous fool'.[1] That was a most telling designation. Iwano, however, was neither hurt nor offended by the criticism. On the contrary, he was flattered by the remark, which he interpreted as praise, and he compared himself with Toyotomi Hideyoshi (1536-98), the ambitious and often foolhardy regent of Japan during the period 1580-98.[2]

From 1908 when he met Masuda Shimoe, in the novel-series the model for the protagonist's mistress, and until his death in 1920, Iwano continually found himself in the middle of some kind of scandal. But he never lost heart; at least he never admitted openly to doing so. No matter how severe the criticism and the reproach, he would defend himself, always energetically and effectively, without ever suffering defeat.

The following quote is from Akutagawa Ryūnosuke (1892-1927)'s caricature of Iwano. The episode is a convincing illustration of the self-confident and proud writer's attitude.[3]

Mr Iwano Hōmei
I believe it was a late Autumn evening.

In the company of Mr Iwano Hōmei, I was on my way to Sugamo on the electric train.[4] Mr Iwano was wearing a cloak and sat resting his elbow on the handle of his umbrella. He was in a good mood and as usual he was telling me loudly and with vigour about various things, such as how to look after Western flowers and of a method he had invented which would help keep your stomach in good order.

I do not remember how it happened, but all of a sudden our conversation hit upon the sale of a novel which was very popular at the time. And then Mr Iwano said quite shamelessly:

1. Ōsugi Sakae was a literary critic as well. Due to his ideology and his political activities, he was much hated by the authorities, and during the chaotic situation after the earthquake of 1923, he and his wife were murdered by an officer's nephew. Cf. Ōsugi Sakae, *Iwano Hōmei-shi o ronzu* (1915), in which he reviews Iwano's book *Kakei hakushi no Ko-shintō taigi* (On Dr Kakei's 'The essence of the old Shintoism', 1915) Also see *MBZ* vol. 71, 387.
2. Cf. Iwano, *Empukuka toshite no Ōsugi Sakae-shi* (Mr Ōsugi Sakae — a gentleman), *HZ* 17, 424-28.
3. The text has at the earliest been written in 1919 and at the latest in 1922 when the book *Tenshin* (The zen-monk's snack) with the quoted text was published. According to Yoshida Seiichi, Iwano was a best-selling author in 1919. Cf. Yoshida, *Shizenshugi no kenkyū* vol. 2, 663.
4. *Sugamo* is one of the northern parts of Tokyo.

'My dear friend, I am aware that this is his first novel, but still it cannot possibly sell that much. My books usually sell about ... copies. And what about yours, how much do they sell?'

I would have preferred not to, but was practically forced to tell him how many copies my book *The Puppeteer* had sold.[5]

'Do you really sell that much?'

Mr Iwano wanted to hear more.

Several first novels had sold more than mine. — I mentioned a couple of novels and told him the number of sold copies, with which I happened to be familiar. But unfortunately it seemed that most of these first novels had sold more than his own books.

'Well, they sell pretty well, eh?'

Mr Iwano frowned, and seemed sceptical for a second. But indeed that was literally only for one second. Before I would even have been able to answer him, the vivid sparks had returned to his eyes. Simultaneously, Mr Iwano ventured the following remark — quietly as if out of compassion for the world:

'But then, they are indeed difficult to read, my books.'

I shall let other people judge his calibre as a poet, novelist, dramatist or critic. But in my eyes, the dear Mr Iwano Hōmei was such an amiable optimist that he almost made me feel exalted.

The mischievous Akutagawa Ryūnosuke presumably exaggerated or twisted the episode to fit his exquisite style. But nevertheless, the caricature may help us create an image of Iwano — the unique, awkward Don Quixote of modern Japanese literary history.

Indeed Iwano's self-confidence or insolence were so enormous that his actions were practically unintelligible and seemed insulting to other people. He did not show any consideration whatsoever for such universal human qualities as courtesy, kindness or modesty. Neither did he care about sophisticated expressions of any kind, and he was often considered both selfish and arrogant, as well as prone to exposing his vulgar nature and to promoting himself. At the worst, he was described as a roaming erotomaniac.

But all the time, he was convinced that his work was not only superior to the work of Akutagawa or other writers making their débuts at the time, but also to the most representative writers of Japanese naturalism, writers whom he actually appreciated highly.[6] It was equally evident to him that his

---

5. *The Puppeteer* (*Kairaishi*, 1919) is Akutagawa's second collection of short stories and consists of eleven short stories written during the period 1917-19.
6. Cf. *Gendai shōsetsu no byōshahō* (Narrative techniques in the modern novel, 1911, in *HZ* vol. 10, 489-505.

work was difficult to read but of a high quality. With identical seriousness, he would furthermore call his *oeuvre* 'the literature *après Baudelaire*',[7] thus seeing it as superior to Western symbolism. He would praise his own novel *Dokuyaku o nomu onna* (The woman who takes poison, 1914), by calling it a masterpiece greater than *Faust*.[8]

So the Iwano who sat erect next to Akutagawa on the train, was neither pretending to be a great writer nor promoting himself. He was just behaving as he always did.

Iwano's immense self-recognition and almost reckless frankness were important factors in the framing of his literary theory and thus played an important role in his work. For in order to understand his literary theory as a whole, it is necessary to look closely at his extravagant, even insane self-estimation and at his primitive and often infantile behaviour patterns, which were completely free from the customs and social norms of the age.

2. The Anti-social Male

> But to Verlaine, happily, experience taught nothing; or rather,
> it taught him only to cling the more closely to those moods in
> whose succession lies the more intimate part of our spiritual life.
> Arthur Symons

Iwano Hōmei's five-volume novel cannot without reservation be classified as a work of Japanese naturalism. Both its composition and style are far too peculiar to allow for such a classification. Admittedly, the central idea behind the work is iconoclastic, the expression is both spontaneous and revealing, and the construction rather loose. The form thus shares qualities with other works characterised as belonging to Japanese naturalism. But the naturalistic writers, with Shimazaki Tōson and his epoch-making novel from 1906 *Hakai* (The broken commandment) as a primary example, mainly focused their interest on the relationship between the individual and society. Their works attempted to describe modern human beings with personal traits. An analogous concern is never found in Iwano's novels. The thoughts and actions of his protagonist are focused on 'the masculine' or rather 'the male' without any regard to social aspects. In this respect, Iwano has nothing in

---

7. Cf. *Jijitsu to gen'ei* (Facts and illusions, 1914), in *HZ* vol. 18, 226-75.
8. Cf. *Danjo to teisō-mondai* (Man and woman and the question of fidelity, 1915), Chapter 11: '*Motto bungei o rikaiseyo*' (You should comprehend better the art of language), in *HZ* vol. 17, 324.

common with the other writers of the naturalistic school, and in order to avoid confusion and misunderstandings, we may consider him an exception within Japanese naturalism.

Iwano's novels attempt a careful study and illumination of the structures of consciousness and the behavioural patterns of the exposed and anti-social male. This is achieved through both inner and outer descriptions of his doings and reactions.

No persons can liberate themselves entirely from the society in which they live, and the one who wishes to survive, must in some way fit him- or herself into the existing system. Further analysis shows that a man's relations to the community are almost always, implicitly or explicitly, reflected in his sexual life. And as far as our 'male' is concerned, sex, being the basis for his existence, shapes his thoughts, governs his actions and forms his personality.

Iwano screens the body of his protagonist, Tamura, with X-rays in order to lay bare the skeletal essence of the male to the eyes of all, that is, in order to visualise the core of the man's intuitive, erotic philosophy of life, which is 'momentariness'. But this operation is used to describe the man only. The protagonist's mistress O-tori, for instance, is portrayed so vaguely and incoherently that the reader only sees her in snapshots. This is also true for the other subordinate characters in the novel. They hover around the man, whereas to him everything exists as a landscape.

When Iwano is busy with what he calls his 'enterprise' — running a factory which produced canned crab meat on Sakhalin — also this project is considered symptomatic of male impulses. Again a viewpoint which would allow us to see the activity of the individual in a larger, social context, is missing.

The further Iwano's protagonist is removed from society and its intricate systems, the more he loses his personality and comes to seem a pronoun-type — an anonymous erotic creature. Few words are needed to uncover the instincts of such a character. But what then does the author wish to express with his work of fiction?

Iwano is basically concerned with abstracting his protagonist to such an extent that he becomes an exemplification of the male by cutting him off from the various social relations in which he is involved. This concern naturally involves the simultaneous search for a method which will render such an abstraction possible, without risking that the work loses in realism.

Of course there is no way for us to know how consciously the author Iwano worked at the structure of his work. But if we limit our examination to the actual result, we must admit that despite certain flaws and short-comings, the composition of the work is excitingly effective and strangely charming. Firstly, we may ascribe these qualities to the fact that contrary to the reader's expectations, the protagonist Tamura Yoshio never changes during the course of the five volumes. He simply gains slightly in experience with new situation that he confronts. Secondly, his way of thought and his actions are so eccentric that few readers will be able to identify with him — an eccentric, a dreamer, a chauvinist, a fanatic and a far too eager lover of women.

With no fears, Tamura Yoshio preaches his principles to anybody he meets. Whenever he is not understood — which unfortunately is far too often the case — he believes this to be a fault on the part of the other person and not his. He also considers other people's criticism and reproach towards him as signs of their own banality. But in the eyes of others, he is nothing but a roaming, dissolute philanderer suffering from megalomania. On the one hand, Tamura Yoshio is a caricature, but on the other hand he is intended to be the incarnation of the fatal impulses of the male. He adheres to no universal ethics which would unconsciously and mechanically differentiate good from bad. To Iwano, it is important to disarm the reader's lubricious curiosity, in order for him to be able to furnish the holy idiocy of his protagonist with a meaning, that is, with a literary reality.

Tamura Yoshio is highly egocentric, and he bares his sexuality to the furthest degree. He completely disregards normative ethics and the eyes of others. He is simple, sincere and strange, and in the greater social context he is cut off from the outside world. Nevertheless, his disregard for other citizens is based upon his principles of 'momentariness' (*setsuna-shugi*), 'semi-animalism' (*hanjū-shugi*) and 'the metaphysics of sufferance' (*hitsū no tetsuri*). Everything is defined in accordance with these thoughts which in the novels (as was true for Iwano himself) function as explanations which were to protect him from possible attacks.

Therefore we may consider Tamura Yoshio's frequent sermons on 'philosophy' not as the author's trivial nonsense, but as a necessity in order that the actions of the protagonist do not appear as sheer idiocy. This is sustained by the author's need to repeatedly call the reader's attention to the fact that Tamura Yoshio *is* a 'philosopher'.

Tamura Yoshio lives quite seriously in his 'philosophical' daydreams, he never doubts himself and never abandons his projects. But it is only when through his actions and not necessarily by virtue of his 'philosophy', that his personal qualities materialise before the eyes of the reader that the description of the man, who is free, at least in his thoughts, from the strictures of the commoners' ethics, gains its reality. Not until then may the reader understand that Tamura Yoshio's attitude towards the various women he has been socialising with as well as his merciless attack on and rejection of common family life, are the unrestrained expressions of the essence of the male.

In order to prevent the reader from getting the impression that Tamura Yoshio merely regards all reproach, slander and insinuation as a snigger aimed at him by the others who remain incapable of understanding his 'philosophy', the author stresses his Quixotic characteristics throughout the novel. When this happens, however, the author never fails to describe the sad and depressing side of his protagonist simultaneously, again either misunderstood or not understood at all by the surrounding world. And as Tamura Yoshio, disguised as Don Quixote, rides or wanders along the road, he gradually changes into the martyr of his own philosophy and thus gains the appearance of a holy man who smiles as he turns to face his pursuers.[9]

When Iwano thus expands the 'philosophical' horizons of his work, it seems to be because he *believes* completely in this 'philosophical' world of his; he lives in it and he lives for it. His 'philosophy' is his *raison d'être*.

It is a unique phenomenon in modern Japanese literary history that a writer bases his work in general and his literary theory in particular on his 'philosophy'. Iwano's 'philosophy' played an important role within his work, not necessarily due to its extensive contents and depth, but because it enabled him to gain a foothold — a point, to which he could always return and in which he could take pride and *believe* intensely.[10]

---

9. During his stay on Hokkaidō in 1909, Iwano had the chance to travel in the areas of Hidaka and Tokachi. On certain stretches he had to ride a horse. While he rode, he would philosophize, in the middle of the unspoiled nature. He did travel alone though, with no Sancho Panza to keep him company.
10. Iwano's attitude towards his theory and its construction is not very rational, but rather evocative and emotional.

3. *The Mystic Semi-Animalism*

> The idea of lyric poetry, certainly, is to be this passive,
> flawless medium for the deeper consciousness of things,
> the mysterious voice of that mystery which lies about us,
> out of which we have come, and into which we shall return.
> It is not without reason that we cannot analyse a perfect lyric.
> Arthur Symons

> It is not words only that are emblematic; it is things which are
> emblematic. Every natural fact is a symbol of some spiritual fact.
> The world is emblematic. Parts of speech are metaphors, because
> the whole of nature is a metaphor of the human mind.
> R.W. Emerson

As in all other fields in which Iwano Hōmei had been engaged, he was also convinced of the worth of his theories within the fields of philosophy and literature. He estimated his own position within the Japanese intellectual world so highly that he regarded nobody as his equal. He was indeed a militant controversialist, and left a number of critical writings, both literary and philosophical. *Shinpiteki hanjū-shugi* (The mystic semi-animalism) from 1906 is the most important of these, since it lays the firm foundation for his theory. Later Iwano would repeatedly return to the book and draw attention to its importance for his work in general.[11]

The year 1906 is worth noticing. One year after the end of the Russo-Japanese war, this was the year in which Shimazaki Tōson published his epoch-making novel *Hakai*. Tayama Katai's '*Futon*' followed in 1907. It should be noticed, however, that in 1906 Iwano had already formulated his aesthetic theory and published it as *The Mystic Semi-Animalism*. At this stage, he was known merely as a 'different' poet and the publication of the book, which was decidedly ambitious, passed almost unnoticed. It was not until three years later, with the publication of *Tandeki* in 1909, that he was recognised as a writer of fiction.[12]

11. Iwano was convinced of the importance of the book to such a degree that when Futabatei Shimei was going to Russia in 1908, Iwano asked him to translate it into Russian. Cf. *HZ* vol. 17, p. 377.
12. *Tandeki* (dissolute living) is Iwano's own translation of the word 'decadence'. Cf. Sōma Tsuneo, *Shinpiteki hanjūshugi shichū*, 20-22, as well as Ishikawa Jun, '*Iwano Hōmei*' in *Bungaku taigai*, 233.

In the opening of his autobiographical novel *Hatten*, Iwano introduces the protagonist Tamura Yoshio, his alter ego, as follows:

Because Yoshio's relations with his father, due to the stepmother, were far from good, he had been independent and lived in his own house for a long time ... [Since] he had with time become famous within the world of letters for his assertion of the active philosophy of momentariness, he would not become the owner of that annoying boarding house.[13]

In *The Mystic Semi-Animalism*, Iwano expounds his theory of the active momentariness. Iwano himself regarded the book as the embryo of his literary and philosophical *oeuvre* and appreciated it highly. Furthermore, whenever he had to answer to criticism aimed at himself, he would open his response by stating that misunderstandings could easily be avoided if only his opponents would read his book — the core of his philosophy — more thoroughly.

In his second collection of critical writings *Shin-shizenshugi* (The new naturalism, 1908), which, as he claimed in the preface, 'could be considered a sequel to *Semi-Animalism*', he developed and amplified his theory by applying it in the discussion of various tangible topics and phenomena. The articles in this second book were mainly answers to criticism of his theory and short, note-like essays intended to elucidate its background. The book did not devote itself to any specific theme as had been the case with the first book. In short, *The New Naturalism* was a supplement to *The Mystic Semi-Animalism*.

In 1906, the foundation for his thought and literature had almost achieved its final form, and in the innumerable essays that he was later to write, he never added any new elements to his basic theory, though the zeal, industriousness and variety of his 'colourful' writings were always noticeable.

In the following, we shall look a bit closer at Iwano's view of literature, on the basis of *The Mystic Semi-Animalism* and *The New Naturalism*, which together form the point of departure for and the source of his extensive philosophical and literary writings.

The Mystic Semi-Animalism is one long essay on literary and philosophical theories.[14] In the preface, the author explains that the book expounds an idea that he has been discussing with and talking of among his friends for more than ten years. In the beginning the idea was naturalistic, it later became more spiritual and finally symbolistic.

---

13. Cf. *MBZ* vol. 71, 169.
14. Ban Etsu, however, regards the books as Iwano's poetics. Cf. Ban, *Iwano Hōmei ron*, 54-66.

His philosophy was not borrowed, but his own — original and distinctive. In the book he had aimed at systematising his philosophy, i.e. at constructing his philosophical system in a theoretical way. According to his own summary given in the supplement *The Misunderstood Semi-Animalism*,[15] the book's contents were as follows:

Initially, the mysticism or the tendency at mystification in Maeterlinck, Emerson and Swedenborg is criticised, then an account is given of the fact that the more Man tends towards idealism, the more inane he becomes, and that the substance of life is found in Man's futile aspirations. The account is based on my particular viewpoint which believes that nature *is* the spirit, i.e. the body and the soul are not two different things, they are not a composite unity either, but rather one and a whole. I also touch upon topics such as love, nation, literature, etc.[16]

Iwano's first philosophical essay was both wide-ranging and varied. We may, however, question the success of his big project and it likewise seems doubtful whether he ever reached his ambitious goal. In any case, it can be claimed that his work remains quite exceptional. He formulated his opinions on almost all the subjects that usually concern philosophers and attempted a systematisation of these, even before he made his more serious efforts at becoming a writer of fiction. This he did in the same way as a philosopher would — by using philosophical terminology and employing a philosophical language, with no reservations — without accentuating the fact that he was actually a man of letters and thus an outsider.

Iwano did admittedly consider himself a philosopher and placed himself on a par with Dr Miyake Yūjirō (1860-1945), Dr Katō Hiroyuki (1836-1916),

---

15. Cf. *HZ* vol. 15, 107-14. The text *Gokai-sareta hanjūshugi* had been written in December 1912, and when *The Metaphysics of Sufferance* (*Hitsū no tetsuri*) was issued in 1920, *The Mystic Semi-Animalism* was included in the book under the abridged title *Semi-Animalism*. In the appendix *The Misunderstood Semi-Animalism*, Iwano gave an account of what had happened to his semi-animalism after the book's publication in 1906 and of the reasons for the deletion of the word 'mystic'. He wrote that his semi-animalism had developed into and been reformulated as 'the new naturalism' by the removal of all its mystical elements. Simultaneously, in the new version he had transformed the designation *reiniku-gatchi* (the union of soul and body) into *nikurei-gatshi* (the union of body and soul). This was to be understood as Iwano's attempt at freeing himself from the influence of metaphysical symbolism. To Iwano, *reiniku-gatchi* was synonymous with symbolism. Cf. Ishikawa Jun, op. cit., 233.
16. Cf. *HZ* vol. 15, 108.

Dr Inoue Tetsujirō (1855-1944) and Nakae Chōmin (1847-1901).[17] There was no reason to discern his author 'I' from his philosopher 'I', because he considered both philosophy and literature to be two inseparable activities in the complete human being. But he *was*, when all comes to all, a writer of fiction, though he was indeed a bit different from most novelists.

It might be useful to attempt a consideration of the reasons that made Iwano, a novelist, develop his own philosophical theory.

First and foremost, we will need to identify the central point in his rather complicated theory and decide what he himself considered the most important elements of *The Mystic Semi-Animalism*. This because, as Iwano writes in Chapter 6, the validity of a philosophical system is determined by the degree of life that the theory gives to its author. To Iwano a theory with no life-giving core was worthless.

So which part of the book did Iwano experience as life-giving?

The Mystic Semi-Animalism consists of 22 chapters. In the first six Chapters, Iwano introduces his reader to the theories of Maeterlinck, Emerson and Swedenborg and analyses the connections between the three. He sees them as the group in the modern European world of letters who share his own point of view (Chapter 1), and acknowledges the fact that their work has informed his own theory.

Iwano was usually arrogant and indulgent when he summarised or commented on other people's articles or theories. Also in *The Mystic Semi-Animalism*, his explanations are full of self-confidence, and his tone is almost

---

17. Cf. the preface to *The Mystic Semi-Animalism*. Miyake Yūjirō was a journalist and philosopher. He began publishing the journal *Nihonjin* (The Japanese) in 1888 and the newspaper *Nihon* (Japan) in 1899. He was a fanatical nationalist and patriot, and fought against the exaggerated tendency at Westernisation in Japan during the Meiji period. He was active within all areas of Japanese intellectual life, and was one of the most influential figures of the age.

   Katō Hiroyuki was a qualified lawyer. Initially, he took part in the civil rights' movement, but he later became the ideologist of the Meiji government. He was also known for his severe criticism of Christianity.

   As a young man, Inoue Tetsujirō went to Germany to study the German idealism. After his return to Japan, he made himself the spokesman of Nipponism and criticised the cosmopolitan atmosphere in the country. He was famous for his ardent polemics, and especially the attacks that he aimed at Christianity in 1891 attracted great attention. In his mature years, he was solely concerned with Japanese philosophy and edited an epoch-making work in multiple volumes on Japanese intellectual history.

   Nakae Chōmin spent the years 1871-74 in France where he studied philosophy, history and literature. After his return to Japan, he became a leading advocate for democracy and civil rights. In 1882 he translated Jean-Jacques Rousseau's *Du contrat social, ou principes du droit* into Japanese, and was himself called the Rousseau of the Orient.

ostentatious. The analysis is difficult to follow, and when he discusses the interconnections between the three thinkers's theories, the logic is often quite vague.

Iwano gives an outline of the theories of the three philosophers in the first six chapters — Chapter 1: Introduction; Chapter 2: Maeterlinck's mystic theory; Chapter 3: Emerson's 'On Nature'; Chapter 4: Emerson's 'On Nature' (2); Chapter 5: The characteristics of and the tendency to mysticism in Emerson's theory; and Chapter 6: Swedenborg the Mysticist. He then concentrates on one topic in order to 'compare the viewpoints and characteristics of the three and put forward his own theory' (Chapter 6).

The problematic theme which he borrowed from the three authors' diverse theories and used in the creation of his own theory, was that of love. This choice bears clear testimony to the field that attracted most of Iwano's interest.

Chapter 7 is thus concerned with the three philosophers' views on love and in Chapters 8-16, Iwano quotes the writings of a series of thinkers, ranging from Western philosophy to Buddhism, in order to attack the various opinions. While undertaking this commentation, Iwano refers to the development of his own philosophy. On this basis, he expresses his own theory — not with any particularly consequent logic, but rather with the help of rather loosely connected associations of ideas, with no further explanations and not in the right order either. The main emphasis is on the severe criticism and/or rejection of the others' theories, which he finds erroneous. Despite the fact that he presents many new viewpoints, one after the other as a matter of fact, they do not lead to anything. He thus argues in a circle, but fortunately never forgets the central topic completely.

At first he defines the word 'mystic', which he understands as 'the condensation of intellectual forces and the transmission of these to the sphere of emotion' (Chapter 8).

Then he claims that 'nature is equal to spirit'. Iwano's theory is thus one of monism, and does not allow for a separation of nature and spirit. He thus opposes himself to Emerson and his monistic theory which regarded the spirit as inclusive of nature. To Iwano this proved that in Emerson nature and spirit are two heterogeneous elements (Chapter 9).

In the following chapter, it is stressed that only the things that change every moment exist. In other words, 'all that exists is the transformation of the symbols'. Iwano disagrees with e.g. Swedenborg, who considers phenomena as the symbols of the spirit (and not vice versa). To Iwano, a symbol may be both a symbol of nature and of the spirit; it may indeed even symbolise any other symbol. This means that existence, that is the symbolic relations between nature and spirit, is always in movement, and has neither a goal nor an end. From this Iwano infers that all existence is futile (Chapter 10).

Contrary to the three mysticists, Iwano finds no regulative forces behind the eternal changing of things. For this very reason, he emphasises the importance of every moment lived (Chapter 11).

'The awareness of the *ego* is born from our life instincts; we may consider the necessity inherent in the instinct as Destiny or Will' (Chapter 12).

The *ego* is thus absolute and autonomous to Iwano. But he rejects every theory which collides with his conviction that 'the Will is the action of the purposeless symbol' (Chapter 12). 'Existence is blind; in moral terms; futile'.[18] 'There can be no purpose in excess' (Chapter 13). Therefore he believes that there will neither be an end in the future nor has there been any beginning in the past; the only thing that exists in this world is the now — the momentary now.

In Chapter 14 Iwano explains the symbol function. The symbols are in constant movement, and the changes become their life. That is to say, no changes — no life.

Then he moves on to the problem of 'intuition' contra 'concept'. He writes that philosophies and religions have ended in failure because they have given priority to concepts rather than to intuition.

'The moments when Jesus Christ or Shakyamuni *intuitively* received holy illumination were surely grand, but as soon as they came under the illusion or *maya* that they should preach to others, the holy illumination became skeleton-like ... To receive holy illumination simply came to mean to embrace a new illusion.' (Chapter 15).

---

18. This may be compared to Arthur Schopenhauer's '*blinder Wille zum Leben*'. Cf. among others Yoshida Seiichi, op. cit., 286.

At this point, Iwano's attitude to life was 'introvert', but it was later 'extroverted', as he strove for Nietzsche's so-called '*mehr Leben*'. Cf. Ōkubo Tsuneo, *Iwano Hōmei no jidai*, 130-32. Simultaneously he tried to achieve satisfaction of his instincts with the result that his life was increasingly characterised by the idea of 'conquest', expressed in his frequent and fervent controversies, his relations to women (serial monogamy) and his nationalism which took the form of Nipponism. More on this later.

In this respect he goes on to talk about sympathy and mercy:

Sympathy is a reciprocal illusion between imperfect humans, and mercy is a tool with which the weak with their own weaknesses embellish the weakness of other people. We will never get rid of our suffering — pathos — in this purposeless cosmos ... It is only our accidental apprehension of symbols by the means of the intuition which in our pathos can keep the vain creatures that we are, alive.' (Chapter 15)

In the following chapter, Iwano amplifies his theory that the symbols make up the baton of destiny, a baton which leads us nowhere. To him, a symbol is simply an instantaneous manifestation: 'When we grope our way in the dark and cry out for help, we only hear our own voice. Out of necessity, a symbol eats up another symbol, which with the help of great suffering, gives birth to a third symbol. We are the children of such passionate births ... We are really the very spirit of pathos' (Chapter 16).

And finally, he gives a rather dogmatic summary of his theory:

My theory states that nature is the same as spirit, and I do not discern the god from the world. There is nothing for us to search for except the very activity of searching and out of inner necessity, we make the symbols our life. And such a life consists of momentary appearances and disappearances (of the symbols)' (Chapter 17).

In Chapter 18, 'The Holy Body of Semi-Animalism', Iwano describes the background for the name of his theory by referring to the Centaur — the mythical creature which is half horse half man. In the Centaur he saw the following: The one half — the man — is a symbol of *anima* (the soul), whereas the other half — the horse — is a symbol of *the animal*.

But his own Centaur has a clear and transparent body. *Anima* and *the animal* have melted together and now create a *semi-anima/semi-animal* whole. From this Iwano's semi-animalism is born.

He was well aware that the abridgement might cause misunderstandings. Therefore he always thought it necessary to return to the stage at which the theory had been named. He knew very well that any philosophy became dogmatic as soon as it was placed in a system.

4. 'Momentariness' and Iwano Hōmei's Views on Love and Sex

> Verlaine was a man who gave its full value to every moment,
> who got out of every moment all that that moment had to give him.
> It was not always, not often, perhaps, pleasure. But it was energy,
> the vital force of a nature which was always receiving and giving out,
> never at rest, never passive, or indifferent, or hesitating.
>
> Arthur Symons

> Only sexual behaviour has the force to disappoint us enough for us
> to change ourselves and thus be open towards a changing world.
>
> Suzanne Brøgger

Iwano Hōmei's philosophy, or rather world view, was concerned with 'the absolute I' and 'the momentary now'. With momentariness — the idea that 'the absolute I' flares up in 'the momentary now' — as a tool, he tried to account for virtually everything under the sun. The theory, however, was not the product of a metaphysical operation, but rather written out of the experience of his own body.

But where did his theory spring from?

He did not change his views on these issues all his life. This must be because his theory was deeply rooted within him.

In order to clarify what a 'life consisting of momentary appearances and disappearances' is like (Chapter 17), he gives a concrete example:

An area in which the fundamental workings of my mind are clearly expressed, and which we all meet with everyday, is that of love and sex. (Chapter 17)

In the opening of *The Mystic Semi-Animalism*, he compared the theories of Maeterlinck, Emerson and Swedenborg, with a special reference to their views on love. Now he returns once more to the discussion of love and sex. Contrary to the other chapters, in Chapter 17, on 'Love and Sex', Iwano is both spirited and convincing. He is obviously on familiar ground here.

Initially he rejects the general idea of love which is based upon the dualism of body and soul, because it is after all both cryptic and hypocritical. He ridicules platonic love and stresses the fact that 'the culmination of love is the embrace'. He goes on: 'No matter how we interpret it, love remains momentary', and 'like everything else in this world, love is a momentary experience'. On this basis, he formulates the substance of love as follows:

Our sexuality is extremely painful. Because our soul knows this very well, it strives for the one moment in which the sexuality within our breast sends out its mysterious flames, fervently and violently. Hereafter the difference between man and woman is forgotten, and the discrimination between *animal* and *anima* suspended, and finally the climax is achieved. After this moment, even the most wonderful love which has lasted more than a million years, is thrown back into the dark. It is in accordance with this point of view that I call my theory that of momentariness. (Chapter 17)

According to Iwano, the substance of love is found in the process during which a man discovers his sexual impulse and simultaneously experiences the sexual act on a physical as well as on a spiritual level. In such a love/sex relationship, Iwano sees the archetype of all human interrelations.

Seen through his eyes, a belief in eternal love is empty and false, and 'the eternal marriage' consequently impossible. 'Monogamy is only true and credible in the moment of sex', he says (Chapter 17). A family, a marriage or a love without sex is completely different from true love.[19]

Only after comprehending this Chapter, does the reader realise that Iwano criticises the accepted theories of love so fervently in order to lay the groundwork for his own theory on love/sex, and that even his worldview is analogous with his views on love/sex.

His opinions on matters related to society and culture as well as his literary theory were expansions and specifications of his views on love/sex. His philosophical system was thus based solely on this idea of love/sex. Chapter 17 of *The Mystic Semi-Animalism* may be considered the point of departure for, and the core of, Iwano's entire philosophy.[20]

The very fact that Iwano had constructed his epistemology on the awareness and experience of love/sex, enabled him to be exceptionally confident and consequent in the creation of his theory. Furthermore, the fact that he was well-grounded within the field of love and sex, allowed him to reject any criticism aimed at him and his theory, and to endure the derision

19. Because of his theory of semi-animalism, Iwano was known all over Japan, but he was nevertheless totally and fatally misunderstood; he was considered 'bestial' and a helplessly dissolute idler. He claims that the ignorant masses had a similar (wrong) conception of the term 'naturalism'.
20. I share this opinion with Professor Tanizawa Eiichi. Cf. 'Iwano Hōmei no bungei shikō' in *Meiji-ki no bungei hyōron*, 139-63.

with which representatives of normative opinions reacted. No matter how severe the attack, he remained convinced that he was not mistaken. He believed that everybody else had to sense and understand the veracity of his theory on their own bodies. Iwano preferred to consider anyone who claimed not to be sharing his experience as liars.

As we have seen in the above, and contrary to his own beliefs, the distinctness of Iwano's philosophy did not lie in any new discovery, analysis or formulation, but rather in the frankness and directness with which he would talk about his own experience of love/sex and of his observations of the enamoured people he had known. He was a child of nature, and knew nothing of vanity or sophistication. Openness and frankness were his inherited characteristics, and these characteristics were unfortunately closely related to his being both egocentric and thoughtless towards other people. He was an unreserved super-individualist. He was on his own, an outsider, but not one of those that find themselves pushed aside, in the shadow. He was in the light, strong and roaring, but not in the centre where he believed himself to be. In the eyes of others, he was strange and different. But this very fact enabled him to remain free of the restraining forces with which most communities check the artist. Due to his favourable position, he was able to construct his philosophical system undisturbed. Because the distance between the community and himself was rather great, he was able to avoid direct conflict with the surrounding world on the level of consciousness. Identity crises and the like were completely unfamiliar to him. He always remained himself and marched directly towards his goal. Even when at times they were far too frank, his words seemed neither mean nor did they cause aversion in other people. This must be related to his almost naive outspokenness.

Since the very beginning of his career as a writer, Iwano had been a stranger to the so-called general opinion of society, and he was thus spared from experiencing isolation because of his eccentric opinions; he did not have to resist or fight against his surroundings. He could do whatever he pleased without having to fear anyone or anything. This is epitomised by his philosophy of love/sex. However, his almost reckless frankness made him unable to measure the distance between himself and the community he lived in. He was indeed aware that his theory was not accepted by the surrounding world, but he would simply endure the ignorance of the banal mob responsible for this rejection. His theory gained impulse and impetus from its own core alone and as such had no foothold in the arena of the established debate. It lacked both in persuasive powers and in the ability to convince. The theory was indeed energetic and passionate, but nevertheless there was no thoroughgoing thread that would allow the reader to follow his way of thought and to comprehend the theory completely.

His theory was enclosed in a circle. It moved fervently around, and ruined much in order to create something new, but it did not develop any further. It changed its exterior almost incessantly, but it stayed firmly immobile. It could not change in terms of *quality*, because it was not allowed to engage in a creative confrontation with the surrounding world.

Iwano's theory was cultivated in a greenhouse, well protected against various kind of exterior obstacles. Consequently it remained the philosophy of an *outsider*; its destructive energies disappeared into the unknown, and never worked as a true rebellious force against the outside world. His almost monotonous attacks on the so-called general opinion was a kind of narcissism and resulted in an eccentricity, which necessarily prevented him from pursuing and elaborating his own theory. His conviction only led to a verbose self-confidence and ended in unfruitful masturbation. As the structure of the theory was simplified, his area of interest became still more diversified.

After having accounted for the background of the term 'semi-animalism' in Chapter 18, Iwano confronts the question of nation and power. He treats the subject insipidly, and writes something like: 'Power is with the individual who realises himself in one moment.' 'If a nation does not have one person who is able to control its fundamental activity, you might as well consider it dead already' (Chapter 19).

In these naive words, we may actually discern the source of the personality cult and Nipponism that Iwano would later glorify and become deeply involved in. The mechanism at work in Iwano is at this stage familiar to us; he was arrogant and excessively self-confident, and disregarded the majority, as if he suffered from megalomania.

In the following Chapter 'The emotional practice — the key to the mystic', Iwano specifies his activism, first and foremost by attacking Schopenhauer's passive negativism, and later by praising Toyotomi Hideyoshi and Napoleon for their momentariness and blind passions, which were according to Iwano, both idiotic and divine.[21]

---

21. He was a free-thinker and formulated his thoughts in his own way. By semi-animalism he thus intended that the life of man consisted in the animal and active striving of the 'body' and not in the vegetative and passive waiting of the 'soul'. He further defines the idea in this way: Life before death; content before form; real striving before empty loftiness; the brutality of reality before the falseness of civilisation; the real strength of man before the god. *HZ* vol. 15, 109 and 111.

5. Iwano Hōmei's View on Literature/Art and 'the New Naturalism'

> Au sens bergsonien, durer c'est changer, changer comme
> on change en vivant, c'est-à-dire en accumulant un passé
> que l'apport du présent modifie constamment.
> Albert Thibaudet

After having formulated his philosophical system in a rather irrational fashion by the means of varied associations of ideas, Iwano Hōmei finally confronts his own field, that of literature. His idea of literature is expressed as follows:

Literature and art are the most individual and most momentary of activities, both capable of bringing to life the symbolic mystic world which every moment changes blindly and in such grand and profound ways. The essence of literature and art lies in their ability to make the soul of suffering, which is resurrected every moment in order to disappear anew, seem active and alive in the way that Toyotomi Hideyoshi and Napoleon I did. In other words: If only a writer succeeds in making the soul which consumes the 'I', seem active and alive, he does not need to have any goal or ideology, and no allegory, consolation or personality either. (Chapter 21)

In Chapter 21 Iwano also bases his argument on criticism of the then current, fixed literary theories, which either presuppose a certain goal or find a pragmatic function in a literary work. His own literary theory, on the other hand, is rather an expression of his dream of the ideal state of mind in which he may bring to life the vital force which is continuously renewed, and which does not tolerate disturbance from the outside.

But the theory is so narrow in its scope that it could hardly have been used by other writers than himself. As we have seen, the theory was an expansion of his views on love/sex. The theory was indeed unique and provided new perspectives. It was certainly well-suited to his own literature, but did, however, never really move beyond this stage. Iwano had little luck in concretizing and elaborating the theory.

In the same chapter 'On momentary literature', Iwano quite unexpectedly discusses the essence of tragedy.[22] According to Iwano, the most important elements to be included in a play (a tragedy), are 'the blind activity of the

---

22. The occasion was Dr Tanimoto Tomi's article *'Kokugeki no shōrai ikan'* (Where is Japanese drama going?) in *Teikokubungaku*, vol. 12-1, 1905.

various symbols and their collisions with each other'. Also since a play (a tragedy) aims at attaining 'the mysterious ecstasy, which no word may express', 'greater importance should be attached to the actors' 'contemplation' than to the 'character' of the roles. The style, however, must be one of thorough realism.

What kind of play was Iwano, who was himself a dramatist, thinking of?[23]

He writes that his momentary play should mainly consist of soliloquy, and that the greater the protagonist, the more the play should resemble a drama of soliloquy. It may even end as a drama of silence. Iwano terms such a play the 'contemplative tragedy'.[24]

Schopenhauer ranged music as the greatest among the various types of art. This made Iwano want to compare his own symbolist, momentary literary theory with Schopenhauer's theory of music. He draws numerous parallels between the function of language as described in his own theory and the function of sound in Schopenhauer's theory. He motivates this parallel by the fact that his own 'language' as well as Schopenhauer's 'sound' are both symbols which on their own have no purpose.

The reason why Iwano has all of a sudden begun discussing music is that he wishes to emphasise the need for the language of the symbolist tragedy to be rhythmical and sonorous in such a way that it may resound, both physically and psychologically, with the audience.

And finally, he concludes that the future kind of literature, like the symbolist tragedy, must provide neither salvation nor solution, but be full of contemplation and melodious language.[25] It may be interesting to note that in this context he expresses sympathy for Strindberg's 'naturalistic tragedies', *Miss Julie* and *The Father*, which he had read in translation.[26]

Because Iwano tended to base his theory on such indefinable, vague

23. His first serious attempt at fiction was a tragedy *Tama wa mayou getchū no yaiba* (The soul wanders and the dagger flashes in the moonlight, 1894) — a combination of Hamlet and Faust, but taking place in modern Japan. He wrote 14 plays in all. Cf. *HZ* vol. 13.

24. There is a certain analogy with the dramatic theories of Samuel Beckett. In Beckett, however, the reduction of speech is caused by a mistrust in language and the kind of information communicated through language, while the silence in Iwano is due to an 'ecstasy', leaving the speaker speechless.

25. At this point in time, tragedy was identical to poetry to Iwano. Cf. Ōkubo Tsuneo, *Iwano Hōmei ni okeru shi to geki.*

26. Iwano's 'new naturalism' is also called 'naturalistic symbolism'. This highly awkward mixture of two very different movements is due to the fact that the two were introduced almost simultaneously in Japan and that they were both accepted uncritically. Furthermore, Iwano juggled with both and fused them in his theory.

concepts as 'momentary', 'the mystic world', 'changing blindly', etc., he never managed to *develop* his theory in any rational way. It remained in a frozen state, and all he could do to prove its validity was to write one short story after the other. His literary method did not concretise his ideas, but was rather a display of his stubborn insistence. His works received their literary realism, not from the content of the ideas, but from the very reference to them — semi-animalism, momentariness, the philosophy of suffering, and so forth. These references became the characteristics of his work.

In the chapter on *The Anti-Social Male*, we saw how the protagonist of Iwano's novel-series became the representative of his own ideas; the protagonist spoke Iwano's words, acted and preached as he would, but his ideas were not structured within the frame of the novel; they were merely introduced and marked. Iwano was content with seeing his protagonist act within the work, representing his own ideas. He did not attempt a personification of his own ideas or the ideas of others. Consequently, the theory never developed. Everything had been locked in place beforehand.

Actually his literary theory was just as vague as his philosophy. It lacked distinct features which might have made it logically consistent. If anything, it was a slogan, so strong and convincing to Iwano that he could continue his work as a writer undisturbed and with unspoiled enthusiasm. This is not to say, however, that his literary theory was banal or insignificant. It did indeed contain something new, inspiring and valuable. More about this later.

Because Iwano's philosophy and literary theory were taking form during the time when Japanese naturalism was being formulated in theoretical terms, he soon became involved in the great controversies that developed among literary critics. He wrote numerous and diverse articles on the topic, and later, in 1908, published these in the book *The New Naturalism*.

The debates that he had with one literary critic after the other, forced him to go over his literary theory again in order to convince himself (once and for all) of the revolutionary nature of his theory. He was different from all other Japanese naturalistic writers because he united naturalism and symbolism in a most peculiar way and called the result 'the new naturalism' or 'the naturalistic symbolism' (*shizenshugiteki hyōshōshugi*).

Contrary to a couple of years earlier, when he had been far too aggressive in his polemics and criticism, this time he was more discreet and took up a more constructive attitude towards the other critics/writers. So when he criticised the work of other naturalistic writers such as Shimazaki Tōson, Tayama Katai and Masamune Hakuchō, he did not deny the validity of their literary methods nor of their good intentions; he was merely dissatisfied with the lack of resoluteness in their attempts to put their theories into practice.[27]

He also demonstrated his friendly understanding of such critics of the naturalistic school as Hasegawa Tenkei (1876-1940)[28] and Shimamura Hōgetsu (1871-1918),[29] when he commented on their critical writings and encouraged them to modify their, in his eyes, imperfect theories. His attitude was, however, entirely different when he addressed the non-naturalistic writers or academics, such as Natsume Sōseki (1867-1916),[30] Ueda Bin (1874-1916)[31]

27. Cf. among others *Shizenshugi zōgon* (Some words on naturalism, September 1907) and *Sho-hyōka no shizenshugi o hyōsu* (Comments on naturalism by various critics, October 1907) in *Shin-shizenshugi*; in *HZ* vol. 15.

28. Cf. among others *Setsunashugi to seiyoku* (Momentariness and the will to life, April 1908) and *Nikurei gatchi = jiga dokuzon* (The union of body and soul = the I is all that exists), May 1908) in *HZ* vol. 15. Hasegawa Tenkei was known for the claim that a description in a work of fiction had to be scientifically exact. (This happens to resemble Arno Holz's '*konsequenter Naturalismus*', which basically strove for mimesis *ad absurdum*. Cf. Lillian Furst, Naturalism, 40.) After the Russo-Japanese War, however, Tenkei abandoned his scientific demands of fiction. He was one of the leading literary critics of naturalism in Japan. His major work is *Genjitsu bakuro no hiai* (The sad revelation of reality) from 1908.

29. Cf. among others *Nikurei gatchi no jijitsu* (Facts on the union of body and soul, March 1908) and *Fugen* (Additions, September 1908) In *HZ* vol. 15.

   Shimamura Hōgetsu studied aesthetics and began his activity as a literary critic in 1895. His critical work was coloured by religion and symbolism. However, when naturalism was introduced in Japan, he joined the movement and he became its leading character and theorist with the book *Shizenshugi no kachi* (The value of naturalism, 1908). His naturalism was passive and contemplative as opposed to the original French movement which was critical and engaged. It is understandable that he later returned to his own mystical symbolism. When naturalism disappeared from the literary arena, he mainly occupied himself with theatre and established the Geijutsuza Theatre, where he put on plays by Tolstoy, Ibsen, Maeterlinck, Wilde and others.

30. Cf. among others *Bunkai Shigi 2* (My private commentary on the world of letters 2, November 1907) in *HZ* vol. 15.

   Natsume Soseki was one of the most important writers in the Meiji and Taisho periods. His début as a writer of novels was the satire *Wagahai wa neko de aru* (I am a cat, 1905-06). His romanticist works which include *Botchan* (Young man, 1906), formed counterparts to the works of the naturalistic writers. After having recovered from a serious illness, he published a series of masterpieces. They were all written in a realist style, and reflected his fears and his depressed existence. The most important novel among these was probably *Meian* (Light and darkness, 1916) — his last and unfinished novel.

31. Cf. among others *Ibusen-ron shiken* (My view on Ibsen, May 1907) and *Bunkai shigi 4* (My private commentary on the world of letters 4, January 1908) in *HZ* vol. 15.

   Ueda Bin introduced the theories and works of the European symbolist poets into Japan. His collection of translated poems *Kaichōon* (The sound of the sea, the sound of the waves, 1905) was of major importance to modern Japanese poetry. His attitude to literature was highly aesthetic.

and Fujioka Sakutarō (1870-1910).[32] Towards their work and theories he remained almost completely dismissive.

This is not to say that Iwano modified his theory. Not at all. He never accepted the method that Shimamura Hōgetsu employed in his analysis of a writer's relationship with the surrounding world, that is the separation of the subjective and the objective points of view in a creating writer.

The reader must remember that there is no other nature than the 'I'. In short, the essence of literature lies in describing the ardent heart of the 'I'.[33] This is exactly what I call to concretise the living and blind life. Nothing is as realistic as this. The fact that Sodō,[34] Hōgetsu and others (is Tenkei among them?) all presuppose the existence of 'the objective', which has nothing to do with the 'I', and regard it as reality, is a sign of dualism — the division between the things and the soul — a dualism which places the ideal and reality in opposition to one another. The 'I' is neither materialistic nor idealistic; real life is the symbolist (that is, living and blind) life of the monistic 'I'. This is no fantasy at all.[35]

After having removed the foundation for Shimamura Hōgetsu's theory, Iwano puts forward his slogan. Due to its *kōan*-like formulations, this may be called a non-theoretical theory:[36]

The new naturalism is neither an ideal nor a goal. It is not a method either. We are used to believing that nothing can be done without the support of such things as ideals, goals or methods, which all restrict us from the outside. (Nothing conceals the truth of the 'I' as much as this habit of thought.) First and foremost we must break with this habit and then give a concrete form to the actively lived life which still remains within the 'I'. This is the essence of the new naturalism.[37]

Contrary to the eclectic and formalistic theories of Hasegawa Tenkei and

---

32. Cf. *Fujioka hakushi no shintaishiron* (Dr Fujioka's theory on poems in the new form, February 1907) in *HZ* vol. 15. Fujioka Sakutarō was a professor at Tokyo University. His major work was *Kokubungaku zenshi, Heian-chō hen* (The literary history of Japan, the Heian period) from 1906.
33. Iwano uses the word *shinnetsu*, his own neologism, for 'ardent heart'.
34. Sodō is the pseudonym of Ogata Ryūsui (1883-?). Due to his theory that literature should serve the interests of society, he was one of the leading pragmatic literary critics of the time. Today, however, he is almost completely forgotten.
35. Cf. *Bunkai shigi 2*. See note 30 above.
36. *Kōan* is part of a catechism in Zen-Buddhism, and is used as the starting point for meditation.
37. Cf. *Sho-hyōka no shizenshugi o hyōsu*. See note 27 above.

Shimamura Hōgetsu, the core of Iwano's theory was made up of life and the impulse of the 'I' alone.

No matter what the subject of the controversy was, Iwano would always return to this core. This enabled him to liberate his 'I' from the yoke of society. At the same time, however, he lost the point of view from which he could have analysed his 'I''s relationship with the rest of the world. As far as his literary method was concerned, it seems natural that he chose to focus on the 'description of the "I"'.

After all, the essence of art is the description of the 'I'. We must not forget that the 'I' cheers up and dwindles away again every moment without possessing the solution to anything at all. It is so, simply because there is no other more natural way of existence. The things that we usually consider objective, that is, the non-'I', and the truth/falseness, goodness/evil and beauty/ugliness of these things as such, are only part of the material that make up the 'I'.[38]

The only method that Iwano found fitting and useful for the composition of his prose works, was thus the theory of the conscious and limited 'description of the "I"'.

In his writing, Iwano embraced very diverse subjects — the cosmos, the world, the community, man and love. He wanted to destroy the various stereotyped, traditional thoughts, but when it came to literary methods, his philosophy knew no other concrete solution than limiting itself to the 'description of the "I"'.

Iwano's 'philosophy of the moment' was founded upon the consideration of the impulse of the 'I' as absolute and on the idea that the true consciousness of man is found in the moment of love/sex. In its entirety, the philosophy was *not a method*, which might have helped one to recognise and modify the relationship between one's own 'I' and the surroundings, but rather *a decision* which alone aimed at a direct linking of the impulses and actions of the 'I' by renouncing all exterior restrictive forces. Considered in this context, it is a matter of course that Iwano saw the 'description of the "I"' as his most important task.

38. Cf. *Nikurei gatchi = jiga dokuzon*. See note 28 above.

6. Iwano Hōmei's Theory of Narration

> ... the Outsider's business is to find a course of action
> in which he is most himself,
> that is, in which he achieves the maximum self-expression.
> Colin Wilson

When Iwano Hōmei's literary method had crystallised in the form of the 'description of the "I"', he posed himself the task of formulating the method theoretically. As is presumably the case with all other writers, his principle of 'the description of the "I"', was the result of his unconscious rationalisation of innate talents and/or abilities that he had acquired earlier. He did, however, firmly believe that the thesis derived from his philosophical theory. We have already seen the theory of the description of the 'I' take shape in the article *'Gendai shōsetsu no byōshahō'* (Narrative techniques in the modern novel, 1911). He further developed his theory through a series of short essays on the literature of the period. But it was not until 1918 that he published his literary theory about 'monistic narration' in its entirety in an article with the long, ambitious title *'Gendai shōrai no shōsetsuteki hassō o isshinsubeki boku no byōsharon'* (My theory of narration which will renew the idea of the novel today and in the future). The formula was thus completed.

Just as Iwano had had no clear perception of the form in which his idea of 'the description of the "I"' was to find expression, he did not really know what his theory of 'monistic narration' would come to produce, and he had no idea of the consequences at all.

When he explains what 'the monistic narration' is really about, he reveals his almost naive dream:

The subjective point of view, which has temporarily been transferred to one of the characters, and the author's own point of view are two sides of the same coin. The author and the chosen character are undoubtedly different, but the author must not differentiate the two in his own world of ideas. He must neither say, for example: 'Even though I am a moralist, I have purposely made my protagonist a non-moralist', nor 'I am an idealist, but I have portrayed a non-idealist'. Even if he has chosen a non-moralist or a non-idealist as his protagonist, he should describe him in such a precise manner that as a non-moralist or as a non-idealist, he [the character] seems coherent in all details and in harmony with his mood. In this way he can bring out that part of human nature which cannot be fully expressed with the particular words 'moral' and 'ideal', or rather the taste of life (we may also call it the profundity of human nature).[39]

At a first glance, this does admittedly seem a theory of narrative *techniques*, but Iwano himself believed the theory to be so fundamental and revolutionary, that he wrote:

Like Baudelaire's method — to see and depict things from within — was born in France and later renewed poetry around the world, I believe, that gradually as our country develops, my theory of narration will renew the writing of novels throughout the world.[40]

What fundamental principle in the theory could make him think in these terms?

During this period his most important task was to prevent common ideas and stereotyped ways of thought from seeping into his own writing. Rather he hoped to realise the 'description of the "I"', also on the abstract, philosophical level, and to give a literary form to the naked and pure 'I'.

But a serious author takes one or two steps forward and tears the clinging fence of abstractions apart in order to give a concrete form to the harsh realities of life. Just as he must confront his own life as his only possible mode of existence, the author needs to choose and limit himself to one single character in his work on to whom he can transfer his subjective point of view or with whom he can share that point of view. Without employing this method, no author can make his narration free of abstract ideas and explanations.[41]

A removal of 'concepts and explanations' from descriptions in fiction, this was the fundamental motive that made Iwano formulate the theory of monistic narration, and which made him believe that he was Baudelaire's equal. Put differently, Iwano's theory was a peculiar method which allowed a writer to isolate himself definitively from the power of 'concepts and explanations' in his description so that he would keep his 'I' in the purest shape. When he thus worked out his theory of monistic narration as the only

---

39. *Gendai shōrai no shōsetsuteki hassō o isshinsubeki boku no byōsharon*, HZ vol. 10, 555.
40. Ibid., 563.
41. Ibid., 554.

possible method, he immediately considered the theory as revolutionary and constantly renewing.

We may call his attitude both manic and naive. His claim was no doubt exaggerated and almost that of a daydream. But his theory was nonetheless concrete and deep in a special way. His theory about the relationship between a writer and the protagonist of his work, contained eternal truth. This should neither be underestimated nor forgotten.

Theoretically, the theory had many weaknesses and short-comings. The most interesting weakness is probably the fact that Iwano did not confront the question of the relationship between 'viewpoint' and 'direct/indirect speech', in this group we may also include 'the (inner) monologue' of a work of fiction. Such a discussion would literally have revolutionised Japanese literature as well as that of the West.

Iwano had actually already attempted something similar to James Joyce's 'stream of consciousness' or Virginia Woolf's 'narrated monologue'.[42] The peculiarity of the Japanese language which does not clearly discern direct from indirect speech on a grammatical level, prevented him from realizing this. This will be discussed in more detail later.

42. Dorrit Cohn's term. Cf. her 'Narrated monologue: Definition of a fictional style' in *Comparative Literature*, 18, 2, Spring 1966, 97-112.

III. The Creation of the Theory

... narrative literature is the most restless of forms, driven by its imperfections and inner contradictions to an unceasing search for an unattainable ideal. It is this terribly human struggle that makes the study of narrative art the most fascinating of literary studies.

Robert Scholes and Robert Kellogg

1. The Point of Departure

The naturalistic creed demanded 'objective narration' of the author, and 'objective narration' was the main characteristic of naturalism.

In Japan the most important part of the naturalistic school was made up of the supporters of the so-called *heimen-byōsha* theory (the theory of flat narration) which had been formulated by the writer Tayama Katai (1871-1930).

'Flat narration' is a technique in which the author does not focus the narration on any specific point. In other words, the author (narrator) keeps each of the characters in the work at the same distance, and an event is thus experienced equally although differently by all the characters.

However, the method was limited from the beginning. It was intended as an 'objective' technique which would allow the naturalistic writer to describe his 'subjective' relations, often in the form of a modified confession. But as a consequence of this opposition between form and content in flat narration, the writer's relation to the work as a whole tended to become more subjective than objective, despite the seemingly 'objective' character of the method. This happens because the authors comment directly on the characters or events that they describe. The bird's-eye perspective allows them to do so. Consequently, however, the author is drawn to the foreground, and the illusion of objectivity is lost.[1]

Although it was as important a theory as that of flat narration, Iwano Hōmei's idea of *ichigen byōsha* (monistic narration), on the other hand, never received support from anyone but himself, at least not in his lifetime.

---

1. The idea of a theory of flat narration was first introduced in Tayama Katai's essay 'Rokotsunaru byōsha' (Uncovered narration, 1904) and was later formulated as '"Sei" ni okeru kokoromi' (The attempt in the novel 'Life', 1908). It was presented finally in the article 'Byōsharon' (On narration, 1911).

For Iwano's writings, not to mention his 'philosophy', the theory was of immense importance. This is clearly reflected in his literary production. Beginning with the novel-series, Iwano wrote strictly in accordance with his own ideas of narrative technique and developed and expanded the possibilities of the theory through numerous experiments.

Before we look closer at the actual theory in its finished form, we shall make a study of the various phases of its creation. The theory was elaborated over a period of ten years and the record of its development is characterised by one intense controversy after the other with a variety of critics and writers.

2. The Creation

> 'Der Erzähler' ist der Bewertende, der Fühlende, der Schauende.
> Er symbolisiert die uns seit Kant geläufige
> erkenntnistheoretische Auffassung, dass wir die Welt nicht ergreifen,
> wie sie an sich ist, sondern wie sie durch das Medium
> eines betrachtenden Geistes hindurchgegangen ist.
> Käte Friedemann

> For the Japanese, the term [Naturalism] meant a return
> to the early concept of presenting a record of one's own life
> over a period of time, sometimes as brief a span as a day or two,
> often including many years or a whole life time.
> It meant reaffirmation of the centrality of the author in the fiction,
> and the sublimation of all other characters.
> It was material based on life but altered, heightened,
> worked with for artistic ends.
> Marleigh Ryan

2.1. The Prerequisites

Iwano's theory of narration was not completed and given the title 'the theory of monistic narration' until October 1918. But suggestions of how the theory was to develop as well as indications of the tendency towards monistic thinking, are present already at the earliest stages of Iwano's literary career. The very first sign of this is the poem *'Sangai dokuhaku'* (Monologue in three worlds) from 1905.[2]

As we saw in the previous chapter, all of Iwano's theories and ideas

---

2. *MBZ* vol. 71, 3-9.

originated in the theory of 'mystic semi-animalism' (*Shinpiteki hanjū-shugi*). The theory of monistic narration was no exception. In 1906, when he published the book *The Mystic Semi-Animalism*, Iwano was still a poet and a second-rate playwright, and had no plans to formulate a proper theory of narration. *The Mystic Semi-Animalism* and the collection of essays which followed it, *The New Naturalism* (*Shin-shizenshugi*) first and foremost make up his poetics and partly his theory of drama/theatre, but when he wrote them, Iwano was not concerned with the art of prose as such.[3] In the article from 1908, Iwano thus says that the question of narration is one of the last to which he might devote his time.[4]

But when Iwano came upon Whitman's prose poems, and fascinated by the freedom and unlimited possibilities offered by the form of the prose poem, he began to compose poetry in prose.[5]

This soon led to the writing of prose proper. Iwano was searching energetically for a new form for his writing.

After having tried his hand at some *études* in prose,[6] he succeeded in establishing himself as a prose writer in February 1909 with the novel *Tandeki* (Dissolute Living). It was during the writing of *Tandeki* that Iwano was seriously confronted with the question of narrative technique for the first time.

It thus makes good sense for us to begin our analysis by considering the novel *Tandeki* more closely and especially by investigating the circumstances under which it was written.

Two noteworthy events are closely connected to *Tandeki*. The one is the publication of the article '"*Sei*" ni okeru kokoromi' (The attempt in the novel 'Life') by Tayama Katai, Iwano's rival. The article was published in the journal *Waseda bungaku* in September 1908 just after the completion of Iwano's novel in August of the same year. In the article, Katai preached the advantages of his method of 'flat narration'. The second event was the polemics that had arisen concerning the relationship Art/Life and which reached its climax when *Tandeki* came out in February 1909.

As far as Iwano's relationship to the technique of 'flat narration' is

3. To Iwano poetry and drama were of equal value. Cf. Ōkubo Tsuneo, *Iwano Hōmei ni okeru shi to geki*.
4. Cf. '*Nikurei gatchi = jiga dokuzon*' (The union of body and soul = the I is all that exists, May 1908), in *HZ* vol. 15, 355.
5. Cf. Kamei Shunsuke, *Iwano Hōmei no sanbunshi to Hoittoman*.
6. Here we may mention among others the following short stories: '*Geisha Kotake*' (The geisha Kotake, March 1906), '*Hinode mae*' (Before sunrise, April 1908), '*Rōba*' (The old woman, May 1908) and '*Senwa*' (An episode from the war, June 1908).

concerned, he had long been critical of Tayama Katai's work in general. Already in October 1907, shortly after the publication of Tayama Katai's epoch-making short story *Futon* which came out in the journal *Shinshōsetsu* in September, Iwano criticised him rather severely and accused him of 'still imagining Nature as being exterior to us', instead of recognising that 'the essence of naturalism should consist in the "I"'s complete awareness of itself in every moment, that is in its mood'[7] and that 'this is why we made demands for a new naturalism'.[8]

While Iwano collected his various essays and published them as *The New Naturalism* in October 1908, Tayama Katai completed his novel *Sei* (Life), which had been appearing in instalments in the newspaper *Yomiuri shinbun* since April of the same year.

Iwano made ironical comments on the novel, and announced that he did indeed find it a 'flat' novel. He pointed to a specific example from Chapter 26; a scene in which the protagonist's mother lies mumbling on her deathbed, surrounded by her family. The text says: 'The mystery of the world beyond moved the hearts of those present.' Iwano did not appreciate the expression. He wrote: 'It is too abstract. You can only talk about the mystery of the world beyond, if you discern art from life, and the "I" from the non-"I".'[9]

In the same article, he identifies his own work as 'literature of action' (*jikkō-bungei*) and goes on to say that 'it is not just naturalistic on the level of narration, in the way that Mr [Shimamura] Hōgetsu and Mr [Tayama] Katai may believe, but also as far as the author's relationship [to the surrounding world] is concerned.'[10]

Prior to the publication of *Tandeki*, Iwano had advanced the theory of 'the literature of action', which was basically founded upon his monistic conception of body/soul. The theory was put forward as an alternative to that of flat narration, despite the fact that the latter theory was really concerned with narrative techniques.

This was the background for the publication of *Tandeki*. Even though

7. In the essay '*Boku no yōgorei*' (An example of my way of using words of foreign origin), Iwano explains that he writes 'mood' without translating it into Japanese because he finds no equivalent term in Japanese. He furthermore notes that 'mood' means something similar to 'the way of being of the I'. Cf. *HZ* vol. 18, 105-7.
8. Cf. '*Sho-hyōka no shizenshugi o hyōsu*' (Comments on naturalism by various critics, October 1907), in *HZ* vol. 15, 252-59.
9. Cf. '"*Sei*" *no hyō*' (Review of 'Life', December 1909), in *HZ* vol. 18, 58-60.
10. Cf. '*Jikkō-bungei to dekadan-ron*' (On the literature of action and decadence, February 1909 — March 1910), in *HZ* vol. 18, 90. Shimamura Hōgetsu (1871-1918) was one of the leading critics and playwrights of naturalism.

Tandeki and *Futon* deal with a similar theme, the methods employed in the two novels are very different.

Tayama Katai, however, wrote an appreciatory review of Iwano's *Tandeki*, at least in February 1909,[11] but in June of the same year he wrote as follows:

The more a work of fiction is related to the ideals of its author — ideals such as those nourished by most men of action: that society should be like this or like that or that the 'I' wishes to be like this or like that —, the more difficult it becomes to reach the aim of narration. This is where the artist differs from the man of action.[12]

It is impossible to know with certainty whether Tayama Katai intended this as a direct criticism of Iwano or not, but there is no doubt that the essay made the debate about art/action reach its climax.[13]

On the one side we find the 'orthodox' naturalistic writers with Tayama Katai and Shimamura Hōgetsu in the lead. They divided art from life and favoured a so-called 'objective' and contemplative attitude towards the surrounding world in their writings. Because of the growing interest in the theory of flat narration and because the debate about art/life (action) coincided with the publication of *Tandeki*, Iwano could not ignore the debate. He was soon involved in the discussions of narrative techniques and stances, a debate in which he could speak as the author of the theory of 'the literature of action', in which art is made equal to life (action). Thus we find Iwano on the other side of the battlefield, all alone, but eager to fight.

During the debate, Hasegawa Tenkei (1876-1940) criticised Iwano's theory of 'the literature of action' with the following words:

According to the theory of Mr [Iwano] Hōmei, art is identical to action; in other words: the actions that are described in a work of fiction are of a kind that the artist [writer] practises in his world of ideas ... his theory can only apply to a minor part of the art [of literature], for instance to lyric writings.[14]

Some months later, in February 1910, Tenkei elaborated his criticisms of Iwano in the article 'Jikobunretsu to seikan' (The separated 'I' and contemplation). He claimed that two major types of the 'I' were developing in modern Japanese literature: 'the confessing I' and 'the contemplative I'.

11. In the column 'Hyōron no hyōron' (A criticism of criticisms) in the journal *Bunshō sekai*. Quoted in Wada Kingo, *Ichigen-byōsharon no seiritsu*, 127.
12. Ibid. As always Tayama Katai chooses his words with little clarity and much ambiguity.
13. Cf. Hirano Ken, *Geijutsu to jisseikatsu* in the *Shinchōbunko*-edition, 1964, 8 ff.
14. In the journal *Taiyō*, August 1909. Quoted in Wada, 128.

He considered Tayama Katai a characteristic representative of the latter group, and Iwano, the author of *Tandeki*, a typical example of a writer employing the 'confessing I'. Furthermore he claimed that Iwano had never practised contemplation and that his confessing 'I' 'was still coloured by old-fashioned romanticism.'[15]

Iwano, the theorist behind 'the new naturalism', could not disregard such criticism. He responded immediately with these words:

No matter whether [Tayama] Katai is inclined towards contemplation and I towards confession, I want us to consider which of the two represents the most profound and genuine attitude; the contemplative non-'I' or the destructively confessing 'I'? ... The so-called 'confessing' attitude allows for a deeper self-awareness.[16]

To Iwano the superiority of his own attitude was obvious.

After having made his début as a novelist with *Tandeki*, Iwano received increasingly concrete and detailed reviews of his short stories, and as the criticism came to focus still more on his narrative technique, he was forced to defend his 'attitude' in theoretical terms. This is not to say, however, that he considered any changes or revisions of his technique. He merely tried to give it the shape of a theory, that is of a systematised whole.

In the preface to *Hōrō* (Wandering) from 1910, the first novel of the novel-series, Iwano writes:

... ideas and illusions which derive from reality, make up the major parts of our lives. If we do not accept this premise, the so-called flat narration (yes, I do admit that in some cases this method may suffice) will often lead to a banal, or rather, meaningless description of useless details. We are already familiar with some such instances. Naturalism should not content itself with the banality of 'objective narration'. Unfortunately far too many prose works do not have the depth that we find in the work of Andrejev or Ibsen, not to mention the novels of Zola. But what is described should be a real and living life, filled with ideas and illusions. I shall leave it to my readers to decide whether such a life has really found expression in this novel [Hōrō] in a genuine way. In any case, I have written the novel with the same attitude as when I wrote *Tandeki*.[17]

The explanation that Iwano offers in the above is not yet concrete. He merely writes that he has preserved his former 'attitude'. But the narrative technique

---

15. In *Taiyō*, February 1910, quoted in Wada, 128.
16. Cf. '*Jikkō-bungei to dekadanron*' in *HZ* vol. 18, 92.
17. *MBZ* vol. 71, 64. The preface is dated May 22 1910. Leonid N. Andrejev (1871-1919) is a Russian novelist and playwright.

in *Hōrō* became the object for multiple analyses and criticisms, and this inevitably made Iwano work seriously on his theory of narration.

In September 1910 a collective review of *Hōrō* was published in the journal *Waseda bungaku*, no. 58.[18] The group of reviewers was made up of Masamune Hakuchō (1879-1962), Yoshie Kogan (1880-1940), Katagami Tengen (1884-1928) and Sōma Gyofū (1883-1950). Among the contributions, Yoshie Kogan's article is the most interesting. He approaches the question of Iwano's narrative technique in an analytical way, making the following three points:

1. ... In the novel, Mr Iwano ... also attempts to describe the ideas and illusions of a single character. To this end he uncritically employs the technique of explanatory narration, despite the fact that writers have up to now been advised against the use of this method. One may wonder whether this method is a necessary means for the description of the characters' serious [social] background ...
2. ... Even in those instances in which a character's actions or opinions may be expressed by the mere rendering of his movements or words, his [Iwano's] narration is imperfect. As a compensation, the author has added his own explanatory remarks. Such explanations are an indication of a lacking narration.
3. ... Under certain circumstances it may be possible to describe the idea of a character separately in a novel, but it is both preferable and more effective to express the ideas or illusions of the character concretely through his actions. Otherwise the character's actions and his ideas or illusions become separated and lose touch ... But in this novel, *Hōrō*, we find an action on the one side and on the other side the idea of the energetic and living momentariness is described as an attempt at explaining or providing the reasons for the action.[19]

Yoshie Kogan's review has evidently been written on the basis of Iwano's preface to *Hōrō*. His choice of words bears witness to this. But it is more important to note that Yoshie has taken the question of explanation/narration as the point of departure for his review. This is the very question that will later make Iwano construct his theory of narration.

Almost simultaneous with the collective review of *Hōrō* is the article 'Byōsha no daizai to byōsha no taido' (The subject and attitude of narration) published in *Tokyo Asahi shinbun* by Chirō, the pseudonym of Abe Jirō (1883-1959).[20] The author of the article does not mention the author of *Hōrō* by name, but there can be no doubt that he is addressing Iwano. He explains his intentions with the article as follows: 'I wish to correct the confused views of art [literature] in our country by pointing to the fact that the contents of

18. *KBHT* vol. 3, 438-41.
19. Ibid., 438-39.
20. Dated September 30 and October 1 1910. Cf. *KBHT* vol. 3, 357-60.

art should be designated by a narrative attitude and a point of view.' And after having distinguished the subjective attitude from the objective one, he writes:

Seen from the point of view of orthodox art, art is concerned with contemplation and description, but not with making claims. The one who claims that an artist should always be the spokesman for the society which he is describing and should put his claims into practice in the real world, misunderstands something and overestimates himself; at least he is seriously confused.[21]

But, 'when all comes to all', he continues, 'contemplation is an action which takes place in the mind. When you choose your material, a work of art based upon that material cannot possibly be created, unless you manage to somehow find some value in it.' From this Chirō infers that:

The question of the material for description and action has a direct relation to the primary question of morality. A work of art which expresses opinions that contradict common sense with regards to the question of the subjects of description and action, will necessarily be persecuted by common sense.[22]

On this background, Iwano wrote the article '*Boku no sōsakuteki taido o akirakanisuru*' (I make my attitude towards the writing of novels clear, December 1910), in which he responded to the criticism that had taken its point of departure in a comparison of his *Hōrō* to Tayama Katai's *Futon*.[23] First and foremost he expresses his disappointment with his opponents' wrong estimation of *Hōrō* in the following way:

When you say that the author of *Hōrō* is more sentimental than the author of *Futon*, this is probably due to your having interpreted my attitude [in the novel] as an ordinary confession ...'

His further counter-criticism is divided into eight points. The sections concerned with the theory of narration may be summarised as follows:

1. The author has felt no vulgar compassion for the novel's protagonist, contrary to what is the case in Tayama Katai's *Futon*. The author is critical and does not

21. Ibid., 359.
22. Ibid.
23. The article is written in the form of a letter, but it is not clear to whom it is addressed. Cf. *HZ* vol. 18, 107-11.

write in a way that may lead the reader to see the protagonist as a marionette epitomising the ideas of the author.

2. Your criticism that among the novel's characters only the description of Hokken is successful, is not correct. Both the protagonist and Hyōhō have been described in a rather satisfactory manner.

3. You reprove me for thinking too much of myself and for being exaggeratedly self-confident, but as far as my work of literary criticism is concerned, I have good reasons for trusting my theory, since it is indeed original. As far as *Hōrō* is concerned, I have taken a critical stance towards the protagonist and not boasted of my thoughts.

4. I have criticised the protagonist sufficiently. Let me make it clear that the protagonist is not [Iwano] Hōmei himself.

5. When you register the weakness of the protagonist's philosophy, you mistake him for the author. The author does indeed criticise the protagonist and his weak philosophy. And it is in this criticism that the philosophy of Hōmei [the author] is expressed.

This is rather a modest tone for criticism written by Iwano. The major points made in the article are that *Hōrō* is not a vulgar novel of confession and that the protagonist is not identical to the author. This brief answer may be considered a general answer to all the criticisms that had so far been aimed at Iwano and his work.

At the very end of the article, Iwano writes: 'My article '*Gendai-shōsetsu no byōshahō* (Narrative techniques in the modern novel) will soon be published in *Bunshō sekai* [a journal].[24] I hope that you will read it.'

So *Bunshō sekai* was to be the scene for a more systematic elaboration of Iwano's ideas concerning narration and for the first formulation of his narrative technique as a theory.

Iwano's theory of narration thus needed the prerequisites that we have considered in the above, as the seeds from which it might grow.

1.2.2. The First Phase

'*Gendai shōsetsu no byōshahō*' was published in *Bunshō sekai* in February 1911. It was written as a counter-criticism and the aim of the article was to defend the narrative technique that Iwano had employed in the novels *Tandeki* and *Hōrō*.

In the beginning of the article, Iwano evaluates all the critical essays in which criticism has been aimed at him. He claims that they are meaningless since the authors behind the essays have not comprehended his art. At the

24. Dated December 1910. Cf. *HZ* vol. 10, 489-505.

same time he aims severe criticism at the disrespect that other naturalistic writers show for the techniques of writing. He also reproves them for stamping their narration with a careless audience-like attitudes.

The ordinary naturalistic authors claimed that a writer should distance himself from his own subjective viewpoints, but Iwano could not accept this opinion at all:

One feels like asking what this 'subjective point of view' is. It can hardly be identical to the authorial I? ... is it at all thinkable that the authorial 'I' should not appear at the surface of a work of fiction? ... the one who hopes to avoid that this happens, might as well quit writing, if I am allowed to express my true opinion.[25]

With this standpoint, Iwano rejected Tayama Katai's works *Futon* and *Sei* as well as Shimazaki Tōson (1872-1943)'s *Hakai* (The broken commandment, 1906) and *Haru* (Spring, 1908), which had all been written with the method of flat narration without any explicit demonstrations of the authorial 'I'. On the other hand, he appreciated Masamune Hakuchō's novel *Rakujitsu* (The setting sun, 1909) and his short stories '*Bikō*' (The quiet light, 1910) and '*Yūjō*' (Friendship, 1910).

Iwano writes further:

The world of letters of today has been confused by the insufficiently developed or misunderstood theory of objectivity, and it forgets to consider what we should do in practise about the subjective opinion. If an author loses his subjective attitude, he is in danger of working merely with meaningless technique ... The authorial 'I' must be explicit throughout the novel.[26]

Iwano believes that the value of a work of fiction is determined by the beliefs of its author, and that this is the very foundation upon which the theory of 'action-is-identical-to-art' should be based.

Without a serious writer's use of a subjective point of view, a genuine description of life is unthinkable. The more serious and grand the writer's subjective point of view is, the more his superficial narrative technique and irrelevant experiences will be destroyed from the inside, and this will result in the birth of a proportionately serious and grand literary work. I call such a subjective point of view — which is, by the way, more important than the question of a writer's objective attitude — the destructively subjective point of view (*hakaiteki shukan*) ... In the literary world of

25. Ibid., 492.
26. Ibid., 497.

today, nobody, not even by utilising a sharp mind, is yet able to implement the destructively subjective point of view completely.[27]

This is how Iwano ends his article. The most interesting point to be made regarding the article is that he is still talking about 'attitude' and not discussing concrete problems of narration. He evidently rejects such discussions seeing them as 'working merely with meaningless technique'.

Iwano's assertion of 'the destructively subjective point of view' remained the trademark of his theory. The theory of 'objective' narration, on the other hand, with Tayama Katai's 'flat' narration in the foreground, was a theory of narrative '*technique*'. The one theory was concerned with 'attitudes' and the other with 'techniques'. There was no chance that these theories might intersect. But Iwano considered nothing impossible. He was convinced that he could unite the two theories. Even though he insisted upon the advantages of his 'destructively subjective point of view', his work was not to be a simple subjective literature; on the contrary, he intended it to become the literature of 'the new naturalism', that is a literature capable of fulfilling the naturalistic creed's demand for objectivity. Debating with the theorists of 'objective' narration thus rendered two things evident to Iwano. Firstly, his 'destructively subjective point of view' had to function in an objective way, and secondly, his theory of 'attitude' would in some way or other have to be applicable to the technical field of writing as well. He realised that he had to solve these two problems in order for his theory to work and for him to be able to develop it further.

In February 1911, the month when the above-mentioned article was published, the critic Maeda Akira (1879-1961) published his review of Iwano's short stories in the journal *Taiyō*. Without having had the opportunity to read Iwano's article, Maeda reviewed Iwano's two short stories, which had both been published in January; that is 'Tsuneko' (Tsuneko, published in *Mita bungaku*) and 'Fumikiriban' (The flagman, published in *Shūsai bundan*), with the following words:

Both the events and the characters are described as the author has interpreted them; this is exactly where we find the uniqueness of his subjectivity. But his continuous insistence upon absolute egoism (*jiga-dokuson*), makes me believe that an objective narration will necessarily be meaningless in the end. For this reason I do not understand why he supports naturalism, whose only demand is that of objective

27. Ibid., 499 and 505.

narration ... In his short stories there are lots of the 'explanations' that naturalistic writers loathe.[28]

This is a severe criticism of Iwano who had declared himself a 'new' naturalistic writer. He immediately retorted in the column 'Danpengo' (Fragments) in the March issue of the journal *Shūsai bundan* with the following words:

The destructively subjective point of view which is based upon my theory of absolute egoism, cannot be separated from the personality of a writer, who is reproducing objective facts the way that they are.[29]

Maeda Akira's next step was the article 'Shunki bundan no ichibetsu' (An overview of our world of letters this spring) in the April issue of the journal *Bunshō sekai*. Maeda Akira reconsidered the question of 'the destructively subjective point of view' in a direct criticism of Iwano's above-mentioned article 'Gendai shōsetsu no byōshahō'.

The question is whether his so-called destructively subjective point of view allows for a copying of objective things as they are at all ... According to his theory of absolute egoism, all objective things exist only as material for the subjective point of view. This is to say that all objective things exist only when they have been modified by the subjective point of view. This again implies that objective things do not exist in any original state. But how are we then supposed to copy them the way they are? He has addressed me with the words: 'According to him and others, objectivity lies in the limiting of one's restricted subjective point of view (shōshukan). But I have avoided using it [the restricted subjective point of view] in my works as far as possible.' But to avoid something is a conscious action. Without him realising it himself, Mr Iwano's restricted subjective point of view has found its way into his destructively subjective point of view, even though he does not want to face this. His restricted subjective point of view works in the very area where he cannot deliberately avoid it. All his works bear evidence of this.[30]

This is very severe criticism and Iwano necessarily made retort. This he did in an article in the newspaper *Yomiuri shinbun* under the headline 'Busshitsuteki byōsharon o nanzu' (I criticise the materialistic theory of narration), on May 23-25 1911:

28. Quoted in Wada, 135.
29. Ibid.
30. Ibid., 136.

The subjective point of view that he discusses is opposed to the materialistically objective point of view. But seen with the eyes of a freely thinking and serious man, the various objective points of view include not only the materialistically objective point of view, but also the spiritually objective view. Furthermore, we find an objective point of view in which matter and spirit or body and soul are united. Because this 'united' objective point of view is identical to the destructively subjective point of view, it cannot be separated from the personality of the author, as long as he incarnates his own absolute egoism. The one who has not understood this, only understands half of my theory, and the result is a terrible misunderstanding. This goes for his review of my play *Ma no yume* (The demonic dream) too. He thinks that the protagonist represents the author and his beliefs. But since the protagonist exists, may it not then be considered a fact that he [the protagonist] 'considers other people to be formalists and rejects them all', the way he does in the play.[31]

According to Iwano's explanation, the restricted subjective point of view, which Maeda Akira accused him of having employed unawares in the play, is really the subjective point of view of the protagonist and for this reason Iwano believes that he has succeeded in maintaing objectivity in the work.

Iwano's theory is indeed valid and he meets no particular problems as long as the protagonist is in the third person ('he/she'), but when the protagonist has been modelled on the author, the beliefs of the two necessarily overlap. In these cases it becomes difficult and even illogical to discern the protagonist from the author.

At that time Iwano did not admit that his theory of the 'united' objective point of view had defects. On the contrary, he even dared give a sharp answer to Maeda Akira's sarcastic comment to Iwano's short story 'Baka to onna' (A fool and a woman, April 1911) in which Iwano described the psychology of a bull. Maeda Akira had written: 'It seems that the destructively subjective point of view will even allow us to gain insight into the mind of a bull!'[32] Iwano's answer was quite simple:

I do not mind accepting his sarcasm. As far as knowledge is concerned, there is no doubt a big difference between people and animals, but if we consider their appetite

31. The same paragraph was, with minor corrections, included in Iwano's great essay 'Setsuna-tetsugaku no kensetsu' (The construction of the philosophy of momentariness) from 1915. The essay was published as a book in 1920. This quotation is from the revised edition, part 3, Chapter 5, section 2, in *HZ* vol. 17, 153-54. The play *Ma no yume* was published in the journal *Mita bungaku* in April 1911.
32. Maeda Akira's words are quoted in Iwano's article 'Busshitsuteki byōsharon o nanzu' (2), published May 24, 1911. It is not known for certain where and when Maeda Akira's essay was published. The quotation is taken from *NKBT* vol. 22, 181.

for life, there is no difference. If this was not true, a male writer would not be able to describe women, and a female writer describe men.[33]

This was a crude formulation. Iwano later realised this and revised his claim in section five of the article '*Gendai shōrai no shōsetsuteki hassō o isshinsubeki boku no byōsharon*' (My theory of narration which will renew the idea of the novel today and in the future) from October 1918.[34]

But apart from the erroneous formulation, Iwano's perception of the destructively subjective point of view shows an aspect of his future theory of monistic narration.

Almost simultaneously with this debate, Tayama Katai published his own theory of narration in the article '*Byōsharon*' (On narration) in the journal *Waseda bungaku* in April 1911. Here he discusses Iwano's novel *Hōrō* and comments as follows:

That the protagonist has a positive attitude towards himself and his actions is all very well, but is it not too naive or even comical that the author himself relates positively to the action of the protagonist and even tries to assign great importance to it?[35]

Tayama Katai also criticised Iwano for not being free from subjective narration in *Hōrō*. Iwano, who was provoked to answer to the criticism, formulated his retort as a supplement to the above-mentioned answer to Maeda Akira in '*Busshitsuteki byōsharon o nanzu*' in *Yomiuri shinbun*. He considered Tayama Katai's 'flat narration' a theory of materialistic narration and elaborated on the criticism as follows:

When Mr [Tayama] Katai refuses to accept it [my narrative technique], because I 'relate positively' [to my protagonist], he merely intends to say that I do not write in a materialistic way. My narration is not flat, but three-dimensional. If it is not three-dimensional, it is at least 'united'. What I have described is what has been perceived and registered by my destructively subjective point of view, but I have not shown any special consideration for other characters than the protagonist himself, and not for other values either. As a proof of this, I may refer you to the scene in which the protagonist is unable to motivate his 'united' point of view and immediately invents an awkward explanation. It is most probable that the author has had a similar experience himself, but it is erroneous to believe that this is the justification or philosophy of the author. But these things cannot really be under-

33. Ibid.
34. The article is translated in its entirety in the following chapter:
35. Cf. *KBHT* vol. 3, 380.

stood if they have not been considered more closely from a three-dimensional perspective or at least from a 'flat' perspective which is not materialistic.[36]

This was a vague formulation, but what Iwano intended to say was basically that the writing 'I' (the author) knew more than the written 'I' (the protagonist) did.

Even though we may here already sense the beginnings of Iwano's theory of monistic narration, he was not yet working on anything concrete within this field. The only theoretical 'weapon' that he possessed at this time was, as we have already noted on more than one occasion, 'the destructively subjective point of view'. But his argumentation was not always logical and certainly not convincing or specific.[37]

Iwano did indeed answer almost all criticisms aimed at him, but he had difficulties communicating with his opponents because of his choice of words. His special language was by the way seen as an expression of his 'dynamic' thinking.

2.3. The Second Phase

Iwano did not proceed to develop the theory further immediately. Instead he chose to expand it by employing it in his criticism of the work of other writers.

He began with a severe criticism of Shimazaki Tōson's short story *'Gisei'* (The victim) in the article *'Shōsetsuka toshite no Shimazaki Tōson-shi'* (Mr Shimazaki Tōson, the novelist) in the journal *Waseda bungaku* in July 1911.[38] Iwano regarded Shimazaki Tōson's suggestive narration as exaggeratedly careful and ambiguous.

But three months later, Tokuda Shūkō (1876-1944, also known under the pseudonym Chikamatsu Shūkō) responded to Iwano's criticism of Shimazaki Tōson, and wrote: 'It seems to me that the essence of the theory of technique which is mentioned in Mr [Iwano] Hōmei's 'Criticism of [Shimazaki] Tōson'

36. Cf. *HZ* vol. 17, 153. Also see footnote 31 in the above.
37. In the preface to his novel *Hatten*, Iwano plainly noted Tayama Katai's reaction to his formulation as follows: 'Tayama Katai said to me: 'All you say is that we should describe things in a profound and sharp manner, but that is not understandable enough. You should probably explain yourself a bit more concretely.' Cf. *MBZ* vol. 71, 167.
38. The short story was published in the journal *Chūōkōron* in January and April and was later used as the second part of the novel *Ie* (The Family, 1911).

and which I do, incidentally, estimate highly, and [Tayama] Katai's 'On narration' are really concerned with the same matter.'[39]

Iwano responded as follows, as always employing and discerning between the materialistic theory of narration and the unified-body-and-soul theory of narration:

There is a basic difference between the insincere attitude of a writer who leaves it to his reader to guess the rest of the action [in a short story], and another writer's efforts to describe life as such in the form of a suggestion. To this we may add that a writer can only manage the former project by the means of a technique alone, whereas he can only fulfil the latter when his thoughts have been annexed to his theory.[40]

Iwano's next article, '*Byōsha sairon*' (On narration once again) in the journal *Waseda bungaku* in February 1912 was, as far as his procedure is concerned, a repetition of his criticism of Shimazaki Tōson. This time he analysed Tokuda Shūsei's novel *Kabi* (Mould) which had been published in the newspaper *Tokyo Asahi shinbun* in August-November 1911. But apart from Iwano's indication of the fact that the novel was written as an autobiographical work with a third-person protagonist, there is nothing in the article to suggest that Iwano's theory had evolved.[41]

Analogous to these theoretical essays, Iwano wrote the novels *Dankyō* (The broken bridge, 1911) and *Hatten* (Development, 1911-12) to complete his big project, the five-volume novel. When *Hatten* was finished, Tayama Katai reviewed it immediately in the essay '*Chikagoro yonda shōsetsu ni tsuite no kansō*' (On the novels I have read recently) in the journal *Bunshō sekai* in May 1912 with the following words:

In *Hatten* there is no difference between the author and the protagonist. Also emotions are described in a way that makes only the feelings of the protagonist seem genuine. All other characters, especially the ones who oppose the protagonist, have been treated cooly as if he [protagonist] has not really noticed them. The author does not even seem to have considered the situation of Chiyoko (the protagonist's wife).

Therefore the strong emotions and severe sufferings of the protagonist and his girlfriend have been expressed very well, but presumably these are simply the

---

39. In the article '*Heimen-byōsha no oshie wa ikanaru han'i made junpō subekika*' (To what degree the teachings of flat narration should be followed) in the journal *Shinchō* in October 1911. Quoted in Wada, op. cit., 139.

40. In '*Danpengo*' (Fragments) in *Waseda bungaku*, November 1911, ibid.

41. Cf. *HZ* vol. 10, 518.

emotions that the writer himself has experienced, and they can all be expressed in terms such as: 'I suffered terribly under this' or 'It tormented me'. The style has not yet reached the stage which might permit one to survey all of humanity and from which both good and bad are surpassed. For these reasons the novel does not have the value that might have made us consider it a work of art. 'The subjective point of view [of the author] has flowed out, but nothing is left!' — after reading the novel my mind has been dominated by such disappointment.

I hardly need to point out that one should not distance oneself from genuine emotion, but I find it quite problematic to treat other characters [in the novel] from the point of view of one single character only. To describe Chiyoko's ugly figure simply by reporting that her figure is ugly, is a so-called 'explanation', and it can hardly be thought that her figure has in this way been described correctly.[42]

This was all centred around an issue which had been discussed several times already, but because it touched the very core of Iwano's theory of narration, he could not remain silent. Since the article had furthermore been published just before *Hatten* was to come out in book form (July 1912), it provided Iwano with an excellent occasion for counter-criticism. First and foremost, he formulated his defence in the preface to the book *Hatten*. After having once more boasted of the advantages of the destructively subjective point of view and the superiority of unified-body-and-soul narration, he stressed the objectivity of the novel. Since Tayama Katai in his criticism had compared Iwano to Shimazaki Tōson among others, Iwano wrote as follows:

In my novel there exists the required coherence, despite the occurrence of 'some passages which remind the reader of a diary', and in contrast to [Shimazaki] Tōson's filmic short stories which contain incoherent diary notes that have inappropriately been inserted here and there. The 'singing passages' in my novel clearly express the mood of the characters described. Contrary to this use, the corresponding passages in Tōson's work convey the author's sentimentalism, which has been cunningly masked and hidden.[43]

Furthermore he reacted with fury to Tayama Katai's claim that 'also emotions are described in a way that makes only the feelings of the protagonist seem genuine' with a: 'Nonsense!'. He himself believed that the emotions had been 'described very well'.[44]

The most important element of this debate was, however, that Iwano had, without realising it, received a good tip from the part of Tayama Katai's

42. Wada, op. cit., 140-41.
43. *MBZ* vol. 71, 168.
44. Ibid.

criticism which was concerned with certain passages in Iwano's novel being mere 'explanation' and not description.

With this background, Iwano concentrated on the question of description/explanation and produced the following rather schematic outline:

According to [Tayama Katai's] one-sided, materialistic theory of narration, narration is not an immediate suggestion of the entire content (though this is genuine narration), but a superficial modification produced with the use of words such as 'like'. The latter identification we better call an 'explanation'.

There are thus four stages into which the ways of expression in fiction may be divided: (1) Explanatory explanation (The domain of the old school). (2) Explanatory narration ([Shimazaki] Tōson's abstract, contemplative narration). (3) Narrated explanation (Tayama Katai's materialistic flat narration belongs here.) (4) Narrated narration (We find techniques similar to this in certain of [Masamune] Hakuchō's short stories and in [Tokuda] Shūsei's *Kabi*.) Whether a narration is sharp or serious, naturally depends on the choice of style, but no sentimentalism is needed [to obtain it]. And I believe that my unified-body-and-soul narration belongs to group 4. (I shall discuss this theory of the four styles more closely elsewhere.)[45]

This preface was dated June 5, 1912, and as Iwano himself had announced, it was developed further in the next article '*Shōsetsu-hyōgen no yon kaidan*' (The four ways of expression in fiction), which was published in the journal *Bunshō sekai* in July the same year. In this article Iwano's theory of narration was, for the first time, formulated quite theoretically (however formalistically rather than systematically), and as we have already seen, this formulation had its point of departure in Tayama Katai's criticism of the 'explanatory' narration in *Hatten*.

Iwano had written '*Gendai shōsetsu no byōshahō*' (Narrative techniques in the modern novel) along with the novel *Hōrō*, but this time, that is after the publication of *Hatten*, he had to publish a more specific theory of narration. This became the article '*Shōsetsu-hyōgen no yon kaidan*'.

2.4. The Third Phase

Almost simultaneous to Tayama Katai's criticism of *Hatten* is the novelist Nakamura Seiko (1884-1974)'s article '*Byōsha no igi*' (The significance of narration, June 1912) in the journal *Bunshō sekai*. In the article Nakamura

---

45. Ibid.

Seiko compared Iwano and Tayama Katai. For this reason, Iwano formulated his article '*Shōsetsu-hyōgen no yon kaidan*' as an answer to Nakamura Seiko's criticism which had taken the following two issues as its point of departure:

1. A narration must be sensuous.
2. An author cannot describe his psychological life as such; he must use either explanations, comparisons or symbols.[46]

It remains a mystery how Iwano and Nakamura Seiko were able to communicate at all, since they both made use of such vague expressions. However, Iwano responded as follows to Nakamura Seiko's criticism: First of all he refers to the mistake that Nakamura Seiko makes when claiming that narration should be sensuous, and points out that 'sensing something is perception, awareness and will to life, all at once'.[47] Iwano believes that narration can also describe what happens on the levels of awareness and will of life. As far as Seiko's second point is concerned, Iwano believes that the mental life of a philosophically disposed human being (here Iwano is referring to the protagonists of his novels) can be '*described*' through '*concrete*' expression without the description turning into an explanation.[48] And he goes on: 'The proper use of symbols in the new literature has nothing to do with "indirect description". I wonder whether the value of metaphors and symbols does not lie in the very fact that they do not create any indirect relationship [between things] as comparisons do?'[49]

According to Iwano, the characteristic traits of styles 2 and 3 [explanatory narration and narrated explanation respectively] are their use of 'comparison', whereas style 4 concentrates on metaphorical and /or symbolical expressions. Hereafter Iwano concludes by identifying the reason for Nakamura Seiko's having misunderstood his theory:

Even though I achieve what he calls 'an explanation of a psychological life' in a concrete narration which penetrates things, it seems that my narration has nevertheless been perceived as an explanation. This because of his erroneous theory of narration which is defined materialistically.[50]

---

46. Wada, op. cit., 143.
47. Cf. *HZ* vol. 10, 524-25.
48. Ibid., 520-21.
49. Ibid.
50. Ibid.

The debate did not cease here. In September 1912 Nakamura Seiko published the article *'Iwano Hōmei-shi ni kotau; yo ga shōchōshugi oyobi byōsharon ni tsuite'* (An answer to Mr Iwano Hōmei; on my symbolism and theory of narration) in the journal *Waseda bungaku*. The most important paragraph in the article goes:

Even though a meditation which belongs to real life in which matter and spirit are one, is concrete, it still becomes an explanation as soon as it is expressed with words. For instance, the life that a person may lead by meditating upon anything in the world, is indeed concrete, but when he receives an enlightenment such as 'nature is eternal', and when this is expressed in language, it has already become an explanation ...

Mr Iwano says that an originally theoretical and explanatory content can be artistically transformed and thus concrete. But I wonder whether it is not obvious that this cannot possibly be done without the use of sensuous elements ...

To express the result of a philosophical or psychological life, only the explanatory style can be employed, and it is only when an author wishes to describe a vague psychological state/process such as an emotion/frame of mind, that metaphors or symbols may fittingly be used.[51]

As the controversy developed, the tone became still more vehement. Iwano's answer to the above was printed in the December issue of *Waseda bungaku* under the headline *'Gendai shōsetsu kontei no gokai; futatabi Nakamura Seiko-shi ni'* (The fundamental misunderstanding of the modern novel; to Mr Nakamura Seiko once more).

Iwano opens the article by claiming that Nakamura Seiko himself reveals how the foundation for his own theory has been shaken, when he refers to metaphors and symbols. As far as the question of 'explanation' is concerned, Iwano writes as follows:

Because the question of rendering the expression concrete ought to occupy a central position in any theory of narration, I have only mentioned what may be concretised and to what extent this can be done, also as far as philosophy or other abstract material or states are concerned. We do not need to spend our time on what he calls insight into eternal nature, which is realised through contemplation — (I consider it unnecessary to say that this is not the contemplative life itself, but rather an explanation, and as such conceptual).[52]

It should be noticed that during this debate Iwano was forced to discern what

51. Quoted in Wada, op. cit., 144.
52. Ibid., 145.

can be described from what cannot: The material for description must, according to Iwano, be 'a contemplation as well as the life which implements the philosophy derived from contemplation, that is the life which loves/hates, develops and constructs/destroys this philosophy. And this is precisely the material for my five-volume novel'.[53] In other words, Iwano believes that in his novel he has written about a '*life*' which can be *described*.

He goes on to stress the fact that some writers when they describe the psyche, are only able to give abstract explanations. Seen from Iwano's point of view, this merely shows that they do not have the sufficient talent to carry through a proper description. However, he warns against drawing the conclusion that mental life cannot be described. On the contrary, he believes that this can be done; mental life can be described in a concrete way by the means of the unified-body-and-soul theory.

Thus Iwano criticised the supporters of flat narration for their formalistic conception of the question of explanation/description. The debate on the unified-body-and-soul description did not develop further in connection with the publication of the novel *Hatten*, apart from a few insignificant comments addressed to Iwano and which he did not consider it necessary to answer.

We must not forget that Iwano's theory of narration was at this stage formulated primarily as a defence of the technique he had used in his autobiographical five-volume novel. He continued claiming that the novel work was a product of an authentic narrative technique. It is, however, interesting to note that the theory was only valid as far as the novel-series was concerned. Between the novels *Hōrō* and *Hatten*, Iwano published about twenty works (short stories and plays), but none of these had any importance for the continuation or development of his theory of narration.

2.5. The Fourth Phase

In the period 1913-16 the controversy over the theories of narrative technique quietened down. This was presumably due, partly, to the fact that the debate had for the time being exhausted the list of problematic points, and partly to the fact that as naturalism waned, Tayama Katai had withdrawn from his position as chief editor of the journal *Bunshō sekai* which had been one of the most important arenas for the polemics.

But it would be wrong to disregard the importance of Iwano's extremely complicated private life when we look at the reasons for the lacking deve-

---

53. Ibid.

lopment of his theory of narration during this period. In the following we shall recapitulate his life.[54]

Immediately after his return from Hokkaidō on December 10 1909, Iwano left his wife Takekoshi Kō in order to live with one of Japan's prominent feminists, Endō Kiyoko. His audacity in the choice of a new partner caused a sensation. Already two days later the newspaper *Yorozuchōhō* wrote about their relationship under the provoking headline '*Rei ga katsuka niku ga katsuka*' (Will the spirit win or will the body?). Iwano's unified-body-and-soul philosophy had been caricatured, as had the active advances he (the body) made to Endō Kiyoko and the passive, almost puritan attitude with which she (the spirit) met his approaches. The situation did, however, end with Iwano's victory.

On September 10 1912 Iwano was finally divorced from his wife and on March 26 1913 he married Endō Kiyoko. On September 7 of the same year, he signed a contract with the publishers *Shinchōsha* concerning the translation of Plutarch's *Bioi Parelleloi*. He started working on the great task around May 1914, and in April 1915 he hired Kanbara Fusae to write out his manuscript. During the work an intimate relationship developed between the two, and Iwano moved in with her in August, a fact that attracted the attention of journalists and resulted in a fervent public debate about marriage and adultery. Iwano had handed in his doctorate thesis *Nippon onritsu no kenkyū* (A study of Japanese rhythm) to the Ministry of Education in April. Partly because of the scandal the thesis was rejected and the publication of his book *Setsuna-tetsugaku no kensetsu* (The construction of the philosophy of momentariness) was postponed for the time being.[55] He spent his time reacting to various critical remarks concerning his person and his views on marriage; his articles and essays from this debate were collected under the title *Danjo to teisō-mondai* (Man and woman and the question of fidelity) and published in October 1915.

In the meantime the children from his first marriage caused him trouble; he was involved in the compulsory sale of the boarding house Hinodekan, which he had inherited from his father and which he had handed over to his ex-wife Takekoshi Kō (June 1915); Endō Kiyoko sued him, demanding that he return to live with her. As a counterattack Iwano sued her for a divorce, but in the end he lost both cases. He founded the journal *Shin-nihonshugi* in January 1916, and Endō Kiyoko sued him again to make him pay for the

54. For information on Iwano's life in this period, see his diaries which are collected in *HZ* vol. 12.
55. The book was published posthumously in October 1920.

upkeep of their children, and as a consequence of his strife with her, his property was sequestrated.

Iwano fought alone against everybody; though he was still as energetic and ill-tempered as always, there were days when he could not pull himself together. One day he wrote in his diary: 'I feel as if I am about to have a nervous breakdown. I have not done any work whatsoever today' (August 29, 1916).[56]

Iwano did not succeed in straightening out the affairs concerning the divorce from Endō Kiyoko until February 8, 1917, and it was not until June 6 of the same year that the sequestration could be withdrawn.

In the middle of this divorce inferno, Iwano's social status as well as his reputation were destroyed, but he remained energetic in his work and during the period from 1913 to June 1917 he published about 40 works, both short stories and plays, in various journals.[57]

During all this time there was no notable discussion of narrative techniques and theories. Not that Iwano gave up on his theory. On the contrary. As we have seen in the above, he had little or no time to discuss narrative techniques, but the most important reason why there were no controversies over narrative theories was presumably the fact that during this period, he wrote no new autobiographical short stories or novels. The publication of these had always caused fervent debates over his method.

One single exception is one of the five novels of the novel-series, *Dokuyaku o nomu onna* (The woman who takes poison) from 1914, which was published in the journal *Chūōkōron*. It may be due to the fact that the novel received good reviews that the publication did not cause the discussion of Iwano's narrative techniques to flare up again; the novel only received minor counter-criticism.[58]

Both Tokuda Shūsei and Morita Sōhei (1881-1949) criticised Iwano for having employed the method of flat narration which he had opposed himself to and criticised.[59] This criticism probably surprised Iwano. He analysed the reasons for their criticism and inferred that it was presumably due to the lack

56. Cf. *HZ* vol. 12, 398.
57. Unfortunately the precise number is not known. Iwano's collected works from 1921-22 are not just incomplete but also full of major and minor errors.
58. One of the positive reviews was written by Masamune Hakuchō in the journal *Waseda bungaku* in December 1914. Cf. Yoshida Seiichi, *Shizenshugi no kenkyū* vol. 2, 313.
59. Quoted in Iwano's article '*Jijitsu to gen'ei*' (Facts and illusions) in *HZ* vol. 18, p. 269. The title of this article has been changed to '*Jijitsu to gen'ei*' in his collected works; it was originally called '*Gen'ei to jijitsu*' (Illusions and facts) and was published in *Yomiuri shinbun*, June 29, 1914.

of moral background in his novel. His acclaimed immoral descriptions were probably interpreted as flat narration. But he rejected any kind of criticism which was based upon the concept of morals/ethics, and retorted as follows:

When art has finally liberated itself from the yoke of morals, from which the new art must escape, it must either work exclusively with technique or become immersed in facts (*jijitsu*). Both Mr [Tokuda] Shūsei and Mr Morita are well aware that I have immediately approached the latter area. But when without any ado, they consider my description of facts a flat narration, all my efforts have been wasted ... They all but close their eyes to facts in mental life and to psychological facts and even though such facts may actually be expressed in a sensuous way, they just judge them superficially, or rather, out of prejudices, and consider them unnatural.[60]

Here we should note the new pair of contrasts that Iwano is using, that of 'technique/facts'. During the debate that followed the publication of the novel *Hatten*, he defined 'life' (*seikatsu*) as the material for description from 'the destructively subjective point of view'. But here he uses the word 'facts' instead. However, the theory of flat narration is not concerned with objective facts in general, but with the psychological facts that Iwano had mentioned in the quotation given above. In that connection he goes on to write:

When my own thoughts have been expressed [in my works], they have not been inserted here and there, but spread all through the work and never put forward as the opinions of the author. They have always been expressed as the subjective points of view of the protagonist or as his thoughts.[61]

The choice of words has changed slightly, but Iwano's theory of narration still moves in the same circles and has not really developed at all from the previous phase.

2.6. The Fifth Phase

Gradually as the problems in Iwano's private life were solved, he began to comment on narrative techniques again, and a new series of controversies arose.

This time the debate was initiated by Hirotsu Kazuo (1891-1968)'s article in the newspaper *Yomiuri shinbun*, in which he wrote that 'an author should not be judged by his principles (*shugi*) or by his affiliation with a specific

60. Ibid., 271.
61. Ibid., 273.

group (*tōha*).'[62] The contribution had no direct connection to the discussion of narrative techniques, but it made Iwano reopen the discussion in the article '*Sōsaku to shugi no kankei*' (The relationship between the art of writing novels and the author's principles, June 1917), in which he described Hirotsu Kazuo's as a 'banal theory', which was always 'propagandised by people with either no or insufficient experience.'[63] He says furthermore:

An author's principles make up his material ... In a novel by an author who has outgrown the stage of amateurishness, you will always find a living trait which is his own. Such a characteristic trait cannot be created through imitation but only through an exposure of the author's inner life. And when this exposure — quiet or enthusiastic — is performed in a state of tension, he will become aware of his own tension. And this constitutes his principle and his life.[64]

According to Iwano, literary principles can be divided into two categories: the principle of narration and the principle of philosophy. And in him these two principles are one and the same.[65]

The question of principles was thus combined with that of narrative theories, and the so-called debate of principles arose.

Furthermore, Iwano stressed the superiority of his realism compared to idealism. He considered it 'far too old-fashioned to discern realism from idealism on the basis of the division of body and soul'.[66] He argued in favour of his realism in the following way:

In a work of realism, the author presents the world with his life, his experiences and his humanity, all of which make up the background for his opinions and beliefs. In this respect, there is hardly any difference between realism and idealism. But writers of realism do not tend to be of one fixed opinion nor to isolate it. In

62. Quoted in Iwano's article '*Sōsaku to shugi no kankei*' (The relationship between the art of writing novels and the author's principles), June 1917 in the journal *Chūō bungaku*, in *HZ* vol. 18, 324.
63. Ibid., 323.
64. Ibid., 325.
65. Ibid., 326.
66. Ibid. The fact that Iwano inserts idealism in his considerations is due to the appearance of the *Shirakaba*-group on the literary stage of modern Japan. Iwano actually quotes one of the representative writers of the group, Mushanokōji Saneatsu (1885-1976), in the same article, and criticises his idea that the future world of letters should attach greater importance to 'quality and quantity', but not to 'principles'. Iwano, on the other hand, believes that quality and quantity are directly connected to principles. Ibid., 324.

idealism, on the other hand, a fixed concept of life or humanity is often created, and consequently a moral dimension is added to the concept.[67]

To Iwano, the realism on which his own works had been built, was by far the better method. With this debate centred around the issue of principles, he developed his theory of narration, in the light of realism, or rather, in the light of 'inner realism' (*naibuteki shajitsushugi*).

Kaneko Yōbun (1894-1985) asked Iwano what he had wished to express in the short story '*Tsumetai tsuki*' (The cold moon, June 1917, in *Bunshō sekai*).[68] Kaneko Yōbun was a writer who was almost didactic in his insistence that authors should express the spirit of love in their work.

In his answer, '*Naibuteki shajitsushugi no rikkyakuchi*' (The standpoint of inner realism), Iwano defines Kaneko Yōbun's demand as 'nonsense, influenced by 'translated' [read: foreign and only partly digested] humanism,'[69] and he defends his own point of view by saying that 'what is expressed in the novel is the reality of a human life, or in other words, the reality of human nature or of humanity.'[70] He is furthermore of the opinion that the formulation of Kaneko Yōbun's question bears witness to his inability to discern idealism from realism. Iwano regards the real aspects of life, that is its movements in the 'now', as movements without any ideal or solution. This is the point of view from which he watches life, and this is where the core of the most serious realism is to be found.[71]

Iwano does not mention the destructively subjective point of view at all in this article. One almost gains the impression that he has stepped a few steps backwards and drawn nearer to the orthodox naturalism of Tayama Katai and Shimazaki Tōson. But actually he has not moved in that direction at all, but rather towards the monistic theory of narration.

Further on in the same article, Iwano writes:

Ever since *Hatten* and *Dokuyaku o nomu onna*, all my work has been deep into realism. To this we may add the fact that the protagonists [of my writings] have been at the centre in a way that creates the impression that they are speaking as 'I's. For this reason, the things that, despite their presence, they did not see or hear, or

67. Ibid., 326-27.
68. Kaneko Yōbun's question stems from an article, published in the journal *Nippon hyōron* in July 1917, and is quoted in Iwano's article '*Naibuteki shajitsushugi no rikkyakuchi*' (The standpoint of inner realism), which was first published in *Nipponshugi*, August 1917. Cf. *HZ* vol. 18, 368 and 371.
69. Ibid., 371.
70. Ibid., 368-69.
71. Ibid.

of which they were not told are not included [in the narration], even though the writer himself knows and is able to write about these things. (This goes for both short stories and novels.) ... This has repeatedly been misunderstood, and readers have thought that the author and the protagonist were the same person.[72]

Then he gave an outline of the following four ways of writing fiction:

1. The author selects one of the characters of the work as his ideal and through the speech and actions of this character, he expresses his idea. (This is the most awkward technique.)

2. The author allows for the events in the work to develop in whatever direction he prefers. (The use of both 1 and 2 are found in the work of writers of the idealistic as well as of the aesthetic school.)

3. Some writers believe that they are able to separate themselves from their work, and that an objective narration without their own subjective points of view is possible. (This is materialistic naturalism.)

4. With the subjective point of view, an author may render an animated life which has neither ideals nor goals, real. The objectivity of the material for a work of fiction is found exactly here. (This is total naturalism or inner naturalism.)[73]

Iwano stresses the fact that his own methods belong under point 4, and then he concludes as follows:

To express universal humanity in a symbolic way — this is a real picture of inner realism.[74]

Iwano expanded the theory in the next article 'Naibuteki shajitsushugi kara' (From the perspective of inner realism, September 1917, in *Shinchō*), and made it clear that 'he would speak the case of inner realism and implement it, right until the end'.[75] Because the word 'inner' was a new term and had not been sufficiently defined in the two articles mentioned above, Iwano wrote a small article formed as a dialogue 'Naimenteki, gaimenteki' (Inner, outer, September 1917), in which he explained that '"inner" was not merely concerned with the

72. Ibid., 370-71.
73. Ibid.
74. Ibid., 372.
75. Cf. *HZ* vol. 10, 540.

demonstration of one's subjective point of view, but also with the way in which the subjective viewpoint was concretised'.[76]

Half a year after Iwano's focusing his theory on inner realism, the discussion of 'principles' burst out again.

In response to an anonymous comment in the newspaper *Jiji shinpō* which had claimed that 'principles are merely a part of art' and that 'the essence of art is man, but not principles',[77] Iwano wrote the article '*Hito no shugi*' (The principle of man) and published it in the same newspaper.[78] The main content of the discussion was a repetition of Iwano's previous controversy with Hirotsu Kazuo in 1917. But this time the debate gained a broader resonance with the result that the journal *Shinchō* published a special issue with the theme 'artist and principle' in May 1918.[79] Among the contributors were Nagayo Yoshio (1888-1961), Akutagawa Ryūnosuke, Ema Nakashi (1889-1975), Hirotsu Kazuo, Morita Sōhei and Toyoshima Yoshio (1890-1955).

With his usual zeal, Iwano criticised their opinions in his new article '*Boku no izumu-kan o nobete shoka no izumu-kan o hyōsu*' (I make my view on various -isms clear, and criticise the views of others), which was published in the June issue of *Shinchō*.[80]

In the article Iwano sums up his own theory while criticising the varied opinions of others, and infers:

When an author's principles do not create any tension, he cannot be producing creative work; a writer cannot exist without this tension.[81]

As a synthesis of his many years as a critic, Iwano finally published a coherent theory of narration '*Gendai shōrai no shōsetsuteki hassō o isshinsubeki boku no byōsharon*' (My theory of narration which will renew the idea of the novel today and in the future), which was mainly based upon his theories of 'principle' and of inner realism. The article was published in October 1918 in the journal *Shinchō*. We may note that it was in this article that Iwano used the term *ichigen byōsha* — 'monistic narration' — for the first time.

76. Ibid., 542.
77. Quoted in '*Hito no shugi*' (The principle of man) in *HZ* vol. 18, 297.
78. According to *HZ*, the article was printed in May 1918. This, however, has turned out to be wrong. The article was really divided into two parts and published in *Jiji shinpō* on March 31 and April 5 1918. Cf. '*Shōwa joshi-daigaku kindaibungaku kenkyū-shitsu*'(ed.), *Kindai bungaku kenkyū sōsho*, vol 19, 255.
79. *Geijutsuka to izumu to no kankei ni tsuite no kōsatsu* (On the relationship between the artist and various isms).
80. Cf. *HZ* vol. 18, 301-10.
81. Ibid., 303.

IV. The Theory in Translation with a Commentary

> Even God sees Satan's inner being through coloured glasses.
> Iwano Hōmei

My Theory of Narration Which Will Renew the Idea of the Novel Today and in the Future[1]

Part 1: An Illustrated Exposition of Authorial Attitudes[2]

When, as I do, one considers the problem of narration in novels,[3] one quickly discovers that the theory is far from fully clarified[4] and that there are still a number of points which, with the single exception of myself, hardly anybody seems to be aware of.[5] It firstly has to do with the *fusokufuri* [neither-identification-nor-differentiation] relation between the author and the protagonist in a work of fiction. The *fusokufuri* relation, which the author ought to have to all the characters in his

1. The article was first printed in the journal *Shinchō* in October 1918, but when it was included in *HZ* vol. 10, it underwent minor revisions. The following translation is based on the text in *HZ* vol. 10, 544-64. With regard to the title, the *Shinchō* version has a subtitle as follows: 'Please read'. The *Shinchō* version can be read in *NKBT* vol. 22, 167-84. (In the following the *Shinchō* version will be referred to without reference to the page numbers in *NKBT* vol. 22.)
2. The *Shinchō* version simply says '1'. It is likely that Iwano edited details in the text when, according to a diary entry dated December 26 1919, he decided to write a larger work about monistic narration. Cf. *HZ* vol. 10, 564.
3. The fact that narrative technique not only has to do with writing techniques, but also with authorial attitude, that which Iwano called *hakaiteki shukan* (the destructively subjective point of view). Cf. *HZ* vol. 10, 489-505, especially 499 and 505. See also III.2.2. for 'Gendai shōsetsu no byōshahō' (Narrative techniques in the modern novel, February 1911).
4. As was seen in the previous section III.2.5 and 2.6., the debate about theories of narration had been quiet during the period 1913-16 and the new debate which was revived in 1917-18 had only just begun.
5. In his essay 'Kyōdo geijutsu to byōsha mondai' (Local art and the question of narration, in *Yomiuri shinbun*, January 1 1915), Iwano writes the following: '...the reason I stopped [working with narrative theory] was because our literary world... is made up entirely of stupid people who did not understand half, no, not a quarter of my theory.' Cf. *HZ* vol. 10, 531.

work has even been mentioned often by Mr Tayama Katai in accordance with his rather weak theory of flat narration. But my theory greatly emphasises the author's *fusokufuri* relation, not to all the characters, but to the most important character, or rather *solely* to the protagonist. This is what distinguishes my theory from others.[6] There are still many problems with this theory of narration, but I will, in the following, deal only with this one issue.

Most people confuse the author's attitude before he chooses his material with his attitude after he has chosen his material. Let us use an example. We have a group of people consisting of A, B and C,[7] and we want to depict either their mood, their daily life or an event which has affected them. When we weigh the possibilities, all the while keeping in consideration both the author's expectations [about his work] and the various theories [that exist], we find that there are three possibilities. The *first* possibility: the author holds an omniscient point of view. He perceives and observes the mood and life of each of the members of the group, equally and directly. This is equal to a 'comparison' and it is identical to a simple bird's-eye view narration or flat narration and can be illustrated in the following manner:

Diagram 1

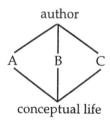

The *second* possibility involves the author feeling his way into one of the member's of the group from the very outset. We assume that A is the protagonist. The author is now in A's mind. He observes the others through A and all that which A does not hear, see or feel, is considered an unexplored world, an uninhabited island and as such it is left undescribed, even though the author has knowledge of it. If there is something he does not want to leave out, he describes it as if the protagonist heard, saw or felt it. This is precisely the attitude which I have insisted upon and practised, both as a writer and as a critic. It can be illustrated by the following:

6. The background for the theory is Iwano's epistemological conviction. It was his belief that one could only perceive and feel through a chosen character, in other words the chosen subject was always at the centre of the narrative.
7. The *Shinchō* version reads: 'A, B, C and D'. Iwano has left out 'D', presumably to simplify the illustration.

Diagram 2

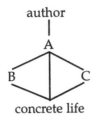

It is easier to understand this attitude if one considers the fact that, even though the author gives A the third-person form (he could just as well have chosen B or C, as long as it was only one of them), he is actually letting him speak just as autobiographically as he might have in the first-person. If A is identical with the author, then the work becomes autobiographical in accordance with the first model of attitudes. However, in this the second model of attitudes, a *fusokufuri* relation exists between A and the author.[8]

Because the author perceives life through a particular person's state of mind,[9] he actually relates, at least outwardly, in an indirect way to life. But this indirect relationship serves to render abstract explanation impossible and the narration concrete. This corresponds to 'metaphor' or 'symbol'[10] rather than to the 'comparison' [of the first model of attitudes]. In a comparison, we say 'you [a woman] are like a flower on a high mountain',[11] and the woman and flower are placed on the same level even though we relate directly to them both. They thus remain two different, distinct things. However, we can remove the word 'like' and instead say 'you are a flower on a high mountain'. The woman is given a depth which makes her identifiable with the flower [despite the fact that we now relate indirectly to the flower]. The direct relation [between the compared objects] renders it impossible for us to free ourselves of ideas and explanations when we employ comparison.[12] On the other hand, a metaphor or that which is even better,[13] makes the objects placed in an indirect relationship appear more concrete, despite everything. If one applies rhetorical and poetical terms to my theory of narration, the first attitude could be described as a 'simple comparison' and the second as a 'complicated, but pure metaphor or something even better'.

8. Iwano considers this relationship to be the guarantee of objectivity. He returns to this subject in part 3.
9. *Kibun*: empathetic state.
10. *Hyōshō*: Usually 'symbol' is translated with *shōchō*, but Iwano always used the word *hyōshō*.
11. *Takane no hana*: An expression for something rare and unattainable. Is also used in other contexts to describe an exceptionally beautiful woman.
12. See III.2.3., page 94 about Iwano's 'four ways of expression in fiction' — explanatory explanation, explanatory narration, narrated explanation and narrated narration.
13. Here Iwano is probably thinking of 'symbol'.

The *third* attitude is a mixture of the first and the second. But like the first, as such, it can only work theoretically. Therefore, it is unavoidable that the illustration will be quite artificial and complicated. The author is not limited to one member of the group which as a whole provide the material for his narrative, but he shifts between A, B and C, observing the moods or lives of the others through the chosen character. He observes through A as well as the others and in the final analysis, he stands at an equal distance from all four[14] elements [members] and maintains his bird's-eye view. This can be illustrated as is shown in diagram 3.

Diagram 3

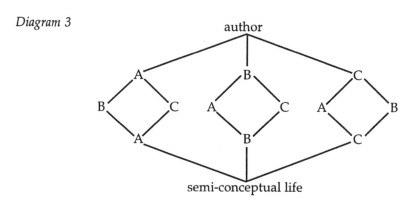

We may take this theory a step further, despite the fact that it becomes quite complicated. We will find that it is possible to move the author one step up and to select either A, B or C from the top line [of diagram 3]. In this way this character alone[15] comes into a direct relationship with the author who is placed just above. This can technically be described as the *fourth* attitude (see diagram 4 below). But the third illustration can actually be reduced to the first and the fourth to the second. I stand on the side of realism in my outlook on life, even as I attempt to make my understanding of reality more thorough and clear, avoiding abstractions and explanations which would obstruct my attempts to probe deeply and purely into reality. Therefore, I reject the first attitude even when it does not consist of 'explanatory explanations' and choose the other attitude which is that of 'narrated narration'.[16]

14. Iwano appears to have forgotten to correct this to 'three'. See note 7 above.
15. In the *Shinchō* version Iwano uses 'directly'. The correction has made the meaning clearer.
16. These two last sentences are a little different in the *Shinchō* version: 'Incidentally, I stand on the side of realism and attempt to make my perception of reality deeper and clearer. Therefore, while avoiding empty discussions, I stay away from abstractions and explanations in my novel-writing. To this purpose I reject the explanatory narration of the first attitude (even when it is not 'explanatory explanation') and I choose the other attitude exclusively which is 'narrated narration'. In the following I will attempt to explain the reason for this.'

Diagram 4[17]

author

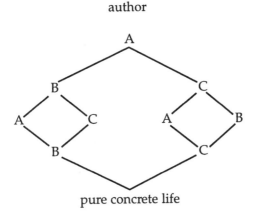

pure concrete life

Part 2: The True Understanding of Life and the Only True Attitude

Generally speaking, it is not possible to grasp life's meaning only through observing it at a distance (this is true both of the 'flat' observer and of the bird's-eye view). One can only grasp it by entering a person's subjective point of view. Only from this angle the view reflects real life. When it is said that one should make one's subjective point of view a mirror,[18] it is only a rhetorical comparison. If the 'I' were like a mirror, it would be a god. If not a god, then its subjective point of view would at least have been made of glass. And even if it is said that one should appreciate equanimity, there are limits. If one goes beyond these limits, then one's subjective point of view is no longer that of a human being. The human being is a burning body wherein intellect, emotion and will-power are mixed without differentiation. Yet when the burning power or the taut perfection is relaxed just a little bit, the intellect, emotions and will-power still function. Despite the fact that, due to the relaxation, they are inclined to become detached from one another, they nonetheless function and although in an awkward way, they colour the subjective point of view. For this reason, it is not possible for a human being to consider life or other human beings without using his or her own body or in some cases his or her coloured subjective point of view.

We can be certain that A and others exist, aside from ourselves, because the proof of this is within the scope of our knowledge. To imagine that beyond this boundary B or C exist, is, if not a fantasy, certainly arrogant — not to mention any discussion of A's or anybody else's emotions, which can certainly never be understood in the way that A and these others actually see themselves. In our own world we cannot include anything but that which we understand by watching,

17. This illustration is not included in the *Shinchō* version.
18. Iwano is alluding to Tayama Katai, the originator of and spokesperson for flat narration.

listening or using our imagination in a realistic way. Therefore [our] world or life
are not the world or the life that all people know of, but something that everyone
in his own way finds reflected in his own subjective point of view. In other words,
it is an empire in which everyone is the emperor and where the sovereignty of other
people is not accepted. Ignorant people often call such a philosophy insolent or
arrogant, but it should be considered the most modest attitude, when one at least
does not want to conquer the territory beyond one's own with the help neither of
one's imagination nor of one's own ruthless logic, and when one does not show the
greed of logic-lovers such as Abe Jirō[19] and others.

With this outlook on life in mind, we turn to think of the case of the author.
An author does not understand other people as well as he understands himself.
Therefore, no matter how objectively he may observe them and no matter how far
from them he may place himself and calmly contemplate them, he is unable to
depict their mood as a whole (that is to say the frame of mind that they themselves
have already experienced). The same is true when the author is a man who must
relate to a woman or when he is an adult who must relate to a child or even when
he relates to an animal.[20] One can only describe that which can be found within the
boundaries of one's own 'colour'. Because of the lacking awareness of this
limitation, an ambiguous and immature narration and/or narrative theory has
appeared in our literary world. For example, once the honourable epithet 'myriad-
minded' was used to describe Shakespeare,[21] but this was a saying that was handed
down from a time when one could accept objectivity without any restrictions. But
according to my investigation, Shakespeare 'coloured' the 'myriad' in his plays with
his subjective point of view in a way which was much less intelligent and much
more flat than that of our Chikamatsu.[22] It is in this case of no use to speak of the
difference between a greater and a lesser subjectivity.[23]

If one applies my theory to modern writers, it appears to fit in such a precise
way that it is almost entertaining. I have earlier written about each of them
indivdually and shown how one can see that Mr Masamune Hakuchō's so-called
subdued subjectivity is no more than an attitude provoked by a melancholy which

---

19. Abe Jirō was a philosopher and a critic. He indirectly criticised Iwano's narrative
    theory in his essay 'Byōsha no daizai to byōsha no taido' Cf. page 83-84.
20. Note Iwano's own words about the depiction of animals later in part 5.
21. Samuel Taylor Coleridge (1772-1834), *Biographia Literaria*, 1817, Chapter 15.
22. Chikamatsu Monzaemon (1653-1724) was a *jōruri* playwright from the *Edo* period. He
    is often called Japan's Shakespeare.
23. *Dai-shukan* and *shō-shukan*, respectively the greater and the smaller subjectivity, are
    Tayama Katai's inventions. *Dai-shukan* — the vast subjectivity of nature— is considered
    to be life's innermost core, while *shō-shukan* — an individual's subjectivity — is
    considered a negative element which ought to be eliminated, also in narration.

is the result of his stomach disease;[24] Mr Tayama Katai's sentimental subjectivity is due to the fact that his contemplative experiences have only come to expression in the eve of his life and he has by contrast spent his youth in a clumsy and sentimental manner;[25] when Mr Shimazaki Tōson appears to be worldly-wise and profound, but his art actually reveals itself to be inane, it is due to the fact that in a mundane way he has experienced far too many mundane problems[26] and finally it would appear to me that the overwhelming eagerness or rather enthusiasm of Mr Arishima Takeo's subjectivity (I have actually not yet dealt with this topic in depth) stems from the fact that even though he has been challenged with serious troubles both intellectually and emotionally, he has not reflected considerably on his experiences.[27]

The reader will have to analyse them on his own, bearing in mind that all the above-mentioned writers employ the first attitude which is illustrated in Diagram 1. The first attitude has been given numerous names — 'pure-objectivity', 'bird's-eye view', 'a distanced position' (bōkanteki) or 'sensuous experience'. But when one first realises that objectivity is no more than an opposing factor, it becomes easy to see why it is impossible for any writer to be purely objective and as such be able to relate equally to A, B, C and D.[28] They choose, because they have given it insufficient thought, an attitude which only God (on the assumption that he exists) can have. Could this not be considered arrogance? We humans are mere pale greenhorns, blunt swords or snobs (even Shakespeare was said to be a thief).[29] To show such arrogance from above; this is the bird's-eye view. The 'distanced position' shows arrogance from the side and if these two are put together, one finally gets 'the flat' [narration]. This has been the tendency of most naturalistic writers. Because none of them have understood themselves as beings of a unified

24. In 1913 Iwano wrote a long essay about one of the leading naturalistic writers, Masamune Hakuchō, with the title 'Ibyō shosan no geijutsu' (Art provoked by stomach disease, Shinchō, June), in which he analysed Hakuchō's short stories. In Iwano's view Masamune Hakuchō's artistic work was based on his indifference, passivity and defeatism which was probably a result of the stomach disease which he had suffered from since childhood.

25. Iwano wrote an essay 'Katai-ron no ittan' (An aspect of Katai's life and art, Bunshō sekai, February 1917) in which he analysed the sentimentality of Tayama Katai's work. Cf. HZ vol. 18, 203-4.

26. Iwano wrote about Shimazaki Tōson's work in, among others, the article 'Shōsetsuka toshite no Shimazaki Tōson-shi'. Cf. HZ vol. 18, 121-42 and this book, page 91-92.

27. Iwano wrote about Arishima Takeo (1878-1923)'s art in an article 'Arishima Takeo-shi no ai to geijutsu ron' (About Mr Arishima Takeo's love and art, Nipponshugi, February 1918). Cf. HZ vol. 18, 332-41.

28. Iwano seems to have forgotten to delete D in his revision of the text.

29. Iwano is referring to an old rumour about the possible reason for Shakespeare's departure from Stratford-upon-Avon for London. According to the rumour, Shakespeare was ordered to leave his home town because he had committed a theft.

body-and-soul,[30] I have criticised them and called them too mechanical or materialistic.[31] And I have considered my own naturalism to be an inner naturalism.[32] This is what I now call inner realism. It avoids all that which is materialistic. 'Whether it happens from the above, from the side, or on the surface, an author can only write what he himself has registered by way of his five senses' — this is what Mr Tayama and his followers once said. (Mr Nakamura Seiko[33] was one of them, but it appears that he has been converted, probably through dishonest means. He has recently accused me [of misunderstanding him][34] and untruthfully claimed that it was a lie that he had said that [what was cited above].) They even said that one can never describe the psychology of a character, neither A's nor the others'. It is precisely such a comment which I would call 'sensuous'.

But nonetheless they guess their way, in so far as it is possible, into the psychology of their characters who are the objects (of their narration), and describe

30. See page 58ff for Iwano's explanation of the unified-body-and-soul philosophy in *The Mystic Semi-Animalism*.
31. In his article '*Busshitsuteki byōsharon o nanzu*' (I criticise the materialist theory of narration, May 1911) he criticises Tayama Katai's article '*Byōsharon*' (On narration, April 1911). Iwano writes the following: 'Mr [Tayama] Katai distinguishes, as ordinary people do, between spirit and thing. He believes that if only he can get a hold of the thing, then the spirit, which he probably thinks is subordinate to the thing, will follow. With regard to his view on life, he is a materialist. If one is an adherent of the unified-body-and-soul theory, then one can, simply by realising one's view of life in a concrete manner, depict life in its entirety, even though one just takes a fraction of it. But if, on the other hand, one follows the theory which distinguishes between spirit and thing and if one concentrates only on materialist aspects, as Mr Katai does, then it is obvious that one's narration will only scratch the boring surface and not penetrate the actual content. Mr Katai usually speaks of art as "entering the brain through the eyes", but his "flat narration" is solely for the eye.' Cf. *HZ* vol. 17, 152. See also page 88ff, as well as the footnote 31 ibid.
32. In and around 1917 Iwano was working with inner naturalism (See page 102 ff). This is a narrative method which the author uses, first and foremost to concentrate on the protagonist and his/her inner world. In the little article which is written as a dialogue '*Naimenteki, gaimenteki*' (Inner, outer; September 1917), Iwano writes that it is a method with which one can 'realise one's subjective point of view in the narration'. Cf. *HZ* vol. 10, 541-43.
33. Nakamura Seiko (1884-1974) was a novelist and critic. He was known as one of the theorists behind 'flat narration'.
34. In his article '*Naibuteki shajitsushugi kara*' (From the perspective of inner realism. *Shinchō*, September 1917), Iwano wrote the following: 'Most adherents [of naturalism] made do with the materialist [naturalism] and uncritically thought that the foreign [naturalism] was also like that [i.e. materialist]. At one point Mr Tayama and even his follower Mr Nakamura Seiko expressed the idea that one could depict the exterior of a person, but one could not depict a person's psychology. (In the August issue of *Waseda bungaku* Mr Nakamura Seiko wrote that I had misunderstood him. I find it very rude that he considers it to be my misunderstanding when he just wants to correct his earlier statement and withdraw it.)'. Cf. *HZ* vol. 10, 538.

them in terms such as 'someone's voice sounded in such and such a way to their ears' or 'somebody's action seemed so and so to their eyes', etc. But that (which they describe) is not the inner life of the actual thing nor is it the actual psychological life. The reason they cannot depict a psychological life with their method of flat narration is that they overestimate the objectivity of their thinking to an almost absurd degree. This is actually a reaction stemming from a convinced belief in the restrictions and limitations of subjectivity. An author's objectivity is significant when he is choosing his material and before he begins to write about (or on the basis of) the chosen material. But when he has initiated the actual writing, he has to feel his way into A or one of the others, whether he wants to or not. This can also be explained with the theory of empathy (the theory of the projection of one's emotion, rationality or will-power unto another) which is said to have been dominant (in the intellectual world) abroad recently.[35] One feels one's way into either A or B, preferably without a restricted subjective viewpoint, but as broadly as possible, to the very boundaries of what appears natural. When the author feels his way into people in this way, the relationship between the writer and the protagonist becomes closer and as a result more limited (even an adherent of flat narration is aware of this); as a result one cannot truly understand anything but the feeeling of A, B, or C. This is the same as not being able to understand other people in real life; if you are A then you cannot understand B and if you are B you cannot understand C. Nobody except for myself has noticed this, neither abroad nor in our country, with the exception of some who have already thoroughly digested my theory.

Part 3: Monistic Narration

In Mr Hirotsu Kazuo's novel *Futari no fukōmono* (Two unhappy people),[36] an event is developed on the one hand, while at the same time another event is developed which actually has no relevant connection to the people involved in the first event, just for the sake of comparison. Such a method has, no matter what objective he (Hirotsu Kazuo) may have, an abstract purpose, that is to say it should explain something; the one event has no concrete connection with the other or they do not

35. Theodor Lipps' theory of *'Einfühlung'* (1851-1914) provided the point of departure for his own understanding of art. According to his theory, the viewer had to project feelings into a work of art in order to understand it. The theory was introduced in Japan in April 1917 by Abe Jirō (see note 19 above) in the book *Bigaku* (a translation of Lipps *Ästhetik* [1903-06]). The book may well have stimulated Iwano's thinking.

36. The *Shinchō* version reads '... *Futari no fukōmono* which was carried as a series two or three months ago in *Yomiuri shinbun*.' The novel was published in the newspaper starting on April 20, 1918 and ending on July 23 the same year. Iwano wrongly cited the title as *Futari no fukōmono* (Two unthankful people), this has been corrected in the translation.

correspond. When I expressed my views on such a method,[37] he said that he agreed with me in the cases where the method had a particular purpose in itself, but if the purpose was to explain something else then he did not understand me properly. Think also of Mr Tokuda Shūsei's short story 'Ikaku' (The threat).[38] Judging from the sequence of events, the protagonist is Asakichi, but most of the content is coloured by Ofuki's mood. Sometimes Ofuki is described as Asakichi sees her, and at other times Asakichi is depicted through the eyes of Ofuki. Because such unstable description is repeated many times, even though this is just a brief short story, the most important element (of the short story), the fact that the woman threatens the man, neither becomes the story's primary 'content' — the threat facing the man — nor its 'mood' — the foreboding mood which the woman provokes. In other words, it [the most important element] is something which from a position exterior to the short story, the author has added as an idea or abstraction. And we would not expect such un-unified (with regard to body-and-soul) works or abstract works from a true literary writer.

When an author writes about a certain material in a particular way, the fact that he has already studied the material from all sides, makes him able to feel his way into both A and B *before* he picks up his pen to write. He can even become C or D.[39] But if he goes further in his reflections, which have not yet taken any definite shape, he will at some point become B, or somebody else, in order to explain A — only to become A again in order to make B and others superfluous. He thus shifts his position frequently according to the circumstances. This is, however, a signal indicating that the author still allows for authorial comments and abstract explanations. One might say that due to his immaturity as an author, he wants to demonstrate the *hayagawari*-trick.[40] Even in a theatre performance, the *hayagawari*-trick is considered a secondary extra show and it is not used very often today because it is regarded as old-fashioned.[41] Despite this, the situation in our literary world is such that most fiction writers, together with writers of more popular literature, boast of such tricks in their work. But a serious author takes one or two steps forward and tears the clinging fence of abstractions apart in order to give a concrete form to the harsh realities of life. Just as he must confront his own

---

37. There was an intense debate in 1917. Iwano responded to Hirotsu Kazuo's essay in *Yomiuri shinbun* (the title and dates are unknown) with the article 'Sōsaku to shugi no kankei' (The relationship between the art of writing novels and the author's principles, June 1917). Cf. page 100ff. Hirotsu Kazuo responded in *Waseda bungaku* in August in an article with the title 'Iwano Hōmei-shi ni kotau' (An answer to Mr Iwano Hōmei).

38. In the *Shinchō* version the following is included: '...in the June issue of *Chūōkoron*'.

39. See footnote 28.

40. *Hayagawari*: This is a trick used in a *kabuki* performance by an actor who speedily changes his costume in front of the audience in order to play two or more roles in the same scene.

41. The *hayagawari*-trick is part of certain *kabuki* pieces and as such it is an 'old-fashioned' trick, but it is still used today in certain performances though rarely in modern plays.

life as his only possible mode of existence, the author needs to choose and limit himself to one single character in his work on to whom he can transfer his subjective point of view or with whom he can share that point of view.[42] Without employing this method, no author can make his narration free of abstract ideas and explanations.[43] The writer must be in the same mood as one of them (his characters) (for example A) and depict life just as he sees it himself. It is only when a writer has come this far that he will no longer simply describe the sensed experiences of a character, but will involve himself in the psychology (of that character) and portray him 'concretely'. If the author wants to become B or C, he is free to do so, but having made the choice, he must not see things from a point of view different from that of B or C, no matter whether this coincides with his (the author's) thinking or not. But many writers are unsure about this point. This is what I meant when I mentioned earlier that many writers make this mistake and have difficulties in working out how to relate to the protagonist 'before' they choose and 'after' they have chosen their material.

The subjective point of view, which has temporarily been transferred to one of the characters, and the author's own point of view are two sides of the same coin. The author and the chosen character are undoubtedly different, but the author must not differentiate the two in his own world of ideas. He must neither say, for example: 'Even though I am a moralist, I have purposely made my protagonist a non-moralist', nor 'I am an idealist, but I have portrayed a non-idealist'. Even if he has chosen a non-moralist or a non-idealist as his protagonist, he should describe him in such a precise manner that as a non-moralist or as a non-idealist, he (the character) seems coherent in all details and in harmony with his mood. In this way he can bring out that part of human nature which cannot be fully expressed with the particular words 'moral' and 'ideal', or rather the taste of life (we may also call it the profundity of human nature). And the same goal is achieved no matter whether we describe a moralist or an idealist. The idealist authors look for this goal in the author's own ideas, whereas the inner realist expresses it through a monistic and harmonious mood in his work.[44] Herein[45] lies the author's outlook on life, his

42. The passage 'or with whom he can share that point of view' is missing in the *Shinchō* version.

43. In his short essay 'Nikurei-gatchi = jiga-dokuzon' (The union of body and soul = The I is all that exists, published for the first time in the newspaper *Yomiuri shinbun*, May 24 1908), Iwano writes the following: 'When all is said and done, the essence of all art is the depiction of the self. One must not forget that the 'I' is enlivened in every moment and then diminished again without having a solution to anything in particular. This is exactly the case because there is no other more natural way to exist.' Cf. HZ vol. 15, 358.

44. Iwano is referring to himself. In doing so he has also explained what his earlier 'narrated narration' is about.

reflection and his criticism. To fulfill this purpose he need not engage himself in anything, but the situation or mood of his protagonist A and never with B or C separately. Yes, he may engage himself in them, but in that case he must not pass his personal judgment on them; he may deal with them to the extent that they are absorbed in A's mood. Because otherwise there is a danger that the needle of abstraction is stuck into the unaffected and natural material in vain.

Part 4: Narrow, but Profound

In comparison with monistic narration, the (narrative method shown in the) first illustration is pluralistic. That I mention this, may make thoughtless people happy and make them say something like: 'Since the old philosophy included both monism and pluralism,[46] it is fun to have the two variations in our narration also'. But 'variation' and this notion of narration being 'serious or not-serious'[47] are two different things. When in their narrative, adherents of the theory of pluralistic flat narration place themselves in both A and B's place, this is because, after having chosen A (as the protagonist), they soon discover that they are dissatisfied with A alone. The reason for their dissatisfaction has to do with the fact that when they choose to transfer, in part or completely, their subjective points of view on to A, they forget that the A which they observe is the whole of A (no more and no less) (an author cannot write of that which he has not seen). If one perceives the whole of A as such then one can make do with that which A observes, with regard to B and the others. Only in A has life taken a concrete shape and to wish (to know, to see) all that which A has no knowledge of, is like wishing to be on an unexplored island. But somebody who is not familiar with this practical theory will not attempt to see life in its entirety in the figure of one of the characters A, B, C or D.[48] He tries to supplement the half which A has no knowledge of with something that the others may know of. But in this way and contrary to his beliefs, he is unable to perceive life in its entirety or, in other words, he is unable to give a concrete shape to life.

The attitude which is shown in the first illustration is a mixture of empty theory and fantasies. The first attitude is an attempt to make the impossible possible; the narration required of this attitude cannot enter deeply into things, it is doomed to float about on the surface. This literature which remains at the level of ideas is welcome to exist at the same level as popular literature, but if with this

---

45. In the text Iwano actually writes '*kotoni*' (especially) which is presumably a misprint. This is why it has been corrected in accordance with the *Shinchō* version which reads '*kokoni*' (herein).

46. For some mysterious reason the word *fubenri* (uselessness) is used in the text. It was corrected in accordance with the *Shinchō* version to *tagenron* (pluralism).

47. The original reads *shinkoku tagenron* (serious pluralism). In accordance with the *Shinchō* version, it was corrected to *shinkoku fu-shinkoku* (serious or not-serious).

48. See footnote 28 above.

attitude, it wants to stand equal to the literature which is the result of the second attitude, it should be regarded as incredibly arrogant. Between the literature which allows for the manipulation of ideas and remains at the level of ideas and the literature which does not, there are immense differences in depth and worth. But this is something that cannot be understood by others except those who have thoroughly digested the ideas and life of our modern times.[49] When I recently met Mr Nakatani Tokutarō,[50] I criticised his short story 'Tsukiyo' (A moonlit night).[51] In the short story, the author is both the one girl O-sato and the other girl O-mitsu, the young man who plays the violin poorly and the other man, and because he shifts the point of view far too often, the mood that surrounds each of the characters becomes no more than the author's explanation. When he writes in this way, little is to be expected of him in the future. Mr Ikuta Chōkō[52] was also present and he thought that my advice was much too narrow-minded. But I think that we ought to choose earnest narrow-mindedness rather than indifferent generosity, regardless of whether we are dealing with life philosophies or narrative theory.[53]

If one compares Mr Tayama with Mr (Iwano) Hōmei,[54] one can really see the differences between the attitudes of the first and the second illustration. He, Mr Tayama, once criticised my novel *Dokuyaku o nomu onna* (The woman who takes poison) by saying that the author, that is me, should have observed the woman O-tori better and that I had only achieved half of what I set out to do.[55] But as I replied to his criticism at the time,[56] I have depicted the woman to the exact extent that the protagonist has observed her. If one sees her from another perspective than that of the protagonist, it is possible to develop another impression of her, but I have deliberately avoided this in order to give a solid shape to the protagonist's nature and life. But he (Mr Tayama) was not able to understand this because he

49. Iwano published two books about this subject. *Kindai shisō to jisseikatsu* (Modern thinking and real life) in 1913 and *Kindai seikatsu no kaibō* (An analysis of modern life) in 1915. Iwano is obviously referring to himself here.

50. Nakatani Tokutarō (1886-1920) was a novelist and a playwright.

51. The *Shinchō* version informs us that the short story was published in the journal *Chūgai* in August 1918. The short story is about two young girls and two young fellows in Tokyo's downtown *shitamachi*. They meet one moonlit night only to leave each other again shortly thereafter. A romantic, but trivial story.

52. Ikuta Chōkō (1882-1936) was a critic, a novelist and a playwright. His theory of social criticism was developed in the journal *Seitō* (Blue stocking) which was the mouthpiece of the women's movement in Japan in the period 1911-16.

53. Iwano's essay 'Gendai shōsetsu no byōshahō' (Narrative techniques in the modern novel, printed in *Bunshō sekai*, February 1911) is mentioned on page 85ff.

54. In his articles Iwano usually related objectively to his own person. This is why he uses Mr Hōmei.

55. In 'Watashi no yonda sōsaku' (About the works that I have read) printed in *Jiji shinpō*, June 7 and 8, 1914.

56. In 'Gen'ei to jijitsu' (Facts and illusions) which was published in *Yomiuri shinbun*, on June 29, 1914.

maintained his erroneous theory of flat narration. When I criticised his novel *Ippeisotsu no jūsatsu* (Executing a soldier by shooting),[57] I asked him the following question: (The day after he has instigated a fire, a soldier goes and looks innocently at the place which was destroyed by fire, all the while maintaining an air of non-involvement. A train incidentally passes close by. The passengers in the train catch sight of the place which has been destroyed by fire and they begin to talk about it amongst themselves.) But what do their words have to do with the state of mind of the soldier? — I still have not heard his answer to this, but it is possible that he was offended (by my comment) and needed to let off steam when he, a while later, in connection with something else insulted me in an essay.[58] In the mind of the author, the soldier and the people in the train can undoubtedly be compared, but this is more than superfluous,[59] to (an understanding of) the soldier's life or psychology; it is simply unnecessary.

But what about plays then? — some will probably ask. Judging by the exterior form, the author of a play has equal relations to all his characters. Because there is no narrative passage (in a play), the author can only write such lines as are directly attributable to a character's state of mind and this is true for both the protagonist and the other characters. It seems as if each time the speech changes from one character to another, the author also shifts his point of view. But this only happens on the surface. Has the author of, for example, *Sendaihagi*[60] related equally to the mother Masaoka and the son Senmatsu? Or my point is probably easier to understand if I ask whether he has portrayed her and her maid in the same way? Let us look at another example where the difference in the importance of the roles is not as great: Have Hamlet and Ophelia been placed in two different situations?[61] Not at all. Ophelia is subordinated to Hamlet's agony and Senmatsu and the maid stand or must stand in the shadow of Masaoka's misery and lamentations. The content of both plays is that which the author observes through Masaoka or Hamlet,

57. Iwano's criticism was written in April 1917 under the title '*Tayama-shi no"Ippeisotsu" ni okeru byōsha-jō no ketten*' (On the narrative mistakes in Mr Tayama's 'A soldier'). Even though Iwano simply called the work *Ippeisotsu*, he was referring to the novel which was published in book form in January 1917. Cf. *HZ* vol. 18, 315-20.

58. In the section entitled '*Hihyō toiu koto*' (On criticism) in the essay '*Enjin no hibiki*' (The sound of the motor) in *Bunshō sekai*, May 1917.

59. In the original he uses '*sokuda*' which is probably a misprint or a writing error. In the *Shinchō* version, '*dasoku*' ('jade-feet') has been used, which is probably Iwano's misprint for *dasoku* (superfluous).

60. A famous *kabuki* play, the full title of which is *Mei-boku sendai hagi*. The piece was written by Nakawa Kamesuke (his years of birth and death are unknown) and it had its premiere in 1777. The best-known scene in the play is in the second act when Masaoka, who nurses her master's son Tsurukiyo, gives her own son Senmatsu a piece of poisoned cake in order to save Tsurukiyo's life. Masaoka does not wince as Senmatsu dies. It is her duty to do everything for her master.

61. Furthermore in the *Shinchō* version, he has written 'or are they seen, each in their own life?'.

but only to the extent that they themselves have been able to observe it. This point is something which to a certain degree we are more conscious[62] of in modern drama, for example in Ibsen and Strindberg, more so than was the case in Shakespeare or Goethe.[63]

Part 5: The Difference Between Putting the Abstractions at the Centre and Prioritizing the Transferred Subjective Point of View

For those authors who wish to create serious, earnest art (literature), there is one single situation in which the attitude described in the first illustration is permissible. This is in the autobiographical work where the author is at the top of the diagram, and where he is also one of the characters and speaks through an 'I'. But this means that the mediator whom the author feels his way into and unto whom the author transfers his subjective point of view, is also the author himself. It is easier to understand the relationship if one considers that the A of the second diagram is the author and A *at the same time*. This *fusokufuri* relationship ought to be established anyway between the author-mediator and the author himself, who must be placed higher than the former, as is the case in the second attitude. Thus I accept only the second attitude. Just as a male author can choose a woman to be the mediator, that is to say the protagonist, so it is possible for an author, a man or a woman, to describe the psychology of an animal.

Once when I had chosen the conditions in a cowshed as the material for a short story, I described somewhere in that story (which is included in my book *Gonin no onna* with a minor revision)[64] how a bull that had been overfed, is twisting with pain. In an article in response to this Mr Maeda Akira posed the question whether it was at all possible to portray the psychology of an animal.[65] I answered

---

62. The *Shinchō* version reads 'more and more' rather than 'to a certain degree, we are more conscious'.

63. The *Shinchō* version is followed by two sentences: 'Just as Gorkij in *The night shelter* describes the surroundings through the eyes of an old man, somebody always functions as the mediator whom the author can feel his way into. This is the case even in plays; what will it not be like then, in novels, where one is free to use as many narrative passages as one wishes?' (The original title of The night shelter is *Na dne* [1902]. The old man mentioned in the quotation is called Luka.)

    The reason why Iwano deleted these two sentences is unknown. The first sentence might just as well have remained, but the formulation in the second sentence was probably problematic.

64. The short story's title is '*Baka to onna*' (A fool and a woman). It was printed in *Shinshōsetsu* in April 1911. Cf. *HZ* vol. 2, 237-69. '*Gonin no onna*' (The five women) was published in 1913 and included five short stories which all had women protagonists. The five short stories are: '*O-shima to teishu*' (O-shima and her husband), '*Geisha ni natta onna*' (The woman who became a *geisha*), '*Tsuruko*' (Tsuruko), '*Baka to onna*' and '*Tentō*' (In front of the shop). Cf. *HZ* vol. 2 and vol. 3.

65. Maeda Akira was a critic and a translator.

that it was possible.[66] That was a time when I had not yet mastered the second attitude.[67] Like Mr Maeda himself, I had such immature and materialist characteristics as 'at a distance' or 'to use bird's-eye view'. Today this is actually equivalent to Mr Arishima ['s technique] in his short story 'Gaisen' (The triumph).[68] Contrary to the materialist tendency of all naturalist writers except myself, Mr Arishima has a tendency towards the spiritual, but seen from my unified-body-and-soul point of view, his over-spiritual tendency cannot avoid approaching its opposite — the materialist tendency. As can be said of all the other works by most authors (with the exception of autobiographical works which have incidentally been improving), this short story too has not become a first-class work because it was not written in the monistic way. The author's subjective point of view frequently shifts from one character to another, in the same way as in regular popular literature; the author (the narrator) is now an old general or a young man in a village, now the driver of a carriage or the horse 'Triumph' itself. When I had pointed this out,[69] he (Mr Arishima) sent me a letter wherein, among other things, he asked why I had not noted the horse alone and that it was the *horse* he had described. He probably meant that the horse was the centre or the focal point in the short story.

This connects with Mr Maeda's aforementioned question. The centre which Mr Arishima speaks of and the 'centre' in my monistic and solid theory of narration are far apart. It is only in a fraction of the short story 'Gaisen' that the author enters the mind of the horse. He is inside of everything but the horse's inner being, despite the fact that he is observing the horse. This being the case, it is a misunderstanding to say that the author has described the horse. He has actually only described the numerous characters that have had close contact with the horse without any criteria or connections. It is true that all the people who are loosely described in this way, have their gaze directed towards the horse and one can furthermore say that the

66. See page 89 and note 32 ibid.
67. This should be understood as follows: Certainly it is possible to portray the psychology of an animal, but if one chooses to do so, the whole narrative must be based solely on this perspective. This was precisely what Iwano had not done in the short story 'Baka to onna'. He had several mediators besides the bull itself. Iwano was thus revising an opinion he had expressed earlier. It is extremely rare for him to declare his mistake in such an obvious manner as is the case here.
68. Arishima Takeo was a novelist and a critic. The short story 'Gaisen' was published in *Bunshō sekai* in October 1917. 'Triumph' is the name of a military horse which took part in the Russo-Japanese War. Now it is old and draws a carriage in the country. Arishima Takeo has depicted the inner world of the horse when it falls asleep after a long and hard days work. The horse is treated cruelly and it is very tired, but there is no one to care for it.
69. In the essay 'Arishima Takeo-shi no ai to geijutsu ron' (About Mr Arishima Takeo's love and art) which was printed in the newspaper *Kokumin shinbun* on November 21, 1917. Cf. HZ vol. 18, 336. The essay was later revised and printed in the journal *Nipponshugi* in February 1918.

horse is placed at the centre of the author's abstract explanations, but seen from the point of view of monistic narration, one can never say that the horse is at the centre. This, because the short story as a whole does not express the horse's state of mind. The author has described the general and the driver of the carriage, as well as the general's sympathy and the driver's heartlessness, not solely from the horse's inner world. If one describes a horse in the way that I recommend, it is not impossible for an author to describe the psychology of an animal by feeling his way into the animal if we assume that he has a realistic imagination. It is likewise possible for a man to depict a woman and for a poor man to depict a rich man.

Part 6: Other Writers' Nonchalant Relationship to the Unaffected and Natural Material

When using this narrative method which is so simple and natural, it may easily come to pass that a work which has probably cost the writer a great effort, nonetheless turns out to be nonsense if the author does not carefully consider each word and every passage that he writes.[70] Think of Mr Tanizaki Jun'ichirō.[71] He strives to achieve a well-developed plot and to polish the surface of his sentences, but he does nothing to turn his ideas inward. In his short story 'Chiisana ōkoku' (A small kingdom)[72] he writes the following, in a passage where he should otherwise have been within the protagonist Kaijima's mind: '*It looked as if* Kaijima was on his way to the wine dealer Naitō in K-cho (K-city).'[73] Even though it is Kaijima himself who is walking, the author writes 'It looked as if ...'. This is nothing but an explanatory explanation on the part of the author. In the same way, he writes '... it is true that he was laughing, but his eyes were alarmingly bloodshot'.[74] The sentence might have been concrete if a third person had been present and observed him. But otherwise, and unless the author had written that the character *himself had felt this way*, this must be perceived as an explanation on the part of the author, who has become involved in the course of action.

Unfortunately most authors commit these sorts of errors without noticing it themselves. For example, even in his autobiographical works, Mr Shimazaki Tōson

---

70. This was the background for serious revisions in Iwano's novel-series. More about this later.
71. Tanizaki Jun'ichirō (1886-1965) was a leading author of the aesthetic school.
72. The short story was printed in the August issue of *Chūgai*. The protagonist Kaijima Shōkichi, who is a primary school teacher, is fascinated by one of the students in his class. The child, Numakura, has mysterious abilities. One day the student produces false banknotes. Kaijima uses them to bring his family out of an economic crisis.
73. This sentence appears towards the end of the short story in a scene where Kaijima leaves the house in order to buy some milk for his child.
74. This line appears a little further into the short story when Kaijima suggests to his student Numakura that they share the false money in order to enjoy themselves together.

carelessly describes looks and facial expressions of the protagonist, as if they themselves had seen them, even though this is impossible.[75] In Masamune Hakuchō's short story 'Rōsō no kyōkun' (The old monk's teachings),[76] the mood of the old and the young monk and the woman O-yoshi have been separated from one another because of the above-mentioned carelessness and as a result the short story has become unstructured and monotonous. Not to mention the works of Mr Kamitsukasa[77] (who is as careless as the others). Many authors copy foreign works or the works of our own writers who have in turn copied foreign works. They blame the writers that they have modelled their work on and never recognise their own stupidities and their own carelessness even when these are pointed out to them. Mr Tokuda Shūsei and Ms Nogami Yae(ko)[78] have said to me that one may be able to write short stories with the method I recommend, but it would probably be impossible, or at least very difficult, to write novels in this way. But that which they cannot write, with their nonchalant relationship to literature, is not novels, but simple, natural works.[79] I hesitate a little when I say this, but at the present moment I relate to my novels in the same way as I have so far related to my short stories.[80] (But because I have found errors in my novels Hōrō and Dankyō, seen from the above-mentioned point of view, I have omitted about 100 pages from the manuscript which has a total of 850 pages.)[81]

Neither Tolstoy nor Turgenev knew about this critical problem. But somebody, who translates works by Russian authors writing after Gorkij into Japanese, told me that these writers have become more or less aware of this complex of problems.[82] But I write exclusively in my own way, concentrating on my own theory of narration, no matter what they may be doing abroad. A precise and strict

75. In the *Shinchō* version Iwano wrote the following: 'That there are not very many of such errors in Mr Shimazaki Tōson's works is probably incidental and due to the fact that most of his works are autobiographical.'
76. The short story was printed in *Chūōkōron* in July 1918.
77. Kamitsukasa Shōken (1874-1947) was a novelist and a journalist.
78. Nogami Yaeko (1885-1985) was a novelist and a writer of essays.
79. Iwano uses the word *ten'i muhō* which literally means 'the heavenly creature's clothes are seamless' which can be taken to mean something untouched, unaffected and natural.
80. Due to misprints this passage is impossible to understand in the original. Therefore, this translation is taken from the *Shinchō* version.
81. In the *Shinchō* version Iwano only mentions *Hōrō* and instead of 'omitted', he has written 'omitted and revised'. Iwano's comment reflects that he was in the middle of revising his novel-series. The new edition of *Hōrō* was revised and shortened and then published in July 1919, and the last part of the novel, from Chapter 25 to Chapter 32 (including 25 and 32) were moved to the novel *Dankyō* as the new Chapters 1-5 of this novel. The revised version of *Dankyō* was published in September 1919. See I.8 page 38ff..
82. In the *Shinchō* version Iwano wrote the following: 'But it appears to me that Russian authors after Gorkij have become more or less aware of the problem.'

outlook on life and a theory of narration like mine have been able to appear simply because the spirit of modern literature has touched upon an aspect of our people's nature, namely persistence and perfectionism. I thank our country for this. Like Baudelaire's method — to see and depict things from within — was born in France and later renewed poetry around the world, I believe, that gradually as our country develops, my theory of narration will renew the writing of novels throughout the world.

Lastly, I would like to mention a few more things.[83] A Russian author (I think it was Artsybaschev) wrote a short story about the group mentality of hungry wolves.[84] In Mr Kikuchi Kan's short story 'Kataki no sōshiki' (The enemy's burial)[85] there is actually no protagonist — it is perhaps possible to consider a group of air force officers as one protagonist. When portraying a flock or the psychology of a group, this should also be done from within, with the aid of monistic narration and one must never employ the simple 'at a distance' attitude. The protagonist A should just be the mediator who ties the life of his friends or life in society to the author; he (the mediator) does not necessarily have to be more active than the other characters in the work. For example, in my short story 'Dokutan kengisha to futari no onna' (The man suspected of being a German spy, and two women),[86] the somewhat sensible, unemployed snob is the protagonist, but the short story is mainly about one of the two women. But her course of action in the story is seen entirely through the eyes of the protagonist and as such it is subordinated to his mood. This is precisely what his position as a mediator consists in.

I hope that my theory will not simply be regarded as my personal point of view, but instead that it will be read with particular care by every writer and critic in order that the literature in our country and art throughout the world may become more penetrating and pure.

[September 1918][87]

83. The *Shinchō* version reads as follows: 'I have already used up the allotted space, but I want to mention just a few more things, very briefly.'
84. Michail Petrovisch Artsybaschev (1878-1927) was a Russian novelist. His principal work is *Sanin* from 1907. Which short story Iwano is referring to is unknown. (Artsybaschev's works about eroticism attracted a lot of attention and made him quite popular during his time, but today he has been completely forgotten. He was actually a second-rate author.)
85. Kikuchi Kan (1888-1948) was a novelist and a playwright. He is known for his popular writing. 'Kataki no sōshiki' was printed in *Shinshōsetsu* in August 1918.
86. The short story was printed in the December issue of *Kuroshio* in 1917. When it was included in the collected works, the title was changed to 'Dokutan to futari no onna' (The German spy and the two women). Cf. HZ vol. 5, 129-99.
87. The *Shinchō* version is a little more precise and dates the article September 11, 1918.

V. Criticism and Practice

Ne te quæsiveris extra.
Ralph W. Emerson

1. Criticism of the Theory

Immediately following the publication of Iwano's article on monistic narration, Nakamura Seiko commented on the theory in the newspaper *Yomiuri shinbun*, on October 9 and 10. He was of the opinion that if a writer limited himself to only one point of view throughout a novel, he would end up feeling suffocated. Nakamura Seiko thought that a writer could easily feel his way into the interior life of several characters at the same time. He ended his criticism as follows:

The advantage of Mr Iwano's theory of narration lies in its monistic background, but he must realise that the weakness of the theory stems from his borrowings from the theory of empathy.[1] If he believes in the theory of empathy, why does he then restrict his use of objects ('mediators' in the terminology of Mr Iwano) to one?[2]

He reviewed Iwano's short story '*Kūkijū*' (The air gun, in *Chūgai*, October 1918) from the same perspective, in *Yomiuri shinbun*, October 17.[3]

Iwano reacted harshly to Nakamura Seiko's criticism and review. First and foremost he wrote a short commentary, '*Nakamura Seiko-shi e*' (To Mr Nakamura Seiko, October 22, in *Yomiuri shinbun*) in which he drew attention to Nakamura Seiko's 'short-sightedness' and 'ignorance'.[4] The comment was followed by a longer article, '*Byōsharon hoi*' (A supplement to the theory of narration), which was published in the November issue of *Shinchō*. As far as

---

1. Theodor Lipps' theory of *Einfühlung*. Cf. IV. Part 2, page 113.
2. Cf. Wada Kingo, *Byōsha no jidai*, 156.
3. An autobiographical short story, based on Iwano's journey to Shuzenji on the peninsula of Izu, in March 1915. Among other things, he describes his relationship to the women that he has known during the years, and to his new wife. The tone is bitter and almost Strindbergian.
4. Cf. Wada Kingo, op. cit., 156.

the issue of limiting the point of view to that of one single character was concerned, Iwano provided the following explanation for the feeling of 'suffocation' that disturbed Nakamura Seiko:

[This is] because he maintains the arrogant assumption that we are able to watch A, B, C and D equally just like God, and he imagines the use of a point of view which is limited to A alone or to one of the others to be the result of a similarly arrogant perception.[5]

As far as Nakamura Seiko's remark regarding the theory of empathy was concerned, Iwano defended his theory with the following words:

The author is free to choose which 'object' in the society or life that he is describing, he will use as his mediator but once he has chosen his mediator, all other 'objects' must be described through him ... If he wishes to employ more mediators for his subjective point of view, we are no longer dealing with a concrete work of art, unless he writes as many novels as he has mediators.[6] ... If you employ more mediators in one work, you end up writing an idea-novel.[7]

In the November issue of *Chūgai*, Ikuta Chōkō published the article 'Iwano Hōmei-shi no byōsharon' (Mr Iwano Hōmei's theory of narration). He opens the article by dividing short stories and novels into two categories: on the one hand we have diaries, accounts of journeys, confessions and autobiographies, and on the other hand works of fiction. He goes on to write that if Iwano's novels belong to the first category, then he is willing to admit that the theory is rather valuable. But if they belong to the second category, there is 'first of all no reason to have a central character or protagonist ...' He continues: 'Secondly; even if there is a protagonist, there is no reason why there should only be one. And thirdly; even if there is only one protagonist, there is no reason why he should be treated as a "primary character".' Finally he says in his conclusion: 'Despite my many re-readings of the article, I still do not understand how anyone can claim that only short stories written in the first person or autobiographical stories can be true.'[8]

In this respect we may mention that Ikuta Chōkō reviewed Iwano's short story 'Kūkijū' as well, in the same issue of *Chūgai*.

---

5. *HZ* vol. 10, 598.
6. Iwano himself experimented with this use in the short stories 'Jisshi no hōchiku' and 'Konashi no Tsutsumi'. More on this in V.2.1, page 140-41.
7. Cf. *HZ* vol. 10, 600-1.
8. Cf. *KBHT* vol. 5, 97-100.

Iwano's answer to the article and to the review was formulated in '*Ikuta Chōkō-shi e no kotae*' (An answer to Mr Ikuta Chōkō) which was published in *Chūgai* in December 1918.[9] First of all, Iwano points out that Ikuta Chōkō's criticism points the debate in a wrong direction because his rough classification of short stories, into two groups; descriptions of the author's direct experience and works of fiction. Iwano goes on: 'An author does admittedly write about his own experience, but we are here talking of such experience as he may obtain by picturing that a certain kind of person is confronted with a certain event, and then imagining what he himself would do or feel were he in the situation of that person.'[10] The method that Iwano is discussing here is of course his own, and he goes on to look at his short stories (novels), which 'are no wretched confessional writing deprived of fantasies'. Rather he defines these as 'the literature of inner experience' (*naibuteki-taiken shōsetsu*), in which he has made 'real life come alive without turning it into a mere idea, even though fictitious elements and/or fantasies have been added to it.'[11] Hereafter he stresses the fact that 'what he [Ikuta Chōkō] has categorised as a literature of experience, in other words, consists of works of the so-called inner realism, in which the technique of monistic narration must inevitably be employed.'[12]

Also Maeda Akira reviewed Iwano's short story '*Kūkijū*'. His review was published in the November issue of *Bunshō sekai* under the title '*Gyōshi to kanshō no seikatsu*' (A life in observation and appreciation). He discusses the relationship between the short story and the theory of monistic narration, and criticises Iwano as follows:

'*Kūkijū*' is an autobiographical short story in which the author and the protagonist are identical. About such instances, Iwano has said that there is a relation of neither-identification-nor-differentiation (*fusokufuri*) between A (the protagonist)

---

9. Ibid., 485.
10. Ibid., 468-76. This claim gains a central importance when later (VI.1, page 168ff) we compare Iwano's theory with *watakushi shōsetsu*. Here we will limit ourselves to quoting one of the greatest writers of *watakushi shōsetsu*, Shiga Naoya (1883-1971) on his relationship to his monumental novel *An'ya kōro* (A Dark Night's Passing, translated into English by Edwin McClellan, 1976): 'The protagonist Kensaku is almost the author himself. The novel is actually a mixture of what I would probably do in a given situation if I were him, of what I would like to do in such a situation, and of what I have done in a similar situation in reality.' Cf. *Shiga Naoya zenshū* (Shiga Naoya's collected works), vol. 8, 1974, 20.
11. Cf. *HZ* vol. 18, 470.
12. Ibid., 471.

and the author. But such a relationship cannot be found in the short story. Rather we find only a relation of *identification-and-no-differentiation (sokufuri)* ... Even in an autobiographical short story ... the author must guide his protagonist. Can we still talk of fiction when the protagonist has simply become the author himself?[13]

On January 14, 1919, Maeda Akira published another article in *Yomiuri shinbun* under the title *'Shokan o futatsu mittsu'* (A few comments). Here he criticises Iwano's theory once more:

The theory [of monistic narration] completely overlooks the psychology which is the prerequisite of any artistic activity. No matter whether the protagonist in a work is identical to the author or not, i.e. no matter whether the work is autobiographical or not, the author must have the ability to 'master' [have a general knowledge of] the world of the protagonist better than the protagonist himself. If the situation is different from this, no art is possible ... Once we have realised that the writer must have this ability beforehand, it becomes evident that he needs not confine himself to describing only the things that the protagonist knows of. [Iwano seems to believe that] in a short story, the author expresses the personality of the protagonist, but a short story is a work in which the author gives direct expression to his own world through the world of the protagonist.[14]

Iwano responded to Maeda Akira's criticism already four days later in *Yomiuri shinbun*. He regarded Maeda Akira's criticism as a result of his 'lacking ability to understand',[15] and gave the following explanation of the relationship between the author and the protagonist as seen from the perspective of monistic narration:

If a writer writes about his own world as seen from his own point of view, the result will be an explanation. Therefore he should avoid doing so. Rather, [the world of the author] should be formulated in such a way that the reader can visualise it directly through the world of the protagonist or through the imperfection of his life (there is indeed something to meditate on here) ... When a writer leaves something out of his work, it is also a way of manifesting his critical attitude. Therefore an author cannot be completely identical to the protagonist in a monistic narration either — not even when the work is autobiographical.[16]

---

13. Quoted in Wada Kingo, op. cit., 158.
14. Ibid., 158-59.
15. This was, by the way, the title of the article, which was in Japanese *'Rikairyoku no fusoku da'*.
16. Ibid.

During the entire debate, Iwano's argumentation remained dogmatic: it was weak and not very convincing. The interesting point is, however, that at this point in time two aspects were touched upon in all the critical remarks that were directed towards Iwano: the criticism of the theory itself, and the criticism of the autobiographical short story 'Kūkijū', which had been published almost at the same time as the theory.

Among the several criticisms of Iwano's theory of narration, Tsuchida Kyōson's article 'Iwayuru ichigen-byōsha o ronzu' (On the so-called monistic narration, in *Bunshō sekai*, December 1918) was the most well-formulated and the one that was most convincing in its argumentation. Tsuchida Kyōson, philosopher and social critic, mainly analyses Iwano's theory from a philosophical point of view. He considers Iwano's argumentation 'too weak', and finds his epistemology 'childish' and 'of the kind that is called naive idealism within philosophical circles'. Quite evidently he considers Iwano's theory erroneous, because Iwano 'bases his theory on wrong epistemology'.[17] In the article Kyōson indicates the following five points as errors or weaknesses in Iwano's theory:

1. An author cannot as a matter of course enter the mood of a protagonist A or B.[18] He has his own world, and he cannot have another world with A or B at its centre.
2. Even if the author succeeds in entering A completely, he is only able to describe B and/or C when A is present. This is a disadvantageous and unfortunate situation, because the author cannot know that which A does not know either.
3. When the author enters A, this can only be done in the present moment, and not in A's past.
4. Even if the author enters A entirely, he still cannot describe him completely.
5. If A is, say, crazy, it is impossible for the author to enter him and describe him at the same time.[19]

Iwano's answer to Tsuchida Kyōson's criticism was published under the title 'Tsuchida-shi ni kotau' (An answer to Mr Tsuchida [Kyōson], 1919) in the March issue of *Bunshō sekai*. Here he goes through the five points, defending his theory. But Iwano's countercriticism was not adequately convincing. For

---

17. *KBHT* vol. 5, 101.
18. A, B, etc. refer to 'characters' in a work. Cf. Iwano's illustrations, in IV. 2, Part 1, page 105ff.
19. *KBHT* vol. 5, 101-3.

instance he writes about the first point, the relation between the author and the protagonist:

Because an author should not give expression to his point of view in the form of an idea or 'the pure I' (*junga*) in his work, he tentatively enters the protagonist of the work or the character that I call the mediator, and from this position he realises his own point of view.[20]

This was simply a repetition of what he had already said. As we have seen earlier, the controversies over Iwano's theory of narration had always arisen with the publication of one of his autobiographical works, and primarily when volumes of the five-volume novel-series, in which the author was identical to the protagonist, had been published. The question of the relation between the author and the protagonist was and remained one of the most important and complicated controversial issues in the debate that accompanied the theory of monistic narration.

But to Iwano, the theory of monistic narration was an already finished and completed circle, and for this very reason he was no longer concerned with developing it further. To him the only possible operations regarding the theory were eventual additions, specifications and the final implementation. After having published the theory in its entirety, Iwano was now more interested in studying its validity in concrete cases than in elaborating its actual form.

On this background he wrote the article 'Ichigen-byōsha no jissai shōmei' (Monistic narration in practice, in *Shinchō*) in 1919. In the article he criticised works of his contemporaries from the perspective of monistic narration. The works discussed included Tayama Katai's *Ippeisotsu no jūsatsu* (Executing a soldier by shooting, January 1917), Akutagawa Ryūnosuke's 'Kaika no ryōjin' (The good man during the age of civilisation, in *Chūgai*, January 1919) and Kikuchi Kan's 'Sōshiki ni ikanu wake' (Reasons for not attending the funeral, in *Shinchō*, February 1919).[21]

In the same article Iwano pointed out that he had gone through his own works to correct the passages that were not in accordance with the theory. Among others he was thinking of the novels *Hōrō* and *Dokuyaku o nomu onna* and the short story 'O-yasu no teishu' (O-yasu's husband, November 1918).[22] But Iwano did not only correct these works; he was working on a revision

20. In Wada Kingo, op. cit., 160.
21. Cf. *HZ* vol. 10, 586-93.
22. Ibid., 583 and 585-86.

of the complete novel-series, which was about to come out in its entirety from
the publishing house *Shinchō-sha*. From July 1919, the novel-series was thus
issued with major and minor corrections and omissions.[23]

While he was publishing his voluminous major work, Iwano was planning
to write a great work about monistic narration,[24] partly on the basis of the
article from 1918, partly founded on his new article from September 1919
'*Tetsurijō no yobiteki chishiki*' (The philosophical prerequisite for the comprehension of the theory), which was formulated as a thorough answer to
Tsuchida Kyōson's above-mentioned criticism.[25] In the article Iwano primarily
explains the epistemological foundation for the theory. After having given
an account of the teachings of Avatamsaka Sutra (*Kegon-kyō*), he discusses the
relationship between the objective and the subjective.[26] He believes that we
can only apprehend that of the objective which is based upon the subjective,
and that pure objectivity with no trace of the subjective is impossible. With
the help of the following illustration, he furthermore demonstrates how we
may only apprehend a subjective view if it has been produced by the
objective — the hatched part of the illustration.

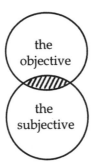

23. Cf. IV. Part 6, page 121ff, and footnote 81 ibidem.
24. On December 26, 1919 he made a note in his diary saying that 'he had begun to write
    about monistic narration'. But because of his death in May 1920, the plan was never
    realised. Cf. *HZ* vol. 12, 564.
25. In *HZ* vol. 10 it appears that the article was written in 1918. This must be a (printer's)
    error.
26. Cf. *HZ* vol. 10, 567-69. It is interesting to note that Iwano considered the theory of
    Avatamsaka Sutra as the epistemological foundation of the theory. This was seen as a
    counterpart to Tsuchida Kyōson's Western sources, Franz Brentano and Edmund
    Husserl. At this point in time Iwano was a nationalist. (He was editor-in-chief of the
    journal *Nipponshugi* (Nipponism).) To him, Japanese (Eastern) culture was superior to
    that of the West and to the rest of the world in general. In the short essay '*Ichigen-
    byōsha to wa?*' (What is monistic narration?, published in *Bunshō kurabu* in October
    1919), he wrote naively: 'A theory of narration as thorough as mine is not known
    abroad. For this reason foreign theories of narration cannot be used as standards.' Cf.
    HZ vol. 10, 596.

He furthermore stresses the fact that the remaining part can only exist as 'presumption',[27] and continues:

[The hatched part] shows the epistemological sphere which I believe can be employed in art ... A classification which sees art as merely sensuous, compared to philosophy which is rational and scientific, belongs to the past ... Most people disagree with me when I consider art as a practice/act on a par with religion, but this is due to their ignorance of the fact that there is a new cultural life or a new art which allows for our entire personality to flare up ... The artistic world which has reached the level of the art of practice/action, is, if considered from an epistemological perspective, a whole new area in which 'apprehension is based upon the intellect which has been filtered through emotion and will' (*jōikachi-teki ninshiki*) ... The part of the subjective point of view, which falls into the objective and which makes up the hatched part [in the illustration], is exactly 'the intellect filtered through emotion and will' (*jōikachi*) or 'the flaring intellect' (*nenshōchi*); or rather 'the flaring up of the heart' (*shinnetsu*), which occurs without separating the intellect, the emotion and the will. I presume it is needless to say that this is exactly the kind of heart that the artist must have.[28]

'But an artist's subjective point of view is of a personal character', Iwano goes on to say. 'If A's subjective point of view is red, also X (the objective) will be reddish to him; seen from the opposite point of view we may say that only this reddish X is true to A. The same goes for B and C of course,' he furthermore explains, with the help of the following illustration:

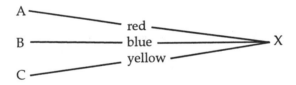

Then he writes as follows:

But there is no need to ask whether this truth is the existential truth or 'Truth'. This because 'the world of the flaring intellect' (*nenshōchi-teki sekai*) which is demanded of the artist, has presumably already been realised in its entirety in the epistemological relationship between A, B, or C and X.[29]

27. Ibid., 569-70.
28. Ibid., 570-72. '*Jōikachi*', '*nenshōchi*' and '*shinnetsu*' are all Iwano's own neologisms.
29. Ibid., 572-73.

In this way Iwano tried to defend his theory of narration also from an epistemological point of view.

During the revision of his earlier works and the clarification of the theory itself, Iwano worked through some short stories which had been written in complete accordance with the principle of monistic narration. This group of short stories included two of his stories from December 1919, '*Jisshi no hōchiku*' (Expelling children from home) and '*Konashi no Tsutsumi*' (Tsutsumi, the childless). In these stories, identical scenes were described from two different points of views, that is, through two different 'mediators'.[30] This was the way in which Iwano experimented with his method in order to demonstrate the validity of the theory in practice.

At this stage Iwano was almost exclusively interested in the technical sides of the theory. He seems to have been imprisoned by his own method, and to have grown dependent upon it.

The theory that was his own creation, began to determine the direction that his writing of fiction was taking. In a way he had become the slave of monistic narration. The original, dynamic 'destructively subjective point of view' had thus receded and been replaced by the more technical 'monistic narration'. The more he removed himself from 'the destructively subjective point of view' and worked on the purely method-concerned side of narrative theory, the less clear did the principal difference between his theory and general naturalistic narrative theory become. Inevitably this led to a discrepancy between Iwano's original intentions and his actual method. And this was presumably the reason why the controversies over the theory of narration no longer progressed in any productive way, but simply continued in an idle fashion.

In the following we shall give some examples of this.

Iwano's short story '*O-sei*' (O-sei, published in *Kaizō*, February 1920)[31] was reviewed by Hirotsu Kazuo in the March issue of *Shinchō*. Hirotsu Kazuo sees

---

30. Cf. page V.2.2., page 141ff in which the overlapping scenes are translated and compared.

31. '*O-sei*' is the first story in the short story series concerned with the female protagonist O-sei, whom Iwano modelled upon his first wife Takekoshi Kō. Cf. page 48). The plot of the series can be summarised as follows: After their divorce, O-sei takes over Taguchi's boarding house, but she is not able to run it properly. For financial reasons she lets her sons live with their father (Taguchi), despite the fact that he had given them up. At this point O-sei has developed a manic fascination for the art of fortune-telling, and she decides to undertake a pilgrimage to the island of Shikoku, in order to begin her life anew. But after some months, she returns with no result, only to return to her old ways. This is of immense irritation to Taguchi.

it as a story in which 'only the outer actions of the idler O-sei are described carefully'. In the March issue of *Waseda bungaku*, the same short story was reviewed by Harada Minoru (1890-1975), who thought it was a story in which the author 'seemed to hold a far too simplistic view of the woman O-sei'.[32]

Iwano responded to these criticisms with the article '*Hirotsu, Harada no ryōshi ni kotau*' (In response to both Mr Hirotsu and Mr Harada) in *Yomiuri shinbun*, March 11 and 12. Among other things he writes that 'for instance the elaborate description of how O-sei caught the lice was actually a description of the woman's inner life and in no way of her outer action'. Then he uses formulations as severe as these:

[They criticise me without understanding that] when a writer employs the technique of monistic narration, he is describing the protagonist's world ... from the *inside*. They call themselves critics, but what ignorance! What qualifications they boast![33]

Even though Iwano aimed furious attacks also at other critics, accusing them of 'ignorance' and of misunderstanding him, the criticism of the short story series about O-sei continued.

Already the day after the publication of Iwano's agitated article in *Yomiuri shinbun*, Eguchi Kiyoshi (1887-1975) reviewed his short story '*O-sei no shippai*' (Osei's mistake) which was the sequel to the story '*O-sei*' which had been published in the same newspaper. Eguchi Kiyoshi found that the 'ugly and lazy side [of O-sei] was far too dominating' in the story, and that this was the only 'explanation for the psychology of the lecherous and indolent woman, written in such insecure language that she seemed like a patient suffering from beri-beri.' He goes on to write as follows:

Also the description of O-sei's mood is far too superficial ... It is most disappointing to see that Mr Iwano's monistic narration has not moved beyond this stage ... If this is where monistic narration is to remain, it is actually no different from formalism.[34]

With these words he backed up Hirotsu Kazuo's criticism of Iwano's short story '*O-sei*'.

The discussion continued in even more fervent terms On March 16 and

32. Both quotations are from Wada Kingo, op. cit., 162.
33. Ibid.
34. Ibid.

17, Iwano responded to Eguchi Kiyoshi's criticism in the essay '*Shōsetsu "O-sei" ni tsuite*' (On the short story 'O-sei') in *Yomiuri shinbun*, in which he actually warned his antagonist against putting forward such courageous statements. Iwano writes as follows:

It is not the exterior aspect of the short story which is 'lazy', but the very content of the protagonist's life. This is what is reflected in the narration ... He [Eguchi Kiyoshi] reproaches me for using 'insecure' language. But if in order to describe a woman like her [O-sei] we should rather employ a clear language, the overall impression would become abstract and the language would not fit the content at all — that is, if the description did not end up as a mere explanation ... Language, like the narration itself, cannot be separated from content.[35]

And he ends the article with the following remark: 'The children who still smell of pee, are worth no more than that stench.'[36]

This was the way in which Iwano rebutted the criticism of the 'greenhorns'.[37] But his attacks upon the young critics/writers did not end here.

On March 27, 1920 Iwano wrote another short essay with the title '*Daisansha to chigau*' (I am not the third person) in the newspaper *Jiji shinpō*. One of the claims that he made here was that 'I was right when I suggested that the greenhorn who smells of pee [Eguchi Kiyoshi] ought to study some more.'[38]

This was too much for Eguchi Kiyoshi. He retorted in an article with the provocative title '*Hōmei-shi ni ichigeki o kuwasu*' (I throw a punch at Mr [Iwano] Hōmei) in *Yomiuri shinbun*, April 2, 3 and 5. He claimed that Iwano's answer was nothing but an attempt to explain away the criticisms, and he then launched his criticism of Iwano's personality in a rather awkward way:

Mr Iwano is simply stupid ... If he wishes to know how other people smell, he must use his nose more attentively.[39]

Of course Iwano did not refrain from responding to this remark. But this time

---

35. Ibid., 163.
36. Ibid.
37. At this point in time, in 1920, Hirotsu Kazuo was 29 years old, Harada Minoru and Eguchi Kiyoshi 30 and 33 respectively, which made them very 'young' according to Japanese standards.
38. Ibid.
39. Ibid.

he was less agitated than had been the case earlier. On the contrary, his tone is almost one of resignation when in the essay '*Eguchi-shi ni kotau*' (An answer to Mr Eguchi, in *Yomiuri shinbun*, April 15 and 17) he writes as follows:

As far as [the theory of] monistic narration is concerned, I am the author behind it, and this goes for the entire world. No one has yet been able to or had the right to comment on it. To me this situation is very sad, but there is nothing that I can do about it, yet.[40]

To Iwano who had written that no one was able to criticise his theory, a continued controversy over narrative theory seemed useless. The vast work on monistic narration which he had planned to write, was not completed either.[41] Even if he had had the time to finish it, it would have been a mere collection of short articles and essays, as had been the case with the book *The New Naturalism*. *The New Naturalism* was nothing but a repetition of his preceding book *The Mystic Semi-Animalism*.

In our passage through the many years of debate on narrative theory, we have seen how Iwano's theory of monistic narration was the product of his attempts at creating a theoretical framework for his writings. This framework would then make it possible for him to make his autobiographical novels and short stories, in which he made the protagonist speak with his own words, appear as works of 'the new naturalism' which used purely objective narration. When during the debate he was met with accusations of writing confessional literature, Iwano invented the concept 'the destructively subjective point of view'. Later when his works employing 'the destructively subjective point of view' were criticised for the use of an 'explanatory' style, he defended his method with the help of the term 'narrative narration'. Then he limited the scope of his narration to events taking place in daily life. With the emergence of the school of idealism, he developed the theory of 'inner realism' and concentrated his energies on the description of an 'inner' life. In order not to confuse the author and the protagonist, he employed the term 'mediator'.

Little by little and during the entire process, Iwano's monistic narration took the shape of a proper literary theory. At the same time, however, it developed into a technical method of writing. Consequently, his 'destructively subjective point of view' was gradually removed from the centre of the theory.

40. Ibid., 164.
41. Cf. footnote 24.

Iwano's novel-series, which had made him formulate the theory in the first place, had originally been opened with the novel *Tandeki* (Dissolute Living), in which 'the destructively subjective point of view' had been the keynote. When after the publication of the theory in October 1918, he revised the novel-series from the perspective of monistic narration, he removed *Tandeki* from the series. This change was an evident indication of where the theory was to end. Also his vehement controversies with the young critics right up to his death were concerned exclusively with the side of narration pertaining to the technical issues of writing.

Iwano the passionate writer had receded and left the scene to his protagonist or his 'mediator', who was concerned solely with the tedious and everyday matters of life. The author's role was thus reduced to registering and 'describing' these matters in as 'objective' a way as possible.

Consequently, monistic narration could not avoid the risk which the naturalistic theory of objective narration had been exposed to from the very beginning; the absence of the authorial 'I'.

From here, the road to *watakushi shōsetsu*[42] was short.

In order to win back the lost authorial presence, all a *watakushi shōsetsu* writer had to do was to play the role of the 'mediator' himself, at the cost of the 'objectivity' of the narration. In this way the author and the protagonist became identical. A 'monistic' relationship is thus preserved, but the writing is no longer concerned with a proper 'narration' because 'narration' always presupposes a necessary distance between the author and the protagonist. The writers of *watakushi shōsetsu* strove to realise the highest ambition of realism, that of verisimilitude, not through objectivity but through subjectivity. Iwano's theory of monistic narration had an indirect but crucial role to play in the development of *watakushi shōsetsu*.

We shall return to this matter below in VI.1.

2. The Theory and Iwano Hōmei's Writings

> Any point of view is interesting that is
> a direct impression of life.
> You each have an impression coloured
> by your individual conditions.
> Henry James

---

42. For the time being we shall define this term as a special kind of confessional writing in which the author appears as the 'I', disguised or not, of his work.

2.1. Short Stories in Monistic Narration

Ever since the publication of his very first short story 'Geisha Kotake' (The *geisha* Kotake) in 1906, Iwano had been inclined to describe the life of only one character in his short stories. This tendency was even stronger in his autobiographical short stories/novels, in which the protagonist is his alter ego. With only a few exceptions, all the short stories that Iwano wrote after the publication of the completed theory in 1918, had been based upon the theory of monistic narration. He worked almost frantically to make his entire production of fiction correspond to the theory. His perfectionism made him correct also already completed works, at least as far as his most important work, the novel-series, is concerned. When he died in 1920 he was still working on a revision of the series.

Among the short stories written just before and after the publication of the theory, the following titles may be listed as representative of monistic narration:

'*Ietsuki nyōbō*' (Woman with a house, in *Chūōkōron*, November 1918)
'*O-take bāsan*' (O-take, the old woman, in *Taikan*, March 1919)
'*Buraku no musume*' (The girl from the slum, in *Shinshōsetsu*, April 1919)
'*Bijin*' (Beauty, in *HZ* vol. 8, March 1919)
'*O-masu no shinjin*' (O-masu's belief, in *HZ* vol. 8, July 1919)
'*Kare no kyū-nikki yori*' (From his old diary, in *HZ* vol. 8, October 1919)

Apart from these, Iwano wrote two autobiographical series of short stories.[43] The first series described his relationship to his second wife Endō Kiyoko and consisted of four stories. We here list these in the order in which the action unfolds:[44]

'*Seifuku hiseifuku*' (The conqueror and the conquered, in *Chūōkōron*, February 1919)
'*Mitsubachi no ie*' (The house with the beehive, in *Yūben*, April 1919)
'*Kūkijū*' (The air gun, in *Chūgai*, October 1919)

---

43. Iwano's five-volume novel-series can be regarded as a love story, describing his relationship to his lover Masuda Shimoe (Shimizu O-tori in the work). If we include the novel-series in our consideration, then Iwano may be said to have written three short story-/novel-series on his love/hate life.
44. These four short stories were published in one volume under the title *Seifuku hiseifuku* in June 1919.

'*Rikon made*' (Until the divorce, published as '*Soshō yori rikon made*' (From the
    trial to the divorce), in *Kuroshio*, March 1917)

In the second series, on the other hand, he described his 'witch,' his first wife
Takekoshi Kō, in the following six stories (listed in the order in which the
action unfolds):

'*O-sei no heizei*' (The daily life of O-sei, published as '*O-sei*' in *Kaizō*, February
    1920)
'*O-sei no shippai*' (O-sei's mistake, in *Kaizō*, March 1920)
'*Kanojo no junrei*'(Her pilgrimage, published as '*O-sei no junrei*' in *Taiyō*, June
    1920)
'*Junrei-go no O-sei*' (O-sei after the pilgrimage; incomplete, published post-
    humously in the book *Onna no shūchaku*, A woman's stubbornness,
    September 1920)
'*Jisshi no hōchiku*' (Expelling children from home, in *Chūōkōron*, December
    1919, published as a book under the title *Jō ka mujō ka* (Mercifully or
    mercilessly, in April 1920)
'*Konashi no Tsutsumi*' (Tsutsumi, the childless, in *Ningen*, December 1919)

In the first series, Iwano's alter ego is called Sekine Kōji and it is through him
that we learn about Iwano's marriage with Endō Kiyoko and their divorce.
The series is consequently autobiographical and written according to the
ideas of monistic narration in its purest and simplest form. There is thus a
relation of *fusokufuri* (neither-identification-nor-differentiation) between Iwano
and the protagonist (or 'mediator').

In the second series, the relationship between the characters changes. The
material is autobiographical, but the narrative method is much more varied
than the one employed in a simple *fusokufuri*-relationship. Seen from the
perspective of Iwano's monistic narration, his second short story series is the
most interesting as far as the possible application of the theory is concerned.

The protagonist in the series is O-sei, who is in trouble because of her
suspicious nature, her jealousy and hysteria. When she is divorced from the
writer Taguchi, she receives the boarding house that he had inherited from
his father, as compensation. She is supposed to run it on her own and take
care of their children. (She and Taguchi had six children,[45] but three of them

45. All in all Iwano had six children with Takekoshi Kō. The first daughter Kiyo (1896-99),
    the second daughter Fumi (1899-1914), the first son Yuzuru (1901-02), the second son

died while they were still infants and their second daughter died from an illness later. O-sei thus had two boys of school age living with her.) But after the divorce O-sei seems to lose her identity and she becomes lazy. She has no idea of what to do with her life. She keeps the boys but teaches them nothing but to hate their father Taguchi.

This is the background for the action in the first story 'O-sei no heizei'. O-sei is jealous because Taguchi has recently found a new young wife with whom he now lives. Her financial situation is difficult as well, because the boarding house has few visitors. She is the only one who does not realise that this is all her own fault. She is not taking proper care of the boarding house. She conceives the idea that she will beg money from Taguchi, using the children as her excuse. This inevitably leads to a terrible argument between Taguchi and O-sei. She is now forced to find another solution. First she tries to better her financial situation with the help of a friend Tsutsumi, who has offered to run the boarding house for her. In the beginning things seem to be going better, but this is only for a while. A scandalmonger called Ōkawa comes to see O-sei and speaks ill of Tsutsumi. Among other things, she claims that he is only helping O-sei because he is planning to steal the boarding house from her. O-sei believes her and in this way her relationship with Tsutsumi is ruined. In the meantime O-sei has allowed her eldest son Yūsaku to move in with his father, because she can no longer afford to pay for his schooling. Her youngest son Masanao stays with her. But O-sei visits Yūsaku, who is now living with Taguchi, far too often, and this is of immense irritation to Taguchi, not just because she visits too often, but also because she talks badly of Taguchi every time she comes to visit her son. In Taguchi's house money and precious objects begin to disappear. Yūsaku and O-sei come under suspicion.

In the second story of the series, 'O-sei no shippai', O-sei gives the boarding house another try. This time she hires a middle-aged carpenter, who later turns out to be Ōkawa's lover. He is engaged to modernise her ramshackle boarding house and is then supposed to take over the daily management. O-sei will pay him a fixed monthly amount for this. But as soon as the house has been repaired, the carpenter moves in with both his family and his lover Ōkawa. This is too much for O-sei. She feels cheated and pushed aside. She is also jealous. She needs a man, but is alone. Nobody is interested in her. She regrets everything. But now it is already too late. The contract has been signed; there is nothing to do. As a last resort, O-sei turns

Kaoru (1903-?), the third son Masao (1906-?) and the fourth son Sadao (was born and died in 1908).

to Taguchi for help. Though he is not happy to do so, he helps her, but only on the condition that O-sei will let Masanao, the youngest son, move in with him as well. O-sei has to accept the conditions. Then Taguchi sends one of his friends to mediate with the carpenter. Difficult negotiations commence. It turns out that the parties may after all arrive at an agreement. But then O-sei becomes suspicious of Taguchi and his friend the mediator. She believes that Taguchi is taking advantage of her situation in order to steal it all from her — first the one son, then the youngest son, and now the boarding house. She is seized by panic. As a consequence of this, she ruins the mediation, and loses everything. It is rumoured that she has gone crazy.

The third story *'Kanojo no junrei'* opens when O-sei, who in the meantime has taken an interest in fortune-telling, goes to her teacher to lament of everything and everybody. But the conversation ends in an argument, and she is thrown out. In despair she decides to undertake a pilgrimage to the island of Shikoku. Some weeks later, dressed in the traditional white dress, she says goodbye to her sons and goes to Tokushima where one of her old friends owns a private hospital. After having stayed and worked at the hospital for some time, she begins her pilgrimage, which consists of walking around the entire island by foot and visiting 88 holy temples in a certain order. During the journey she has visions and believes that she meets the incarnation of Kōbō-daishi.[46] But she has merely been passed by a young monk. She suffers from the desires of her flesh. Finally she returns to the hospital in Tokushima. But because of her physical unrest she cannot bear to stay there. She is thinking of Taguchi and hates him still more, while she becomes more and more jealous of his young wife.

In the fourth story *'Junrei-go no O-sei'*, O-sei is back in Tokyo. She talks to all sorts of people about her 'great' journey. But nobody believes her story of Kōbō-daishi. At the same time she takes to visiting her sons more frequently than ever. Furious arguments break out between her and Taguchi, because she begs shamelessly each time she is with the boys. He scolds her, but she keeps begging. Furthermore, Yūsaku, the eldest son, begins to steal from the house more frequently than he used to.

(Here we move to the next story *'Jisshi no hōchiku'*.)[47] First only small amounts are stolen, but the thefts soon escalate and Yūsaku takes to stealing still bigger amounts, as well as some of the precious objects of Taguchi's wife.

---

46. The Buddhist monk Kūkai (774-835), the founder of the *Shingon* sect in Japan.
47. *'Junrei-go no O-sei'* and *'Jisshi no hōchiku'* actually overlap in certain instances. More about this later.

and finally his dictionaries and collections of journals. Taguchi is infuriated, because he is absolutely convinced that O-sei is directing Yūsaku and perhaps Masanao as well. He summons the boys to a talk, but they remain silent and confess nothing. Taguchi considers this a declaration of mistrust and threatens to expel them from the house. When this threat is of no use either, Taguchi decides to apprentice them both to a trade. Therefore he sends them both to the above-mentioned Tsutsumi, hoping that he will teach them how to behave as apprentices. But then Taguchi is reported to the police and accused of mistreating the children. This comes as a shock, and Taguchi almost goes mad. He immediately sends a letter to Tsutsumi and breaks off his friendship with him. The following day the boys return home, accompanied by a policeman. Taguchi has to receive them. But he does not give up his plan. Never again will he put up with the boys living in his house as marionettes and money providers to O-sei. After having given the boys a final chance, which they unfortunately waste as well, he throws them out of the house. He is deeply depressed by this, but regrets nothing. While he watches the boys walk away from the house, he thinks of O-sei. He hates her more than anything in the world.

The action in the last story 'Konashi no Tsutsumi' is parallel to 'Jisshi no hōchiku': The two boys arrive at Tsutsumi's house with a letter from Taguchi. Unforeseen by Taguchi, the boys lament and tell Tsutsumi how badly they have been treated at Taguchi's house. In the meantime O-sei arrives on the scene and joins the boys in their lamentation. Together they decide that the best solution is to report Taguchi to the police and have the children returned to him. The same evening Tsutsumi receives another letter from Taguchi. He learns that Taguchi is furious. He visits him the following day to explain things to him and better the situation, but to no avail. Their friendship has ended.

In the first four stories, O-sei is the 'mediator' and everything is described from her point of view. Taguchi is the 'mediator' in 'Jisshi no hōchiku', and in 'Konashi no Tsutsumi' Tsutsumi acts as 'mediator'. This means that the scenes in which both Taguchi and Tsutsumi are present, are described from two different points of view; from Taguchi's and Tsutsumi's.

The same goes for the ending of 'Junrei-go no O-sei' and the opening of 'Jisshi no hōchiku', in which the same events overlap and are described from the point of view of both O-sei and Taguchi.

Iwano's theory of monistic narration and especially his demand that a work of fiction should have only one single 'mediator', has been put into practice.

2.2. Concrete Examples

In the following we will compare overlapping scenes as they occur in the progressing plot.

(1) The first piece is taken from the beginning of '*Jisshi no hōchiku*'.

'Come down here!', his wife O-kane shouted[48] as she came noisily up the stairs. She then seated herself by his desk and as she rested both her hands on the edge of his porcelain brazier, she said, 'She has a lot of nerve that Kōda.[49] I thought she was finally going to leave, but then she stuck her head into the hall again and exchanged looks with her children! Then Haruko[50] tumbled unsteadily past them and finally fell. But they just laughed at her and enjoyed themselves. They were actually gloating!'
'...'

Gosuke[51] did not believe that they had really gloated. No, that was not the reason for his sudden, but usual fury.

When he generously allowed her to spend the night in his house every once in a while, it was out of concern for the children and to fulfil her wish - despite the fact that he had once thrown her out of the house because he could not stand her any longer and because she was having an affair, she was after all the biological mother of the two children. But this time she had already arrived yesterday morning and had spent the night. The children were home because it was Sunday today and so she had been able to stay with them until just after dinner. She ought to be happy. Despite all his kindness, she was reluctant to leave the children when she had to go. They were exchanging glances with one another as if they were about to take each other's hands and make a big scene out of it.[52]

When he began to think about these things, he became obstinate and hateful. Suddenly he rose from his desk and went down the stairs faster than his wife and shouted, 'Are you still loafing about?'

48. O-kane is the writer Taguchi's new wife. Kanbara Fusae, Iwano's third wife, provided the model for O-kane.
49. O-sei's surname. Cf. Iwano's first wife's firstname was Kō.
50. Taguchi and O-kane have two children. The eldest is Hatsuo, O-kane's son from her first marriage, and the other is this child Haruko. Iwano actually had two children with Kanbara Fusae. The eldest was the daughter Miki (1916-?) and the youngest was the son Yuzuru (1918-?) who was given the same name that Iwano had given to his first-born son. Kanbara Fusae's son by her first husband was called Masahide. In other words, Haruko is modelled on Miki and Hatsuo is modelled on Masahide.
51. Gosuke is Taguchi's firstname.
52. This short section is a typical example of 'narrated monologue'. Cf. V.2.3.

'As you can see, I'm on my way out.'

'Get out! Now!' Gosuke felt like giving the oldish woman a slap in the face, but he steadied himself and expressed his anger in words and looks only.

He had become very angry when he had found out that she had been going around saying that she was absolutely sure that he would come back to her some day. Back to that mad, hysterical woman! He had also heard that his neighbour's wife and her sister had been so curious to see what she actually looked like that they had peeped through his windows yesterday. It also irritated him greatly that people went around believing that he still made love to her every time she visited him.

'Get out of here! Now!'

'Yes, yes, I'm leaving.'

Kōda looked frightened, but she also looked as if she was going to stay on and exploit his generosity because she wanted to annoy his young wife.

'I just wanted to ask you to take good care of the children, all right? I will be back.'

'No, a hag like you need not come here again!'

'But that's impossible!'

All at once she moved aggressively towards him.

'Shut up! I don't want to hear your story again!' His loud, angry voice shut her up. He lowered his voice and tried to explain the matter to her in clear language:

During the time when he had let her take care of their three children, he had never visited them. Not even when their eldest daughter was ill[53] and wanted to see him. Shortly after she had died, but he had not even gone to the funeral. Kōda went around telling everybody that he was a heartless father, but he had his reasons. First of all he did not want to see the old hag's face, secondly he did not want to confuse the children who were still living with her by letting them come between their parents who hated one another. But last year she had lost the house that he had given her and that she was supposed to earn her living with because of that stupid idea of hers. He had brought the children to live with him on that occasion. Now that they were living with him, she ought neither visit him nor the children as often as she did.

'Every time you come you make the children feel insecure. Not only that, but some unnecessary argument always develops. And that annoys us immensely!'

'Don't you think that it might be your own fault?' Kōda replied.

'Shut up, you hag!'

It was his wife O-kane who said these ugly words that she had actually never

---

53. Iwano's second daughter Fumi was the model for Taguchi's eldest daughter. Cf. footnote 45 in the above.

pronounced before. She was standing next to him and was probably very angry. She continued, 'This would never happen to anyone else. A divorced wife who is shameless enough to come and visit her ex-husband!'

'...'

This seemed to hit Kōda effectively because she looked stiffly and reproachfully at O-kane for a few seconds. Then she turned her uneasy gaze upwards and said, 'Oh? Now I really must go.'

She was very angry. She was just about to step over the threshold of the front door when she suddenly launched her final line, 'Obviously I look like an old woman when you compare me with a young one. I'm worn down and I've been treated harshly.'[54]

This same scene is described from O-sei's point of view in '*Junrei-go no O-sei*':

It was Sunday, at about one in the afternoon. Kōda had spent the night with the children and now she was going to take leave of them. She was standing on the earth-trodden floor in the hall. She did not really want to leave the children yet, so she seated herself on the step and as she supported herself on her elbow, she leaned over on the *tatami* mat in the hall to see how Yūsaku and Masanao were taking care of Haruko together with Hatsuo.[55] Haruko was growing into a nice little girl. She could already stand up, although she was still a little unsteady.

'Do you want to try standing up once more?' Yūsaku asked as he lifted the girl up by her hands. Haruko stood up and began to walk unsteadily. But she tripped over the edge of the *tatami* mat and fell down with a wallop. Everybody laughed out loudly and then Haruko began to cry.

At that moment O-kane stepped out of the living room and threw a quick glance at us in the hall. The next second, she was rushing up the stairs to the first floor with a horrified expression on her face. Soon after, she could be heard saying to Taguchi, 'Come down here! She has a lot of nerve that Kōda. I thought she was finally going to leave, but then she stuck her head into the hall again and exchanged looks with her children! Then Haruko tumbled unsteadily past them and finally fell. But they just laughed at her and enjoyed themselves. They were actually gloating!'

'...'

Who had laughed? Who had exchanged looks? Surely there were limits to what she would do to suck up to him, to the number of lies she would tell.

Even her shrill voice seemed loathsome to O-sei.

When O-kane was fond of her children, was it not natural that also she would

---

54. Cf. *HZ* vol. 8, 2-5.

55. Yūsaku and Masanao are about 14 and 11 years old respectively. Hatsuo is a little younger than them, and Haruko is just a few years old.

be fond of her children? And Taguchi was the father of both sets of children. When O-kane took to lying just because she was young and could suck up to him, then she was certainly going to give an explanation herself that was appropriate for her age.

But when she caught sight of Taguchi who came rushing down the stairs noisily with O-kane at his heels, she could already imagine his formidable anger and she quickly lifted herself up from the step.

'Are you still loafing about?' he asked staring just as angrily at her as she had expected.

When she answered, 'As you can see, I'm on my way out', she had already opened the glass-door and placed one foot outside the threshold. She was quick because she wanted to avoid being hit, but she still held the door with her left hand and looked up at him to hear what else he had to say.

'Get out! Now!'

His anger was much worse than she had expected. His little eyes that were usually so gentle, were flashing and flaming. His shortly clipped moustache seemed to quiver as if he were in a cramp.

'The neighbours laugh at us because you come here.[56] Get out of here. Now!'

'Yes, yes, I'm leaving.'

O-sei pulled herself together and tried to appear calm as she said, 'I just wanted to ask you to take good care of the children, all right? I will be back.'

'No, a hag like you need not come here again!'

'But that's impossible!' she answered and without knowing what she was doing she put one leg back in on the earth-trodden floor. As long as she had her children in the house, he would have to allow her to see them every now and then.

'Shut up! I don't want to hear your story again!' Taguchi scolded her as if he wanted to make her shut up before she went on to say what was on her mind. Then he lowered his voice in such a way that it seemed almost artificial, and said, 'During the time that I let you care for our three children, I never visited them. Not even when my eldest daughter was ill and wanted to see me. Shortly after she died, but I did not even go to the funeral. You went around telling everybody that I was a heartless father, but I had my reasons. First of all I did not want to see your face, secondly I did not want to confuse the children that were still living with you by letting them come between their parents who hated one another. But now you've lost the house that I gave you because of your stupid idea. That is why I have brought the children to live with me. But there is no reason why I should also have you here. Even though the children are living with me now, you

---

56. This line is not found in direct speech in 'Jisshi no hōchiku', but it is expressed in Taguchi's inner monologue.

should not visit us so often. Every time you come you make the children feel insecure. Not only that, but some unnecessary argument always develops. And that annoys us immensely!'[57]

'...'

O-sei stood listening to his long speech, but found nothing reasonable in it. Therefore she said, 'Don't you think that it might be your own fault?'

'Shut up, you hag!'

It was O-kane who broke into the conversation and said these ugly words. She stood with Haruko in her arms. O-sei's words had obviously also been directed at O-kane, but ... O-kane continued, 'This could never happen to anyone else. A divorced wife who is shameless enough to come and visit her ex-husband!'

Even O-sei remained speechless at her sharp words. Especially because O-sei's mistake had been one of the reasons for the divorce. She stared stiffly at O-kane for a few seconds with reproach in her eyes. Then she said, 'Oh? Now I really must go.'

She wanted to ask them to take good care of the children, but she stopped herself in time and instead pretended to be angry as she stepped over the threshold of the front door. But secretly she still did not want to leave.

'Obviously I look like an old woman when you compare me with a young one. I'm worn down and I've been treated harshly.'

With these words O-sei slammed the glass-door shut with a crash.[58]

(2) The following examples are taken from a. 'Jisshi no hōchiku' and b. 'Konashi no Tsutsumi' which were actually written simultaneously.[59]

i) *The first scene takes place in the evening of the day when Taguchi has sent his two sons to Tsutsumi. Taguchi visits Tsutsumi with his wife to play* hanafuda[60] *with*

---

57. With minor changes, Taguchi's response is expressed in 'Jisshi no hōchiku' in indirect speech and in an inner monologue.
58. Cf. *HZ* vol. 8, 642-45.
59. Iwano had written about half of the short story before he reached this point, according to 'Shiobara nikki' (dated November 1919 and printed in *San'esu*, January 1920), which he wrote from the health resort in the form of a letter addressed to his wife Fusae. He finished the short story there *while* he worked on the second short story 'Konashi no Tsutsumi'. More precisely, Iwano finished 'Konashi no Tsutsumi' on October 30 1919 and then the remaining part of 'Jisshi no hōchiku' on November 2 1919. Cf. *HZ* vol. 8, 185-206.
60. *Hanafuda* is a Japanese cardgame which consist of 48 cards. The twelve months of the year are represented by four variations of a flower which is typical of the particular month. The name *hanafuda* means the 'flower-card'.

him and his wife O-take. This is nothing but an excuse. He cannot relax at home. He is eager to know how the boys are doing.

a.

The gate was always locked because there were no servants at Tsutsumi's house. For this reason, he [Taguchi] entered through the back door.

'Are you in?' he asked.

'Yes', was the reply. Taguchi smiled and immediately pushed aside the *shōji*-door[61] to the kitchen. The other *shōji*-door, which separated the little kitchen from the dining room, was open. The light fell in such a way that he could see Yūsaku draw his legs up under himself. He was sitting across from the host.

'...'

All of a sudden Taguchi's expression became one of anger as he stepped into the dining room.

'Are you still here?', he asked rather sharply even though he was not as irritated as his voice sounded.

'I have come to hear the rest of what Tsutsumi told me this afternoon.'

'...'

Taguchi stared at Yūsaku. He thought it strange that his son answered him so despondently and therefore he did not answer with his usual 'Yeah'. The next moment he thought that the poor boy might have been frightened by his terrifying facial expression. At this point he became aware that the back door was quietly being opened. He also thought that he heard the door creak as it closed again. It always creaked because of the weight that was hanging on the door. Unable to see anyone out there, he soon realised that the hysterical ghost[62] had been there as well. That must be the reason for the odd behaviour of the others. His inner anger grew stronger and stronger because of this. It spread throughout his body.

'So you brought Kōda with you,[63] but why? Was that necessary? Go home at once!'

'Yes, you had better go home now', Tsutsumi said to Yūsaku, and then turned to Taguchi and said, 'I have not finished telling him about the things you asked me to teach him.'

Taguchi could not settle down as long as his son was present. Still standing in the dining room, he said to Tsutsumi, 'But ... you don't have to do it so thoroughly. Once is enough.'

61. *Shōji* is a typical Japanese sliding door made of a wooden frame with wooden lists and covered with rice paper.
62. The 'ghost' that he is referring to is O-sei.
63. Cf. footnote 49 above.

'I understand that, but ...'

'I'm leaving now. Good-bye.' Yūsaku said. He had been shifting his legs about restlessly, but he now pulled them up under himself once more. He put both hands on the *tatami*-floor to support himself and rose quickly, lifting first his behind and then the upper part of his body.

'...'

Taguchi looked at him and said nothing. The boy seemed discouraged. He went alone to the entrance hall and disappeared.

All the while Taguchi stood thinking of one of his old friends. Taguchi had once asked him, 'Why do you have to bow like that both when you take leave of your father and when you receive him?' His friend used to go out to the hall every time his father came or left the home. He would bow in a sitting position and rise in exactly the same way that Yūsaku had just done by first lifting his behind. To his question, his friend had simply answered, 'Well, he becomes angry if I don't present myself in the entrance hall'.

Taguchi was not a strict father who demanded that his children should be correct in such superficial things. If he did not want something from his heart then he would not ask his children to do it, no matter what. With this feeling in mind he turned towards Tsutsumi. With a bitter smile on his lips, he sat down on the *tatami*-floor and said, 'Well, shall we play a table?'

His hand slipped in under his clothes to his breast, but he did not pull out the cards. He had lost interest in the game from the moment he had stepped into the room.

'Yes, let's,' Tsutsumi answered, but he did not really seem to want to either. And as if he wanted to change the subject, he asked Taguchi: 'Where is your wife?'

'She will probably be here soon.'

Taguchi did not care whether she came or not or whether they played *hanafuda* or not. So Tsutsumi began to talk about something else.

'Have you heard that Yūsen's stock exchange quotation has risen again?[64] It is probably going to rise even higher. If you have the money, you should buy their shares now. There is a lot of money to be made on them.'

'Yes, who wouldn't want to earn a lot of money?'

But if he had had enough money he would rather have spent it on sending the children to a good boarding school and then let them come home once or twice a year to show how much or how little they had learnt at school. But even if he had the money now, there was no certainty that he would continue to have it in the future, then his plan would fail and he would only be able to educate them half-way. In this way they would never be able to become academics, but

---

64. Yūsen is short for Nippon Yūsen, a firm which was founded in 1885. It is still Japan's largest shipping company.

on the other hand they would not want to work either. Taguchi was not interested in increasing the number of so-called well-educated loafers or to help create more idle intelligence in society.

Tsutsumi the stockbroker changed the subject again. From shares to something else all the while trying not to mention the children or Kōda. He looked as if he had something on his conscience about the same matter, but in the end it suited Taguchi just as well.

Meanwhile O-kane showed up with Haruko wrapped up warmly under a padded nursing-coat. As soon as she caught sight of Taguchi she said,

'You know I've just seen Yūsaku outside. I'm sure it was him. I looked at him, but he pretended not to notice me and hurried away.'

'...'

He simply sent her a look without answering. But Tsutsumi turned his face away and looked bitter.

'Has he not been here?' O-kane continued.

'That sounds strange,' Tsutsumi's wife, O-take, answered from the kitchen where she was washing the dishes.

'...'

O-kane said no more. She sat down silently a bit away from Taguchi. She made a face. He also thought it odd that O-take had answered insincerely without reason. Why had she not been honest and said that Kōda had just been with them? Or it would have been even better if she had just kept her mouth shut. But why had she said something which might reveal Tsutsumi? Did she not know that her husband was sitting here looking bitter? She probably said it because she thought she could succeed in keeping the fact hidden that not only Yūsaku, but also Kōda had been with them. But even though she had not revealed it, Taguchi had already guessed and was convinced of this. But he did not dare to tell O-kane this. Because then O-take would lose face in front of everybody.

A little later O-take came into the room while drying her hands. It was as if a shadow fell on the gathering. It was in many ways embarrassing for all four of them.

'Now that you are here, let us at least play one year,'[65] Tsutsumi suggested just to be polite.

'Yes, perhaps,' Taguchi answered. No matter what the others were thinking about, he was ready for a change of mood and wanted to return to the original plan and play *hanafuda*. He turned towards O-kane who still carried Haruko on her back and who neither knew what to do nor say. To be on the safe side he asked her, 'Do you want to play?'

---

65. A game of *hanafuda* consists of 12 rounds or rather '12 months', thus the expression 'a year'.

He did this because experience had taught him that he could not really enjoy the game if there were not four players involved.

But she answered quite rudely,

'No, I am no longer interested.'

'...'

Taguchi felt sorry for the Tsutsumi couple. So he sat smiling awkwardly for a while. But when he realised that it was actually O-kane who had made an unfortunate situation worse, he became very irritated. After some time he said, 'Well, I think I had better be getting home.' Then he got up and left the house alone.[66]

The same scene is described from Tsutsumi's point of view in 'Konashi no Tsutsumi'.

b.

Unfortunately, at that very moment, Taguchi came in through the backdoor and said,

'Are you in?'

'Yes,' Tsutsumi answered, gruffly on purpose. Although Taguchi always behaved this way, this particular evening his manner seemed unusually impolite to Tsutsumi.

Before Taguchi had had time to push aside the *shōji*-door in the kitchen and enter the dining room, O-sei, who was very pale, ran into the entrance hall, but Yūsaku missed his chance and remained seated. He was immediately caught by Taguchi's sharp eyes.

'Are you here again?'

'Yes, I did not have time to hear everything this afternoon,' Yūsaku said. Tsutsumi greatly admired this ingenious explanation and thought that Yūsaku must finally have decided to leave his father. Tsutsumi looked at Taguchi who still stood and looked down at his son in the dining-room. Trying to pretend that nothing had happened he said,

'I actually had more to tell him about what it is like to be an apprentice.'

O-take greeted Taguchi in the usual manner by bidding him 'Welcome', all the while trying not to reveal anything. But it was already clear from his face that he was suspicious, and without paying particular attention to what Tsutsumi had just said, he shouted,

'Go home at once! You brought Kōda with you, didn't you?'

'...'

66. Cf. *HZ* vol. 8, 83-8.

Tsutsumi thought: 'Taguchi must have sharp ears, probably because he's so worked up. He must have heard the back door open gently just now and then he must have realised that O-sei was hurrying away.' He then said to Taguchi, in a soothing voice,

'Do not speak so harshly to him. He is after all your son.'

'No. When he won't confess to anything and continues to deceive his father then I don't consider him my son!'

Tsutsumi suggested to Yūsaku in a friendly and discreet manner, 'You had better go home now.' There was nothing else he could do for the boy.

'I'm off now. Good-bye.' Yūsaku greeted his father politely from his sitting position on the *tatami*-floor with his legs pulled up underneath him and his hands on his knees. Then, lifting his behind first, he quickly rose and left. Taguchi pretended not to see his son's still child-like movement. Instead he turned towards Tsutsumi and said,

'Well, shall we play a table?' as he smiled and sat down on the *tatami*-floor. He was about to pull out the *hanafuda* cards, but he stopped. When Tsutsumi looked at him, he could see that Taguchi was hiding fatherly tears in his eyes. Tsutsumi thought to himself that things would work out for now, when the police began their inquiry. Tsutsumi smiled and said, 'Yes, let's,' even though he felt a little disconcerted, but there seemed to be little to do about it in the present situation.

They did not play a serious game. They did not play for money or for anything else. Every time he played with Taguchi and his wife, he felt as if they were a royal couple requiring special attention despite their poor playing. He was becoming quite tired of this. Thinking of it, he realised that without being found out, he had better suggest that they should not play if O-kane did not come. He asked Taguchi,

'Where is your wife?'

'She will probably be here soon,' was the answer.

From his voice, Tsutsumi could sense that Taguchi was somehow cool towards his wife. He thought that it was likely that his wife had been upset again because of the children.

'…'

It suited him well if O-kane did not show up. He really preferred not to play tonight. He began to chat and told Taguchi about the stock exchange quotations that he had read about in the paper in the morning. He felt he had to say something in an attempt to save the situation. Meanwhile he recognised the clattering sound of a pair of shoes that he was familiar with. The back door opened and O-kane appeared in a way that reminded Tsutsumi of a *geisha's* entrance. 'Good evening,' she said as she stepped into the room without any ceremony as if it was her own house. But as soon as she caught sight of her husband she said, with her usual shrill voice,

'I've just seen Yūsaku outside. I'm sure it was him. I looked at him, but he pretended not to notice me and hurried away. He has just been here, hasn't he?'

'Maybe,' O-take said, speaking with deliberate ambiguity before anyone else could answer. It was clear to see that O-kane was angry at this response. Her otherwise delicate face became distorted and her always open expression disappeared as she seated herself. But she still carried the child that she had brought on her back wrapped up under the wadded nurse-coat.

'Don't you want to put Haruko down and play a round with us?' Tsutsumi said in his best winning voice. But she did not want to.

'No, I am no longer interested,' she said and looked offended.

'...'

Tsutsumi sat and smiled bitterly, but it suited him better if they did not play. He also thought that the only reason why Taguchi had preferred to speak of something else and had not told O-kane that he had seen his son, was that Taguchi did not want O-take to lose face for her incautious words.

Everyone sat looking embarrassed or irritated, each in their own way.

They took leave of one another without having played.[67]

ii) *In the following scene Taguchi is furious because a police officer brings his two sons back to the house again. Taguchi even receives a warning from the police.*

a.

... [Taguchi] Gosuke certainly did not feel that he ought to refrain from once more sending a sharp answer to Tsutsumi.

'...'

Even if Tsutsumi wanted to recommend them [Kōda and Yūsaku] to do this [to report him to the police], he could at least, if he was his friend, have come to him first, to make sure he knew what was really going on. Then he might have been able to understand the situation better. Even if he [Tsutsumi] would not have been able to understand, it would not have mattered as much if he had then let them report him to the police [after having spoken to Taguchi]. A disagreement could arise between them. Surely the report would not have become dated, if he had just waited a short while!

Taguchi's pen seemed to write almost of its own accord, 'As you must have been expecting, the children have just returned home escorted by a police officer,' and he continued, 'When I sent them to you, you were supposed to tell them what to do as apprentices and to prepare them for their future. I did not send them to you in order for them to report their father to the police.'

67. Ibid., 132-35.

He also wanted to ask Tsutsumi why he had done it and he was able to formulate this as he had thought it out yesterday.

He added, 'To me there can be no other solution but to send them to be apprenticed. But you must promise me that you will never receive them in your home again.'

He even repeated all of two times that Tsutsumi 'had not behaved like a friend'.

b.

There are certain small differences between Taguchi's letter to Tsutsumi as it is cited below, and as it is rendered by Taguchi himself in the above section. We can only wonder whether Iwano did this on purpose, perhaps to make Taguchi's account more convincing (Taguchi had to have a copy of the letter to be able to reproduce it in such precise terms).

As you must have been expecting, the children have just returned home escorted by a police officer. But I sent them to you because I wanted you to tell them what to do as apprentices and what to do when they became businessmen one day. I did not ask you to teach them how to report their father to the police. Why did you do it? For the children's own sake, I had arranged that they could follow the right path, step by step. But you interfered only to ruin it all. I thought there was something strange going on at your place last night. Now I see clearly how the two of you must have sat there and taught them the plan. I thought you were my friend! As I am sure you understand, parents have to send their children far away in order to make them strong. In the future, I hope you'll keep from meddling in our affairs and telling half-lies.

The end.

Gosuke.

iii) *The same evening Taguchi receives a letter in response from Tsutsumi.*

a.

That same evening O-take arrived with an answer from Tsutsumi, but O-kane did not go to the entrance hall to greet her this time either. Therefore Yūsaku went out with Masanao and Hatsuo and spoke in whispers with O-take. O-kane tried to hear what they were saying and finally shouted, 'Yū and Masa, where are you?' But O-take continued whispering with them for a while.

'...'

While he was reading the letter from Tsutsumi, Gosuke thought about O-take. She seemed to be a stubborn woman. But the letter contained no particular reaction such as he had expected. It merely said boring things such as, 'You must forgive me. I did not do it with any wrong intention,' or 'What is good for the children should also be good for you,' and similar cheap moral teachings.

'How can I be satisfied with such a letter?' Gosuke said flinging the letter at O-kane to show her clearly how angry he was.

'...'

She read it through and laid the fairly uninteresting letter on the wooden top of the brazier. Then she said, 'He's mocking us!'

'Yes. He writes that he will come here tomorrow. Then I will have to tell him a few things in a more severe tone.'

He ought to have come tonight already, but he was probably trying to distract our attention from the event deliberately. But he had used that trick himself when [Tsutsumi] had been angry with him [Taguchi] in connection with the model-case,[68] so he would probably have to forgive him for it. He also wrote in the letter, 'It worries me if our friendship of many years will end because of this.' It was easy for him [Taguchi] to see why.[69]

b.

'...'

If Tsutsumi visited him [Taguchi] now, he would not be able to avoid getting the sharp end of Taguchi's tongue. He would have to send him a letter first.

Employing a style, he was accustomed to using in his business letters, he wrote the following:

'I have seen your letter. I'm very sorry that you are so exceptionally irate. But I did not mean any harm in recommending them to go to the police. Since what is good for your children must also be good for you, I thought that it would be the best for all the involved parties. I apologise deeply for having displeased you and brought on your anger. I beseech you to accept my apologies. It is unfortunate for both of us if our friendship of so many years should end because of this. I intend to visit you tomorrow to explain the situation more fully, but for the moment I hope that you will receive my letter and my apologies.

Yours

Bantarō[70]

68. Somewhere else in the short story, Iwano mentions that he had used the couple as a model in another context.
69. Ibid., 102-3.
70. Ibid., 144-45.

iv) *On the morning of the following day, Tsutsumi pays a visit to Taguchi at his house.*

a.

Yūsaku and the other children had already left when [Taguchi] Gosuke rose the next morning. He had risen earlier than usual because he remembered his friend's message from the evening before. Tsutsumi arrived while he [Taguchi] was bathing. He could hear him say 'Hello' in the dining room. It sounded as if he was trying to overcome his embarrassment. He must have greeted O-kane who had just bathed, but it seemed as if she did not answer him. She must either be busy with her make-up or simply irritated.

'...'

While Gosuke thought of these things in silence, he felt a special satisfaction in bathing at home this morning. At the same time he remembered the episode when Tsutsumi had come to ask for help. At that time he had told Taguchi that the price of coal and of tickets to the public bath had risen. He had then suggested that he would pay to Taguchi the amount that he and his wife normally paid for tickets to the public bath in order to cover the coal bill in exchange for being allowed to bathe at his home.

'It will be good for both our families. It does not matter if we bathe after you,' Tsutsumi said.

But Taguchi had been unsure what to answer, 'Yes, maybe it is not such a bad idea, but ...'

Even though Taguchi and his wife kept the right to bathe first, they wanted to be able to take a bath both in the morning and in the evening.[71] Sometimes even three times a day. And what was to be arranged with regard to the children and the maid? He did not want this arrangement to result in emotional disparities between them. Also it would not be entertaining if this would restrict Taguchi's family's freedom to bathe whenever they pleased, but the most serious problem that could be imagined in this connection was the thing which prevented Tsutsumi and his wife from having a child even though they sincerely longed to have one.

'If it continues in this way, we'll never be healthy again,' Tsutsumi had once confessed to him, thus hinting at their illness. If Taguchi's family only consisted of adults, they could be as careful as they were when they went to the public bath. But what were the children to do? It was obvious that they were unable to look out for themselves. If they were infected and finally became blind — who

---

71. Please note that in Japan the bath-water is only changed once a day. For this reason, it is of importance who bathes first. You do not wash in the bathtub, but outside. You only sit down in the bath to get warm.

would be responsible for them for the rest of their lives? Nobody. It was the saddest thing Taguchi could imagine because many years ago he had tried it himself. A mistress had infected him.

Therefore he had said to Tsutsumi, 'I've always been this way. I would not even take a bath after my father because I was annoyed by his lack of caution.' In this way he had mildly rejected Tsutsumi's suggestion.

His [Taguchi's] father was infected and had suffered from the illness at the prime of his life. At that time Taguchi was not involved with prostitutes, and he had not been with any for the last ten years or so either. But he still feared gonorrhoea and syphilis and other such malignant diseases. Maybe Tsutsumi knew this too. If that was the case then it would be twice as unpleasant. While he had suffered from gonorrhoea he had always politely refused offers to bathe at his friends' houses. Except once, many years ago, when he had accepted a bath at Tsutsumi's house. Taguchi had not even known himself that he had contracted the illness then ...

It was doubtless because O-kane did not know how terrible the disease was that she later said, 'Poor them. I think you should do as they have suggested.'

The very same O-kane must have stepped into the dining room now because he could hear her say, 'Why on earth did your wife behave so stupidly?'

'She was embarrassed and felt unable to speak directly. You have to forgive her,' Tsutsumi said. He seemed very tame today.

'And then that business of letting the children report us to the police!'

'But it was not just us that had thought of it. I have heard that your neighbours suggested the same solution.'

'Oh ...?' O-kane's voice changed. 'Like yourself and my husband, the man next door was raised by his step-mother and is therefore of a suspicious and jealous nature. I know that much, but ... that means that the boy has been talking to the neighbours?'

'...' — Taguchi thought that it was probably because she was upset that she said such strange things.

'Yūsaku has been there, yes. According to what he told O-take yesterday.'

'You don't say? She really is insolent, your wife! Has she really been here to hear that from the boy?'

'I don't want to hear anymore about it!' Taguchi shouted while drying himself. His words were not only directed at her, they were also meant to provoke Tsutsumi.

'The children said that they had not yet eaten. We felt sorry for them having been expelled from the house without any food. So we gave them a lot to eat, so much that there nearly wasn't food enough left for ourselves ...'

'What an insult! Yes, I am their stepmother, but surely you can understand that I am not so stupid as to not feed them properly!' she said. She lowered her voice and continued, 'We obviously had no knowledge of this. So we gave them plenty to eat as soon as they returned home, before they left again.'

'They eat well, don't they?' Tsutsumi said in a voice that indicated that he was relaxed now.

'...' Taguchi was amazed that Tsutsumi had misunderstood them so completely also in this matter. But he was also furious that the children had stuffed themselves without restraint. He tied the belt of his quilted robe and greeted Tsutsumi with a tired and quiet voice, 'Hello.'

'You!' O-kane shouted at Taguchi across the dining table. She was sitting in the corner of the dining room by the brazier. The *miso* soup simmered deliciously on the brazier. She looked at him strangely and said, 'He says that the boy went to the neighbour for advice.'

'...' Without answering her, Gosuke walked past Tsutsumi who was seated on the *tatami*-floor. He sat down at the dining table across from O-kane and turned over the soup and rice bowls. [The food is served.][72] As usual, he apologised and began to eat immediately despite Tsutsumi's presence. Purposely turning his face half-way towards him, he said, 'Aren't you a little officious these days?'

With this he also meant that Tsutsumi was being officious in light of the two new facts that he had just been informed of.

'I'm sorry. You must forgive me. But I did not do it with any wrong intentions.'

'I suppose when you say so yourself, but ...' he said and laughed briefly. But no — he was not supposed to smile now. 'It is not that simple for us. We *are* very bothered by this situation.'

'I'm sorry. Forgive me.'

'Do you know what? You are simply bungled. It appears as if the man next door is bungled too and for the same reason as yourself, but ... you need not bungle my sons! You made exactly the same mistake when you reported your own father to the police. It is possible that your case was a little different from mine because you had had problems ever since your childhood. However, both during your court case and during our scandal in connection with my stepmother, all parties were able to reach an agreement without anyone becoming suspicious or jealous of the other. For my own part, I was thrown to the ground during a fight with my father. The only thing I achieved was that my father's fist brushed my former wife's face and hit the child she was carrying on her back. It later turned out that we had both been trying to protect our wives, both my father and I. The situation did not develop any further because as long as we were not living under the same roof there were no grounds for new problems And ... our

---

72. When the table is laid, the bowls are placed upside-down. When you are seated and the bowls have been turned around, the food is served.

innocent baby that was hit by her grandfather later died from diphtheria. Even my stepmother cried at the thought that the child's death might have been caused by the blow she had received as a little baby.'

While he was telling this story, he remembered that he had once protected Kōda from his father and stepmother just as he was now protecting O-kane from his sons. But the thought of this no longer seemed real. He returned to Yūsaku's case and said,

'My son is still childish. He has not yet grown up. In addition, you seem to have overlooked a very important point. This problem is no longer between stepmother and children, but between the children and myself.'

'I did not realise that.'

'Exactly,' he raised his voice, 'and that is why I don't want you meddling ...'

'They are not at home, are they?' Tsutsumi wanted to change the subject and talk about the children.

'No,' Taguchi answered. O-kane served him another helping of rice and he realised that it was not really necessary to pester him [Tsutsumi] anymore. However, he was still a bit annoyed so he said, 'It is your fault that I now have to find apprenticeships for the boys myself. Right now they are out asking if anyone can use them as apprentices. They have to be looked over anyway so they might as well apply directly themselves.'

'Is it really your intention to apprentice them?' Tsutsumi wanted to be sure. But it was also a clear sign that he had not understood his [Taguchi's] purpose.

'Naturally.'

'Oh, well, then I guess there is no more to be done about the matter.'

'Do you know, Yūsaku and Masanao had something to eat at Tsutsumi's place as well,'

O-kane, who had been eating with a serious expression on her face, suddenly broke her silence.

'...'

Gosuke had already told Tsutsumi what he wanted to tell him so he did not wish to return to the subject. He reached out his bowl towards O-kane to request a third helping of rice and said, 'Yes, they were born of the greedy Kōda.'

'Surely they have inherited a little of your nature too?' O-kane said quite superfluously.

'...'

Yes, yes, he knew well enough that he was a gourmand ...

'Well, I'm going to have to leave you. I'm going to work,' Tsutsumi said and left. As usual, Gosuke merely replied with an 'Yeah.'[73]

73. Cf. *HZ* vol. 8, 103-9.

b.

He [Tsutsumi] did not really feel like visiting Taguchi, but he went nonetheless. He stepped into the house, without ceremony as usual. He caught sight of O-kane, who had just put on her make-up. She was straightening her clothes in front of the mirror. He greeted her with a 'Hello' and went into the dining room pretending not to have seen anything. Taguchi was still having his bath. He shouted from the bathroom,

'Is that Tsutsumi?'

'...'

As always Taguchi's voice sounded uninviting and therefore Tsutsumi answered in the same tone, 'Yes'.

Last year he had had quite an unpleasant experience which had involved Taguchi and his bath. As the prices in general had risen, so had the price of tickets to the public bath. Even though O-take and himself made do with a visit to the public bath every second day, it still cost them about one *yen* a month.[74] Therefore, after having spoken with O-take, he had asked Taguchi if they could be allowed to have their bath at his house, even as the very last in line every night. He offered to pay the amount they would otherwise spend on tickets to the public bath in order to cover the price of the coal.

To this Taguchi had answered, 'I'm very sensitive about who uses the bath and when. I did not even bathe after my own father in his house.'

But he always let his children and wife take their baths before him. Surely one could not compare a friend with one's father. Anyway Taguchi's father, unlike his own, had been far too lenient. But he knew that there was another reason why Taguchi mentioned his father. Taguchi was probably scared of the illness which had made O-take and him unable to have children. This was precisely why he had offered that they would take the last bath. If Taguchi wanted to talk about the past, then he might as well mention that Taguchi himself had bathed for five days in a row at his home when he had visited him in Osaka. He had done this without knowing that he had the gonorrhoea which he had contracted in Kyoto the year before. Taguchi ought to have been told how long he [Tsutsumi] had been disgusted by the thought of it.

Speaking of selfishness and egoism, Taguchi was not its only representative. O-kane entered the room without saying 'Welcome' to him. She passed by the brazier in the corner and seated herself at the dining table where several bowls were standing and immediately said, 'Why on earth did your wife behave so stupidly? She was so easy to see through.'

Tsutsumi had himself felt that she had behaved stupidly and had scolded her later that evening. But what was O-kane doing accusing him in this way? After

74. This is the old kind of *yen*.

all she was not the half-crazy O-sei. He had only come to apologise, 'You have to forgive her. She was embarrassed. She did it with no mean intention.'

'I hope not. But the children came with a police officer and they said they had been instructed by you.'

''No, not just by us. I have heard that your neighbours suggested the same solution.'

'Oh ...?' she said, as she looked towards the bedroom as if she wanted to stare straight at the neighbour.

'...'

Tsutsumi noticed that her anger was being redirected away from him so he said, 'Yes, they [the children] had lunch with us and then they returned to Shiba.[75] They visited O-sei and brought her with them to my place. They then went on to visit your neighbours.'

'But when they returned from your place, they ate a big lunch before they left again.'

'Oh, I did not know ...'

So he had been mistaken when he had thought ill of O-kane with regard to the boys' appetite. No, she was not an ignorant mother without an education. Tsutsumi had not been able to contain his amazement at the boys' gluttony. He was almost flattering when he said, 'They eat well, don't they? ... Kids!' She did not laugh with him, but maintained her serious face and answered, 'We did not know. So we told them they could eat as much as they wanted since it was their last lunch at home.'

Suddenly she looked up and said, 'You, he says that the boys went to the neighbour as well.'

'Hello,' Taguchi greeted him as he stepped into the room. He was tying the belt of his quilted robe. 'Aren't you a little officious these days?'

'....'

Tsutsumi was entirely aware of the fact that Taguchi was referring not only to the police report, but also to the lunch which he and O-kane had just been talking about. He simply said, 'I'm sorry if I have upset you, but as I wrote in the letter yesterday, I had only the best intentions.'

'I suppose when you say so yourself, but ...' Taguchi answered as he passed by him and finally sat down at the dining table across from O-kane. Taguchi thus sat with his left profile turned towards him and continued to speak in a rather haughty voice, 'I thought that you were my friend. But you have behaved very foolishly. Both you and your wife have thought that we treat our children as all stepmothers and stepfathers in the world usually do. I have also heard that you

---

75. Shiba is an area in Tokyo. Kōda O-sei's house is in Shiba.

think that O-kane treats Hatsuo like a stepchild because she often scolds him.[76] I don't want to hear that you go around spreading such false rumours so carelessly.'

'...' While Tsutsumi was listening to this, he was struck by the fact that Taguchi and his wife had begun to eat a very humble meal. They had not forgotten that they had once been poor. This impressed him. So he said, 'Yes, it was my fault. You must forgive me.'

'I would like to if only you would try to understand us a little better and not provoke the children ...'

'They are not at home, are they?' Tsutsumi said in an attempt to change the subject, because now both his wife and him were being criticised. But he did not succeed.

'It is your fault that I have to find apprenticeships for them myself. I have sent them to all the places that had notices in the paper. They have to be looked over sooner or later so they might as well apply directly themselves.'

'It is your intention to apprentice them then?'

'Naturally.'

'...' Tsutsumi realised then that there was little to be done about it and felt almost relieved. 'I suppose you'd better do as you want.'

'Yūsaku and Masanao also had lunch at Tsutsumi's place. Can you imagine? They are so greedy!' O-kane said wanting to talk about it again. But she was stopped by Taguchi's reply,

'Yes, they're bewitched by Kōda!'

'Well, I guess I'd better be on my way. I have to go to work.' Tsutsumi said. He was finally able to get away from this unfortunate, uncomfortable situation. As usual no one accompanied him to the door, but this particular morning he did not feel as if he could simply regard it as the habit of an old friend. Taguchi's lazy voice that had simply answered with an 'Yeah,' sounded neither comforting nor friendly in his ears as it usually did.[77]

2.3. A Few Grammatical Problems

In this section we will study a few grammatical problems which are related to the theory of monistic narration. For example, the choice of pronoun, and the use of direct/indirect speech which is of great importance when the narrator chooses one particular person to be the mediator and tells the whole short story/novel from the mediator's point of view.

When Iwano refers to his mediator (the protagonist), he either uses the

---

76. Hatsuo is O-kane's son from her first marriage. Cf. footnote 50 above.

77. Cf. *HZ* vol. 8, 147-52.

person's name or a peculiar Japanese pronoun-equivalent *kochira* which actually means 'this side'. It *can* be translated with 'I/my/me'. The author relates objectively to the mediator when he refers to him by his name (i.e. the point of view is explicitly held by the narrator). Whereas the point of view is held by the mediator when he uses *kochira*. Iwano's narrator moves between two poles — the narrator himself and the mediator; objectivity and subjectivity; the outer and the inner.

We can best illustrate this with a couple of examples:

The scene begins when Taguchi enters the dining room to have breakfast. This section is translated in iv), b. It is taken from '*Konashi no Tsutsumi*' — the mediator is Tsutsumi.

'Hello,' Taguchi greeted him [*kochira*] ...[78]

Kochira in Japanese indicates that the narrator's point of view is identical with the protagonists. A little further on we find similar examples:

'I suppose when you say so yourself, but ...' Taguchi answered as he passed by him [*kochira*] and finally sat down ... Taguchi thus sat with his left profile turned towards him [*kochira*] ...[79]

A little further down, however, we find the following lines:

'...' While Tsutsumi was listening to this, he was struck by the fact ... 'They are not at home, are they?' Tsutsumi said in an attempt to change the subject ...[80]

Here the point of the view of the narrator is external to the protagonist.

It is possible to use both methods in Japanese without creating stylistic or semantic confusion. This is due to the relaxed relationship between grammatical 'persons' and pronouns in Japanese. Throughout time, without being aware of it, Japanese authors have used this narrative technique, which is called narrated monologue in the West, precisely because of this characteristic of the language.

Narrated monologue is also called '*erlebte Rede*' or '*style indirect libre*'.[81] It is usually used to describe a reflective mind. It is most often characterised

78. Cf. *HZ* vol. 8, 150.
79. Ibid., 151.
80. Ibid.
81. Dorrit Cohn, 'Narrated Monologue: Definition of a Fictional Style', 1966.

by the following: it is told in the third person, in the past tense, in direct speech and in idiomatic language.

This can be illustrated by three comparisons:

direct speech	He said, 'I am happy today.'
	He said, 'I was happy yesterday.'
indirect speech	He said that he was happy that day.
	He said that he had been happy the day before.
narrated monologue	He was happy today.
	He had been happy yesterday.

Dorrit Cohn characterises narrated monologue in the following way:

By allowing the same tense to describe the individual's view of reality and that reality itself, inner and outer world become one, eliminating explicit distance between the narrator and his creature. Two linguistic levels, inner speech with its idiosyncrasy and author's report with its quasi-objectivity, become fused into one, so that the same seems to pass through narrating and figural consciousness.[82]

To Western writers this new 'technique' was a destruction of the grammatical 'norm' which they had inherited. But to Japanese writers, fluid boundaries between different 'persons' have always been a matter of course.[83]

One can *actually* read a text, which is written in accordance with principles of monistic narration, as the mediator's own account. For example, in a text where Taguchi is the mediator, we can change the word 'Taguchi' and/or the pronoun which refers to him (*kochira*) to 'I/my/me'. This includes changing the pronoun 'they' to 'we'. This changes the text from a 'description' to an 'account'. In other words, with the change described above, the mediator also functions as the narrator. This is excluded from Iwano's narration because it must be objective — the narrator must relate objectively to the mediator.

82. Ibid., 99. This problem was further explored from a structuralist point of view by Ann Banfield in her article 'Narrative Style and the Grammar of Direct and Indirect Speech', 1973. See Otto Jespersen's *The Philosophy of Grammar*, 1924, for a discussion of grammatical problems related to narrated monologue, in particular in its relation to direct and indirect speech. Jespersen calls narrated monologue 'represented speech' (290-92).
83. This narrative method can be seen as early as '*Genji Monogatari*'. Cf. Suzuki Kazuo, '*Genji monogatari no hōhō, buntai: shinnaigo no mondai*'; Mitani Kuniaki, '*Genji monogatari ni okeru katari no kōzō*; Amanda Mayer Stinchcum, 'Who tells the tale? *Ukifune*: A study in narrative voice'.

The flexibility exhibited by Japanese pronouns can also be seen in adverbials signifying time, e.g. *kinō* (yesterday), *kon'ya* (tonight), *kyonen* (last year). We will give a few examples:

From ii), a., a scene where Taguchi is writing a letter of protest to Tsutsumi.

He also wanted to ask Tsutsumi why he had done it and he was able to formulate this as he had thought it out yesterday [*kinō*].[84]

Here *kinō* means 'the preceding/previous day' in relation to the narrated time. The word *kinō* is used because the protagonist has the point of view, not the narrator.

The next example is taken from a section in 'Konashi no Tsutsumi' in ii), b.

It suited him well if O-kane did not show up. He really preferred not to play tonight [*kon'ya*].[85]

Like the example above, *kon'ya* means 'that night'. Since this is the protagonist's thought, the description is made from his point of view, also with regard to time. Yet another example from iv), b.

Last year [*kyonen*] he [*kochira*] had had quite an unpleasant experience which had involved Taguchi and his bath.[86]

If one were to write the 'the previous year', then the point of view would be moved to the narrator.

Attention is drawn to the fact that the cited lines could *just as well* have been told from the point of view of the narrator in Japanese. If that had been the case, then we would use other adverbials: *mae no hi* (the previous day), *sono ban* (that night) and *sono zennen/mae no toshi* (the previous year) respectively. However, this would mean that the text would no longer be an example of monistic narration.

There is another interesting aspect, which is worth noting, in the second example. This has to do with the verbal suffix '*-tai*' which signals the expression of will or desire. The original reads '... *kon'ya wa yame ni shitakatta*'

84. Cf. *HZ* vol. 8, 100.
85. Ibid., 134.
86. Ibid., 148.

(He really preferred not to play tonight). The suffix '-*tai*' is in the preterite tense thus '-*takatta*'. The suffix '-*tai*' is of interest for our analysis because it can *only* be used when the speaker is expressing *his/her own* will or desire. In other words, one can only use '-*tai*' when expressing one's own will or desire and one cannot express the will or desire of somebody else (in the second or third person) with the help of '-*tai*'.

So, we can say:

Watashi wa nihon e ikitai (I would like to go to Japan)

But this sentence:

Kare wa nihon e ikitai (He would like to go to Japan)

is actually impossible. At least it cannot stand alone when a desire is expressed on the behalf of somebody else. We would have to add a *no desu* in order for the sentence to make sense.[87] Then the sentence will be complete and as such it means what is expressed by the English, 'He would like to go to Japan'. The phrase '-*no desu*' is a copula whereby 'his' statement (wish) of 'I would like to go to Japan' is noted by *the speaker*. Thus the speaker is *referring* to 'his' statement (wish).

When a third person *describes* 'his' wish from an exterior position, then another verbal suffix is employed — '-*tagaru*'. It is often used in the form '-*tagatte iru*' which denotes 'state' in the case of 'he', but never with 'I' or 'you' as the grammatical subject. Thus, one cannot say:

Watashi wa nihon e ikitagatte iru (I want to go to Japan)

unless the intention is to be funny by speaking in an impersonal and incorrect manner. But,

Kare wa nihon e ikitagatte iru

is an objective observation of the fact that 'he wants to go to Japan'.

The verbal suffixes '-*tai*' and '-*tagaru*' exclude one another. They stand

---

87. In his article 'Where Epistemology, Style and Grammar Meet: A Case Study from Japanese', 1973, S.Y. Kuroda analyses the connection between 'grammatical persons' and the verbal suffix '-*garu*'. This article inspired my analysis. In the third section of the article, he investigates the problem of '-*no desu*'. Cf. 379-81.

sharply opposed in their practical usage. Due to this characteristic, it is possible to use the opposition between '*-tai*' and '*-tagaru*' to determine whether a statement is 'subjective' or 'objective' — whether the statement is an 'account' of a subjective view point, or an objective 'ascertainment'.

The given example is thus (in Japanese) a direct rendering of the protagonist Tsutsumi's desire not to play cards that evening, i.e. from his point of view.

2.4. Revisions

In this section we will look at Iwano's novel-series in order to see how and where Iwano revised his works in accordance with his theory of monistic narration.[88]

The plot of the novel-series can be summarised as follows:

Tamura Yoshio inherits his father's boarding house 'Hinodekan' together with his step-mother and his wife. Before long he meets Shimizu Tori. She has come to Tokyo to look for work. First she lives at the boarding house, but when she and Tamura initiate a relationship, he has to find a room for her. He finds one and his double-life begins. Shortly thereafter he runs into financial problems. This becomes one of the reasons why he launches the crab-cannery project in Sakhalin.

But when Tamura goes to Sakhalin to direct the venture, he discovers that the project is about to go bankrupt due to a lack of capital and labour. He cannot return home because O-tori (Shimizu Tori's pet name) has become a burden to him. She has also contracted gonorrhoea from him. When he finally returns from Sakhalin to Hokkaidō to visit his old friend, Arima Isamu, Tamura owns nothing but the clothes on his back. He has known Arima since high-school. They also taught together at the same intermediate school in the town Otsu. Arima is a poor teacher at a folk high-school for girls in Sapporo.

Tamura lives with him for about a year. He looks up another old acquaintance, Shimada Hyōhō, who is the editor-in-chief of *Hokkaidō jitsugyō zasshi* (Hokkaidō business magazine). He goes to see him in an attempt to obtain some money. But whenever Tamura has money, he visits Susukino, the part of town where the brothels are located. In his despair he falls in love with the *geisha* Shikishima. Meanwhile he has one idea after another. He tries to initiate several projects even though he has no money. He wants to do

---

88. Cf. I.8., page 38ff about the development and working process of the novel-series. The novel *Dokuyaku o nomu onna* is not mentioned in the following analysis. As was noted earlier, Iwano did not have the time to revise this novel before his death.

something so that he can obtain enough money to pay back what he has borrowed and what he has lost — and to restore his vitality. But he is without success. The only positive and productive experience that he has during his stay on Hokkaidō, is a two-week trip through the southern part of the island together with a member of Hokkaidō's county council.

O-tori is waiting for him when he returns from the trip to Sapporo. A very unpleasant surprise. She still suffers from gonorrhoea and as soon as she sees him, she shouts, 'Make me get well! Do something about my illness! Or I will leave you!'

Tamura scrapes enough money together to have her admitted to a private hospital. Even though she pretends to hate him, she actually loves him and trusts him. When there are rumours that Tamura has gone crazy during a lecture at an intermediate school, she rushes to comfort him.

Tamura's future looks dismal and O-tori can no longer stand her painful illness. One night she tempts and convinces the desperate and despairing Tamura to commit suicide together with her. They jump into the darkness from a bridge over the Toyohira river. But they land safely in the snow on the river bank. Their attempt at suicide has failed.

A few days later, Tamura borrows some money from his friends in order to return to Tokyo. But the money can only buy them two tickets to Sendai. All he is carrying is the manuscript for the article 'Hitsū no tetsuri' (The metaphysics of sufferance). He has no luggage. O-tori experiences strong pains during the trip. They are forced to get off the train in Morioka, and O-tori is immediately admitted to the hospital in the town. Tamura hurries on alone to Tokyo to try to locate some money. He has no desire to return to his wife. On the other hand he is unable to send money to his mistress whom he has left in Morioka. Meanwhile, Tamura discovers by accident that O-tori has called her new lover to come to Morioka. A telegram written by her new lover is mistakenly returned to Tamura's address. Tamura sends the telegram back to O-tori thus signalling the end of their relationship.

The most important of the corrections that were made in *Hatten* are those which occur in the sections describing situations where Tamura had not been present. These include the last fifth of chapter 6 where O-tori describes an experience from her past from her point of view;[89] the middle of chapter 11 where O-tori is alone and misses Tamura — something Tamura had no opportunity to observe — ;[90] the first third of chapter 12 where Haraguchi

89. Cf. *MBZ* vol. 71, 199-200.
90. Ibid., 215-16.

Seizō, one of the residents at the boarding house, appears although Tamura is not present;[91] a little way into chapter 15 where O-tori experiences pain in her abdomen and consequently stands up abruptly and an inner monologue follows,[92] and a similar monologue by O-tori in the middle of chapter 17.[93]

The text of *Hatten* was not only revised to harmonise with the principles of monistic narration. Revisions were also made of what were then thought to be provocative expressions in the book. Some passages had appalled the authorities to such an extent that the publication of the book had been prohibited in 1912.[94]

In some cases Iwano felt that the third-person account was absolutely necessary for the development of the plot or for coherence. Then he allowed the protagonist to report the experience of the third person in the manner that the protagonist *himself* had understood it, thus allowing for the addition of interpretation and/or commentary. The best example can be seen in chapter 20 in *Hōrō* where Tamura recounts how his friend Hyōhō had met a twenty-two year old girl at a restaurant.[95]

A whole section has been removed as a result of Iwano's revision of the novel *Dankyō*. This section describes O-tori reflecting on her problematic relationship to Tamura. With minor corrections, the whole piece was made into a short story of its own with the title 'O-tori no kurushimi' (O-tori's suffering), which was published in 1910.[96]

Finally two corrections made in *Tsukimono* should also be noted.

The first correction occurs in the scene where Tamura walks hand-in-hand with O-tori through the snow-covered Sapporo as they look for a place to commit suicide together. They finally choose a railway bridge over the Toyohira river. On the way Tamura reflects on all the railway bridges that he has seen up till then.

91. Ibid., 220-22.
92. Ibid., 235-36.
93. Ibid., 241.
94. For a further discussion of this, see Yoshida Seiichi's analysis. Cf. Yoshida, *Shizenshugi no kenkyū.*, 426 ff.
95. Cf. *HZ* vol. 1, 589-97.
96. Cf. Ban Etsu, *Iwano Hōmei ron*, 212 and *HZ* vol. 2, 184-211. The year is taken from *HZ* vol. 2 (Ban Etsu does not name it in his book), however, this does not really agree with the fact that *Dankyō* was published as a serial in January-March 1911. There may be a misprint in *HZ* or otherwise the short story was written in 1910 and then later incorporated into *Dankyō*, only to be removed from the novel again later. For a discussion of other corrections in the novel, see Ban, op. cit. 210-13.

He imagined nearly all the landscapes that could be seen from the window of a train in Japan as a last vision of life.

It was as if he had suddenly fallen from a very high place and the memory of his whole life flared up momentarily.

'I am going to die,' he said as he walked slowly onwards, but he did not walk to show himself the path to death. It was to show the way to another who wanted to die. But he thought he might as well make use of this favourable opportunity and die with her. After all he had to keep her company to the very last moment. In this way he was prepared for his death which was approaching, but ...[97]

This whole passage does not exist in the first version from 1912 where the same scene is described more vaguely.

When the illusion became a thought and disappeared again, it was the sure sign of an unselfish death. But when he realised that he did not feel the mood of death yet, he became irritated and felt disturbed by O-tori's shuffling steps behind him.[98]

A comparison of these two passages reveals conspicuous differences. In the revised edition (the first passage), Tamura's mood is established though an inner monologue (which may indeed seem a little artificial). Tamura holds the point of view whereas in the second passage we find that his thoughts and feelings are almost 'explained'. This explanatory tone is especially distinct in the first sentence, where the statement is actually the narrator's comment which reveals that the point of view is held by the narrator, not the protagonist. In addition, in the revised version we find that Tamura is ready to die unlike in the first version. This evidence shows that Iwano also revised the text to include changes in the protagonist's development, in his thoughts and feelings.

The other interesting change which has been made occurs a little later in the text, when Tamura and O-tori fall from the bridge.

'Be careful!' [Tamura] Yoshio shouted and embraced her. But he realised that it had already happened and that he was going to die now.

The two people held each other and fell into the twilight.[99]

97. In the last of chapter 9. Cf. *HZ* vol. 5, 477.
98. Cited in Ban, op. cit., 215.
99. Cf. *HZ* vol. 5, 482.

In the first version from 1912, Tamura does not really know whether he wants to die or not. The scene is as follows:

'No! It can't be!' [Tamura shouted]
'I'm going to die!' O-tori screams.
They were each wrapped in their own thoughts with their eyes wide open in the dark. They thought at once of all the things each of them had experienced in their lives.[100]

It is obvious why this passage was unacceptable to Iwano. The protagonist Tamura could not have known what O-tori was thinking at that moment. It is the narrator's comment (Iwano usually called it 'explanation') and as such it does not reflect the theory of monistic narration.

100. Cited in Ban, op. cit., 216.

VI. The Theory in a Broader Perspective

> Don Quixote is merely the protagonist of a work of fiction.
> Cervantes was not Don Quixote. How do these Japanese writers
> conceive of this strange idea of wanting to be the protagonist
> of their own work?
> Mishima Yukio

> The outsider problem is essentially a living problem;
> to write about it in terms of literature is to falsify it.
> Colin Wilson

1. Iwano's Theory in Relation to that of *watakushi shōsetsu* — Japanese Confessional Writing

In a work of *watakushi shōsetsu*,[1] a writer's daily life is described, and only from his own point of view. 'Daily life' should be understood broadly; it may include anything that a person experiences everyday, but a typical characteristic of the sort of 'daily life' described in a *watakushi shōsetsu* is that it is cut off from real life and thus bears no actual connection to it; in other words, it has been more or less 'manipulated', for the sake of 'art'. *Watakushi shōsetsu* is an autobiographical fiction, but not an autobiography. Even though a work of *watakushi shōsetsu* meets the 'demand for truth' that is made of any work of fiction by the author's own presence in the story, with or without a mask, the story still remains a work of fiction. This is due to the closed universe which the work constructs and which has no direct connection to the real world. As far as the relationship between the writer and the protagonist is concerned, in *watakushi shōsetsu* we may indeed talk of a monistic relation in which not only the author (the one who writes) and the protagonist (the one who acts) but also the narrator (the one who narrates) are one and the same. But these three elements have different functions and their mutual relationship can

---

1. On the development and problematics of *watakushi shōsetsu*, see among others Miroslav Novák, '*Watakushi shosetsu* — The Appeal of Authenticity' in *Acta Universitatis Carolinae, Philologica* 2, Orientalia Pragensia II, 1962, 25-41; Irmela Hijiya-Kirschnereit, *Selbstentblössungsrituale, Zur Theorie und Geschichte der autobiographischen Gattung 'Shishōsetsu' in der modernen japanischen Literatur*, 1981; Edward Fowler, *The Rhetoric of Confession, Shishōsetsu in Early Twentieth-Century Japanese Fiction*, 1988.

never be unambiguous because only one of the three functions can be filled
at a time. A *watakushi shōsetsu* writer always runs the risk of losing the objectivity of his work, because of this monistic relation between writer, narrator
and protagonist; he runs the risk of turning his work of fiction into either an
essay, an autobiography, a documentary, a diary, or something of the like.

Instead of avoiding the danger and finding a purely literary solution,
certain writers have chosen to eliminate the boundary between the real and
the fictitious worlds by playing their 'fictitious roles' in the real world. They
then attempt to reproduce their experiences in the form of a literary work.
In order for the work to achieve its full effect, the reader is assumed to have
knowledge of the life of the author *beforehand*. That is to say that a work of
watakushi shōsetsu presupposes an *extra*-literary connection to reality/the surrounding world.

Japan has known two kinds of *watakushi shōsetsu* writers, who have acted
out their roles in real life in order to collect material for their writings. They
may have done this deliberately or not. One group of writers, the martyrs
filled with a sense of guilt, specialised in spiritual masochism. This group
includes among others Kasai Zenzō (1887-1928) and Dazai Osamu (1919-48).
The other group of writers sought harmony of the spirit by striving to live a
quiet, idealistic life or by living as eremites in the middle of nature (or in
their own interior), alone with their senses. This group includes Shiga Naoya
(1883-1971) and Kajii Motojirō (1901-32) among others.

In the following we will compare Iwano Hōmei's autobiographical works
with *watakushi shōsetsu* in general, in order to elucidate the relationship
between Iwano's theory of monistic narration and the works of the *watakushi
shōsetsu* school. We shall take Iwano's novel-series as our point of departure.

The most noticeable difference between the novel-series and *watakushi
shōsetsu*, is the fact that like the cast list in a play, Iwano presents the reader
to his characters in the opening of his novels *Hōrō* and *Hatten*. The protagonist
Tamura Yoshio is thus introduced as an 'active metaphysical philosopher of
momentariness' (*setsunashugi no jikkō tetsurika*) and as a 'contemplative poet'
(*shisakuteki shijin*) respectively.[2] These cast lists tell us better than anything
else about the peculiarity of Iwano's autobiographical works, especially as far
as the relation between the author and the protagonist is concerned.

Inspired by the confessional style that Tayama Katai had employed in the
short story 'Futon' from 1907, Iwano discovered in what direction he wanted

----

2. In the revised editions Iwano has removed these cast lists. But this is merely an outer
   change. All the characters in the novel-series are introduced to the reader, each with
   his own label glued on his forehead.

to take his prose writing. In contrast to Tayama Katai, who had described an unmotivated, nonchalant everyday existence in his novel-series, Iwano attempted to describe the deliberate, dynamic actions of one who is controlled by his thoughts and ideas. Iwano did this by fixing the point of view with his alter ego. In this way he achieved a clear and intense perspective in the work.

After the publication of '*Futon*', the development of *watakushi shōsetsu* was in a certain sense characterised by the disappearance of the 'I' in the works. With time, the 'I' ceased to belong to the surrounding world; it became increasingly abstract, and merely had the function of being a witness;[3] the 'I' thus lost its substance. The surrounding world and one's own 'I' could not be described at the same time from the point of view of the 'I'. A choice had to be made. Based upon a consideration of which of the two elements was thought to be the most important, the *watakushi shōsetsu* writers fell into two groups; the egocentrics on the one side, and on the other, those who were seeking to balance the two elements. While the former find their identity in their 'acting "I"', the latter find their identity in the 'telling "I"'.

In Iwano's novel-series, the identity of the protagonist (Iwano's 'acting 'I') Tamura Yoshio is guaranteed from the beginning as a fixed frame, no matter whether 'cast lists' are presented or not. That his life and actions seem alive and trustworthy, despite the lack of self-criticism or of any thorough analysis of his interior world in the novels, is due to the fact that the protagonist is in reality a vital man of action. Furthermore, Iwano's technique of writing is effective and creates a strong sense of reality. Iwano's method, which first and foremost consists of the 'neither-identification-nor-differentiation' relation between the author and the protagonist,[4] here creates the background for his compact, vivid style.

Those of Iwano's short stories/novels that are written according to the principles of monistic narration, create a peculiar universe. In these works only the consciousness of the protagonist is described and only that part of the surrounding world which is reflected in his consciousness exists for the protagonist; all that exists for him is thus his own consciousness, which reacts to the surrounding world. Explanations are given, but no development takes place in his inner world, because we can only talk of development when a

3. A witness cannot act and watch himself at the same time.

4. The *fusokufuri* relationship. The critic and writer Ishikawa Jun considers Tamura Yoshio and Iwano as inseparable, and does not see their relation as one in which Iwano is the original and Tamura Yoshio a recreation. Tamura Yoshio is almost a symbol of Iwano himself and makes up an essential part of Iwano's life. Cf. Ishikawa Jun, 'Iwano Hōmei' in *Bungaku taigai*, 1976, 236-38.

character's consciousness in its entirety is confronted with reality/the surrounding world.

In the unsuccessful story 'Gimeisha' (The man with the false name, published in *Taiyō* in April 1912), Iwano tried to take the issue of 'consciousness vs. the surrounding world' to the extreme. The story is concerned with Kosuge Teiichirō, whose first surname was Motono. After committing a murder and robbing his victim in his native town in the area of Osaka, he escapes to the USA where he hides as a missionary. After a considerably long period of time, he returns to Osaka, where he lives as a priest under a false name. One evening he has a nightmare which is followed by strong pangs of conscience.

Iwano describes the man's nightmare and his streams of consciousness from when he is half asleep and until he wakes up again. It is a weird story which at the same time constitutes a unique attempt in modern Japanese literature, if we take into consideration the moment in time at which it is written.[5]

The past and present of the protagonist overlap, while the narration is consistently written in the present tense. But the style is not sufficiently 'streaming'; it is more 'telling' than 'showing'.[6] The intention to describe the desperate soul of the protagonist when his inner world and the outer world lose contact, is indeed very original, but the picture of the protagonist's consciousness does not develop in a convincing way. His psychology is not analysed sufficiently, and his monologue (inner thought) thus never becomes 'streaming'. This means that the content of the story does not seem probable, and for this reason we must consider the story a failure. The short story remained Iwano's first and only attempt in this area.

In the short stories that are based on monistic narration, Iwano neither analyses nor relates to the 'I' in a critical fashion. What he describes, is a mixture of the results of the actions of the 'I' *and* the 'I's view of the surrounding world as it is seen from a distance.[7] In Iwano's stories 'the others' exist only in the consciousness of the 'I'; the protagonist himself relates directly to 'the others' and 'life', while the writer has an indirect

---

5. Cf. *HZ* vol. 2, 272-89. Without wanting to compare Iwano's unsuccessful attempt with the work of James Joyce, we may note that as far as the aspect of form and style is concerned, the attempt resembles Joyce's method. As regards the idea, again with no comparison, the story reminds us of Dostojevski's novel *Crime and Punishment* which is a drama of the interior world of a human being who is cut off from the surrounding world.

6. Cf. W.C. Booth's discussion of 'telling' and 'showing' in *The Rhetoric of Fiction*, 1969.

7. Notice that this is not an 'either-or' relation, as is the case in *watakushi shōsetsu*.

relation to 'life', which makes it possible for the author to avoid abstraction and explanation and instead employ concrete expressions and metaphors. In other words, things are 'shown' rather than 'told'.

In Iwano's novel-series the protagonist is self-confident and arrogant but capable of neither self-analysis nor self-criticism. What lends a dimension of literary reality to the novel-series is firstly, and as mentioned above, the unusual vitality of the protagonist, and secondly, the exquisite and exciting narrative technique. Monistic narration has here enabled Iwano to solve the problem of point of view which was so closely connected to autobiographical works in general.

For the sake of comparison we shall look at Iwano's novel *Tandeki* (Dissolute living, 1909). This story exemplifies the passage from his earlier bird's-eye perspective to monistic narration. In *Tandeki* the protagonist 'I' has a double identity. According to Iwano's theory of monistic narration, a writer must not relate directly to the world that he is describing in his work; he must not move out of his mediator, who is usually the protagonist. But in *Tandeki*, the 'I' acts both as an acting 'I' in the past and as a telling 'I' in the present.

For instance in the first paragraph we may read as follows:

All of a sudden he [the boy Sho-chan] said:
   'One of our *geishas* says that she would like to take [English] lessons with you too.'
   'No, I can't be bothered,' *I* answered, but *when I think back on it now, I see* that already then that *geisha* intended to make a fool of me.[8]

Here the 'I' is not independent, that is it has not been sufficiently objectivised. This is, by the way, the mechanism upon which *watakushi shōsetsu* is constructed.

In those of Iwano's autobiographical stories which were written after the publication of the theory in 1918, on the other hand, the protagonist is independent and described in an objective way. This is connected to the fact that Iwano has consistently removed all description in the present tense concerned with present arguments from his works.[9] This means that in his last stories

8. Cf. *HZ* vol. 1, 114-15.
9. In Japanese the present tense first and foremost serves the purpose of denoting that an event takes place at the same time as either the enunciation itself or as the other events specified in the enunciation. The form of the present tense may thus carry meanings of both the preterite and future tenses, dependending on the context.

which are written in accordance with the principles of monistic narration, we never find a sentence such as the 'when I think back on it now, I see' of the quotation above. The writing 'I' (the author) has thus been removed from the narration.

Iwano's theory of monistic narration came to its full expression in his novel-series. Here the method proved itself of excellent use for the description from the inside of the almost heroic but also high-flown (and therefore at times also comical) protagonist; it enabled him to describe both his enthusiasm and his melancholy from his own point of view. In the novel-series Iwano's narration is both symbolic and concrete, and the structure of the work is multi-dimensional. Iwano's attempt was successful, at least as far as his autobiographical works, in which the protagonist is his own alter ego, are concerned. But Iwano was mistaken when, intoxicated with his own fancied success, he believed his theory to be universal. He believed in the truth and validity of the theory right until his death in 1920. It is indeed a paradox that he himself became the one who would prove the shortcomings of the theory, or rather, its narrow-mindedness and flatness, when he wrote the two connected short stories 'Jisshi no hōchiku' (Expelling children from home, 1919) and 'Konashi no Tsutsumi' (Tsutsumi, the childless, 1919), some parts of which have already been introduced in the previous chapter. Together the two stories were to create a whole, that is to say that neither was complete on its own. This very 'wholeness' is what we call reality, concrete life, the objective world or 'nature', and it was for this very purpose that Iwano had created the theory of monistic narration. Iwano would probably have added the consideration that reality as such does not exist, and that we can only speak of the personal reality of the individual human being.

Iwano's theory was not effective either, when the protagonist was no longer the vital man of action that we know from the novel-series, Tamura Yoshio. Despite this Iwano experimented untiringly with his theory. He wanted to create 'wholeness' in his art on the basis of monistic narration. He took his theory to the furthest extent and the result was the two connected stories mentioned above. The attempt was interesting, but came to expose the limited validity of the theory which had been intended as a patent solution to all 'objective' description of 'life' in its 'entirety'.

The writers of *watakushi shōsetsu* did not share this striving for objectivity. They were content with their subjectivity, also as far as narration was concerned. The issue of point of view was unknown to them for the comprehensible reason that to them it was always evident who was the narrator, whom they wrote about, and how the relation between the narrating and the narrated was to be perceived. What interested them mostly was what they were writing about, and whether their experience was true and whether the resulting narrative was genuine and finally whether their relation to both, that is to both the experience and the narrative, was honest. Sincerity was the primary priority, and during and after the act of writing, their subjective world was heightened within their emotion to become a part of 'nature' itself. *Watakushi shōsetsu* thus came to have a function of catharsis for the writer.

With the introduction of naturalism into modern Japanese literature, a group of writers began to take a serious interest in daily life and in the objectivity of narration. In their attempts at embracing the entire surrounding world in their narration, the adherents of flat narration (*heimen byōsha*), including among others Tayama Katai and Shimazaki Tōson, became prone to producing voluminous, but tepid and superficial works, in which the bird's-eye perspective of the narrative functioned in a centrifugal way. Iwano, on the other hand, went in the opposite direction with his theory of monistic narration. He tried to describe the entire surrounding world by concentrating on one single character, who was to be considered a symbol of the world according to his theory. His theory of narration was centripetal.

If we look at *watakushi shōsetsu* in the light of traditional Japanese naturalism, we may justly argue that Iwano's theory of monistic narration was of great importance. This goes not only for the theory itself, but also for its application in practice, in the form of Iwano's five-volume novel-series and his other autobiographical stories. But *watakushi shōsetsu* is not a mere continuation of Iwano's literature. Considerable modifications, including a series of misinterpretations of his theory, have been made. We have discussed some of the most important differences in the above. But if we must mention one single aspect in which *watakushi shōsetsu* differs significantly from the art of Iwano, we may look at the tendency in *watakushi shōsetsu* to subjectivise at the cost of the objectivity of narration. The *watakushi shōsetsu* writers are no longer concerned with the surrounding world/life, but with the 'I', and only with the 'I'. Their tendency to subjectivise may almost be called a romantic inclination. As far as the theory of point of view is concerned, the works of *watakushi shōsetsu* are primitive repetitions of the *emotion* of the authorial 'I'. The art of writing has here been subjected to the demand for 'honesty'. Iwano, on the other hand, was concerned with restructuring the perception of the surrounding world/life on the basis of his philosophy, that is his concern is with 'intellectual' work.

When Iwano's theory was published, it immediately caused a stir within the world of letters, and a heated controversy followed. The theory was criticised by various critics and writers. But Iwano had no doubts regarding its worth and validity. He did not live to see that modern Japanese literature did develop in the very direction that he had predicted and which he was to follow himself. Most Japanese writers have, to a greater or minor extent, and consciously or not, each in his own way re-examined the theory and tried to employ it in practice. On the position of the theory within modern Japanese literary history, the writer Funabashi Seiichi (1904-76) writes in *Iwano Hōmei den* (Iwano Hōmei - a biography):

Following the decline of Tayama Katai's naturalism and his method of flat narration, the psychological, inner narration arose; from the minute but monotone and superficial description of nature, we see a move towards monistic narration. This was the main tendency within the literary world. This because the exaggerated realism was questioned, as was the demand for precision in narration, which merely turned into the report of some situation.

To be brief; a new method of narration was needed after the failures of naturalism. Idealism, which in a reaction to naturalism had moved towards the opposite extreme, had found itself at a dead end. The great waves of the period brought literature from ideas to 'concrete things' and from logic to psychology. Even though Iwano's theory was received as poorly as was the case, it fitted very well with the tendency of the time. Neither should we disregard the fact that in its depths, the theory actually decided the direction for and controlled Japanese literature.

This monistic tendency did indeed lead to a change in the kind of novel that was being written; from the psychological novel, over *shinkyō shōsetsu* [an essay-resembling novel in which the author's state of mind is mainly described] to *watakushi shōsetsu*, and even on to a kind of novel which only treated the most trivial matters from the author's everyday existence. Parallel to this change, monistic narration degenerated and stagnated. Nevertheless, the core of monistic narration — the development from logic to psychology and from ideas to 'concrete things' — was put into practice not only by [Iwano] Hōmei himself, but also by the majority of the most important Japanese writers after him.[10]

Contrary to his intention, Iwano's theory of monistic narration was manipulated and came to form the foundation for the development of *watakushi shōsetsu*. That was the destiny of the theory.

---

10. Cf. Funabashi Seiichi, *Iwano Hōmei den*, 2nd edition, 1971, 321. The book was first published in 1938. Funabashi was probably thinking of Shiga Naoya as one of the most important Japanese writers within the realist school. Naoya's masterpiece, *An'ya Kōro* (A Dark Night's Passing) had been written during the years 1922-37.

2. The Theory in Relation to Point of View Theories in General

> He [Henry James] put into the mouth of Lambert Strether,
> the middle-aged hero of *The Ambassadors*, a speech that begins:
> 'Live, live all you can, it's a mistake not to.'
> But Strether's own attempt to 'take the world into his soul'
> is miserably unsuccessful.
> Colin Wilson

2.1 Henry James and Iwano Hōmei

Henry James died in January 1916. Iwano Hōmei died in May 1920. Apparently Iwano knew nothing about Henry James, despite his otherwise wide knowledge of the literary world of the West. At least James is never mentioned in Iwano's voluminous writings.

At this time the Japanese world of letters was strongly influenced by French literature. Both naturalism and symbolism had been imported to Japan directly from France. If we take this circumstance into consideration, it becomes understandable that Henry James was not known in Japan; he wrote in English, was an emigrant writer and his contemporaries considered him a minor writer. Only *Daisy Miller* (1879) found a wider audience.

But if Iwano had heard of Henry James' point of view theory, he would probably have been surprised. Iwano always thought that the theory of monistic narration was his own unique invention and that he was the first in the world to have conceived it. But Henry James had put his own point of view theory into practice already in 1903 with the novel *The Ambassadors*. Even if Iwano had known of this, we may well imagine that he would have denied the validity of Henry James' theory and underestimated his experiments with narrative technique in *The Ambassadors*. Iwano's self-confident and polemic nature would probably have prevented him from accepting that Henry James held the authorial rights to the theory of point of view. This is the degree to which he was convinced of the validity of his own theory and of its revolutionary character.

Ibuse Masuji (1898-1993) writes in the essay '*Hajimete atta bunshi*' (My first meeting with a man of letters, July 1935) about his first meeting with Iwano:

The first man of letters I met was Mr Iwano Hōmei. It was at the very time when Mr Iwano was engaged in frequent controversies over the theory of monistic narration. When I visited him for the first time, he said ...:
'A man who has knowledge of the theory of empathy, but does not under-

stand that of monistic narration, is hopeless. The artist to introduce monistic technique within the visual arts, was Cezanne. The first to employ it in poetry was Baudelaire. In the art of drama Gorkij was the first. And in the art of prose, Iwano Hōmei from Japan.'

But abroad both Chekhov and Maupassant used a method of expression, which involved a focus for the narration. I was not sure whether they were aware of having employed the monistic method, but in some of their works the method is used in such a consistent fashion that one would think that they did so consciously. Therefore I said to Mr Iwano that also Maupassant employed monistic narration. Then Mr Iwano burst into laughter and said: 'Are you serious? But try to read one of Maupassant's stories first, and then my short stories on O-sei. Then you will understand the character of monistic narration better. The artist to have introduced monistic narration in the art of writing, is Baudelaire.'[11]

At the time Ibuse Masuji did not know that Iwano had taken the technique of point of view one step further than Chekhov and Maupassant, but on the other hand Iwano did not know that before himself Henry James had developed the technique to its furthest extent.

To make sure that Ibuse Masuji is referring to an actual event, and that his account has not been distorted by his well-known irony, we will quote Iwano's own comments on the importance of the theory:

By now I have published many essays on the use of monistic narration in the art of novel writing. I also plan to publish a book about the subject in the near future. My theory may renew the art of fiction fundamentally, not only in our country but in the whole world.

Both Tolstoy and Dostoevsky based their works on explanations and their narration remains superficial. This is not just true for Tolstoy but also for all the other famous writers from different countries. Therefore it is useless to mention Tolstoy or Flaubert or D'Annunzio, in a criticism of my theory of monistic narration. Such an attempt is almost equivalent to trying to link the new literature to old-fashioned examples ...

A narrative theory as thorough as mine has never been seen abroad. Therefore foreign narrative theories cannot be used for comparison. Only in the future, when foreigners will study modern Japanese literature, and not until they discover my work, will they learn that a whole new narrative method exists. Some do not take my theory of monistic narration seriously, and they think that it is merely concerned with narrative techniques in ficiton. But narration is not just an outer

---

11. Cf. *HZ* vol. 9, 148. On the theory of empathy, see IV. Part 2, page 113, and note 35 ibidem.

form. It also regards the issue of the subject matter of a work. Try to sit down, read a story written as monistic narration and then another story which is not written in this style, and then compare the two. You will have to find that there is a difference in the depth of the stories. Or put more precisely; in the short story which is not written with monistic narration, the narration remains superficial. In short, monistic narration is an 'inner' narration.[12]

As we have seen earlier, Iwano concluded his narrative theory from October 1918 with the following words:

I hope that my theory will not simply be regarded as my personal point of view, but instead that it will be read with particular care by every writer and critic in order that the literature in our country and art throughout the world may become more penetrating and pure.[13]

There is no doubt that Iwano was a nationalist, but we must not forget that where his own theory of monistic narration was concerned, he really believed in its universal validity.

In the following we will compare the principal points of Iwano's theory with Henry James' point of view theory, which was closely connected to his strivings to depict a deeper psychology in the novel, and which laid the foundation for the literature of the stream of consciousness.

Contrary to Iwano, who had written a series of articles on monistic narration, Henry James did not treat the issue of point of view in a systematic way. We may read about his theory only in fragments — here and there in the prefaces to his short stories and novels or in his essays. When we compare his theory to Iwano's, it may therefore prove useful to quote from Percy Lubbock's *The Craft of Fiction* (1921) in which Henry James' method is summarised and developed.

Interestingly enough, like Iwano, but in a more controlled manner, Percy Lubbock was convinced of the universal nature of Henry James' point of view theory.

When the whole volume is full of a strongly-marked idiosyncrasy, quite unlike that of anyone else, it is difficult to distinguish between this, which is solely the

---

12. Cf. '*Ichigen byōsha to wa?*' (What is monistic narration?, 1919), in *HZ* vol. 10, 594-96.
13. Ibid., 564.

author's, and his method of treating a story, which is a general question, discussible apart. And thus it happens that the novelist who carried his research into the theory of the art further than any other — the only real 'scholar' in the art — is the novelist whose methods are most likely to be overlooked or mistaken, regarded as simply a part of his own original quiddity. It should be possible to isolate them, to separate them in thought from the temperament by which they were coloured: they belong to the craft, which belongs to no man in particular.[14]

In the book, Percy Lubbock 'isolates' Henry James' 'method' in various ways, but the best and most concrete description of Henry James' point of view theory is probably the section in which he analyses the point of view of the protagonist Strether in the novel *The Ambassadors*.

But though in *The Ambassadors* the point of view is primarily Strether's, and though it *appears* to be his throughout the book, there is in fact an insidious shifting of it, so artfully contrived that the reader may arrive at the end without suspecting the trick. The reader, all unawares, is placed in a better position for an understanding of Strether's history, better than the position of Strether himself. Using his eyes, we see what *he* sees, we are possessed of the material on which his patient thought sets to work; and that is so far well enough, and plainly necessary. All the other people in the book face towards him, and it is that aspect of them, and that only, which is shown to the reader; still more important, the beautiful picture of Paris and springtime, the stir and shimmer of life in the Rue de Rivoli and the gardens of the Tuileries, is Strether's picture, *his* vision, rendered as the time and the place strike upon his senses. All this on which his thought ruminates, the stuff that occupies it, is represented from his point of view. To see it, even for a moment, from some different angle — if, for example, the author interposed with a vision of his own — would patently disturb the right impression. The author does no such thing, it need hardly be said.[15]

In this we find the essence of Henry James' point of view theory. We may compare it to Iwano's persuasion:

14. Cf. Percy Lubbock, *The Craft of Fiction*, London 1921, Jonathan Cape Paperback Edition, 1965, 186-87.
15. Ibid., 161-62. Dorrit Cohn characterises the typical narrative situation preferred by Henry James and not least by Percy Lubbock, and in which narrated monologue occurs, as follows: '... in which [in the narrated monologue] the viewpoint coincides as closely as possible with that of one character, while the knowledge of the narrator is limited to the psyche and field of perception of that character at the moment of narration.' Cf. 'Narrated Monologue: Definition of a Fictional Style,' in *Comparative Literature*, vol. 18, 1966, 106.

We assume that A is the protagonist. The author is now in A's mind. He observes the others through A and all that which A does not hear, see or feel, is considered an unexplored world, an uninhabited island and is as such it is left undescribed, even though the author has knowledge of it. If there is something he does not want to leave out, he describes it as if the protagonist heard, saw or felt it. This is precisely the attitude that I have insisted upon and practised, both as a writer and as a critic.[16]

As Iwano himself states, he put his theory of monistic narration into practice in such a consistent and thorough way that he was no longer satisfied with merely writing his new works in agreement with the theory. He also went through his earlier writings in order to revise the passages that were not in accordance with the theory. To Iwano the theory was an axiom.

But with Henry James the case was different. As mentioned earlier he never composed a systematised theory to describe his method. After some fumbling in the dark and many stylistic attempts, he finally arrived at the method that he employed in the novel *The Ambassadors*. But even this method did not become a point of departure for the narration to which he could return and which he could have worked in accordance with.

'... the point of view *appears* to be his [Strether's]', but 'there is in fact an insidious shifting of it', even though few readers notice this. Strether is 'the watcher', but the next moment he becomes 'the watched'. This is not to say, however, that the point of view in the novel is *explicitly* moved to another character or to the author himself. Thanks to the flexible point of view which has been given to Strether, and which enables the author to go in and out of Strether without ever leaving him completely, the reader is able to see the man Strether directly and objectively.

If Percy Lubbock or Henry James had been able to read Iwano's theory, they would have considered it both rigid and narrow-minded. Probably neither Percy Lubbock's theory/analysis nor Henry James' work would probably have seemed sufficiently profound from the viewpoint of Iwano. Iwano would even have said that this was due to an insufficient depth in their world view. As we already know, Iwano gave the second section of his theory of narration the title 'The true understanding of life and the only true attitude' (*shin no jinseikan to yuiitsu no taido*) and wrote as follows:

In our own world we cannot include anything but that which we understand by watching, listening or using our imagination in a realistic way. Therefore [our]

16. Cf. *HZ* vol. 10, 545.

world or life are not the world or the life that all people know of, but something
that everyone in his own way finds reflected in his own subjective point of view.
In other words, it is an empire in which everyone is the emperor and where the
sovereignty of other people is not accepted. Ignorant people often call such a
philosophy insolent or arrogant, but it should be considered the most modest
attitude, when one at least does not want to conquer the territory beyond one's
own with the help neither of one's imagination nor of one's own ruthless logic
...[17]

No matter whether Iwano is insolent or arrogant, he does in this way declare
his intention of renouncing the so-called 'objectivity' and 'omniscience'.[18] And
it was the very notions of 'objectivity' and 'omniscience' which also Henry
James turned his back on definitively. We may also say that Iwano and Henry
James basically held the same life and worldview, apart from one difference
which was the consequence partly of their cultural backgrounds, partly of
their natures.

The difference in their attitudes to the surrounding world may briefly be
defined as the opposition we find between dualism and monism; i.e. Western
dualism as opposed to Japanese monism. In the figure of Henry James,
Western dualism had reached its almost pathological extreme, and it lent him
a tinge of schizophrenia. While Iwano, who on the whole seemed both
healthy and naive, was obsessed with Japanese monism in an equally
pathological way.

Iwano's almost manic relation to the monistic world view culminated in
an episode which took place in a secondary school at Hokkaido, where a
friend had encouraged him to give a lecture. The episode was later related in
the novel *Tsukimono* (The posessed one, 1912-18) where Tamura Yoshio is the
protagonist.

Almost intoxicated with his own voice, in the middle of his speech,
Tamura Yoshio shouts: 'I am the emperor of the Cosmos — No, I am the very
Cosmos!' But the audience burst into laughter. In their eyes Tamura Yoshio
was simply a comical character. Thus rumours spread that Tamura Yoshio
had gone mad.

This episode tells us something of the degree to which Iwano was taken
with his monistic philosophy.

17. Ibid., 549-50.
18. But Iwano did not renounce the objectivity of the narration itself.

Henry James' dualism came to its extreme in the figure of the protagonist of the short story 'The Jolly Corner' (1908). The protagonist Spencer Brydon returns to the USA after many years in Europe. But in his old residence he is surprised by his own double.

Just as Tamura Yoshio's outburst was typical of Iwano's manic tendency to monism, the superstitious belief in the double was a *basso continuo* in Henry James' *oeuvre*. Just as Iwano's monistic narration drove him to an extreme, Henry James took his dualistic view to a maximum. Their writings were very different, but they had both arrived at a method which used a monistic (single) point of view throughout a work. Can we call this a coincidence? No, not quite. This was almost a necessary consequence of one and the same development which had taken part first in Europe and then in Japan. Henry James' and Iwano's writings had the same background. But here we are only discussing the point of departure for their writings, and not influences or the like. Even though the foundation was the same, Iwano's theory did not develop quite as Henry James'. This was mainly due to the specifically Japanese elements in the modern Japanese literature of Iwano's day; the very uniqueness of Japanese naturalism inevitably lends a peculiarly Japanese touch to Iwano's theory. For instance, he put a far too exaggerated emphasis on theory and form, and also the subjective tendency, which almost approached idealism and romanticism and was a typically Japanese element.[19] So in his own zealous and consequent way, Iwano took also this tendency to an extreme.

Whether it was Iwano's or Henry James' narrative theory that came to 'renew the idea of the novel' then and later, is open to debate. Iwano himself claimed that his theory was universal, and similarly Percy Lubbock never doubted the universal character of Henry James' method. But in this case we are only concerned with method. We may indeed consider their methods as 'models' for their writings. But we cannot separate their methods from their fictional writings and give an independent status to them. The methods of both writers were closely connected to their temperaments and talents, to such a degree that it would be meaningless to discuss their methods as abstract, general rules that all writers should follow. We know that Iwano was not even able to explain why his *oeuvre* was supposed to be so fascinating. Similarly Percy Lubbock was unable to analyse the charm of

19. A similar peculiarity is found in German naturalism, with smaller modifications. Cf. Lillian R. Furst and Peter N. Skrine, *Naturalism*, London 1971, 37-41.

Henry James' writings. But one thing is certain: the interest that their writings attracted was not caused by methodology alone.

As far as Iwano's *oeuvre* is concerned, it was his theory that gave a unique touch, a literary identity, to his work. The uniqueness of his 'literature', on the other hand, consisted in his manic striving for 'the monistic', which was to exceed even the frame of the theory. In his fanaticism he lived out his momentariness through the figure of Tamura Yoshio; in the same moment he could experience the ecstasy of momentariness and disillusion. When he shouted: 'I am the emperor of the Cosmos', he cried out his 'Eureka!' And when afterwards he cried: 'I am the very Cosmos!' He simultaneously declared, consciously or unawares, that a 'Cosmos' does exist. In the same moment the writer Iwano disappeared. All that was left was the cosmos, which was really the 'I', Tamura Yoshio. The epistemologist Iwano became an ontologist. It is this ecstatic metamorphosis which may move the reader, and in which the reader may identify with the writer. But neither Iwano's theory of narration nor his worldview was able to describe this process. Or put differently; this ontological leap in his literature broke the framework of his literary theory.

As far as the relation between Henry James' literature and his literary theory is concerned, we may notice its inherent contradiction. The subject matter of the novel *The Ambassadors* does not really fit its form. The fictitious world that has been described in the novel, is created only as what the protagonist Strether sees. All other characters in the work are coloured by his fear, joy, doubt and faith. All that happens in the world of the novel is what he himself believes is taking place. There is no way in which the reader may verify whether the characters are in reality as they have been described, and whether the episodes have actually taken place or not the way they have been described. Nevertheless, the reader keeps telling himself, with a certain undefinable irritation or unrest in his mind, that this is not the real world, not reality itself — or that reality must be concealed behind this fictitious world.

Through the thoughts of Strether, we learn about his philosophy, but the reader finds these thoughts and his world view meaningless compared to 'reality'. At the same time we discover that behind these thoughts and beyond this worldview, 'something else' is to be found. When Strether complains about his useless view, he calls this 'something else' the 'darkness behind darkness'. Strether does not shout out his 'Eureka!', but the reader is nevertheless moved by his quiet whisper: 'I have not found it!'. Why? Even if Strether has not found 'it', he does at least suggest one reality — his own reality, which is to say that he had almost found it anyway. The novel *The*

Ambassadors is thus constructed upon a dualistic assumption, even though the point of view relationship in the novel is monistic. Henry James' monistic point of view is based upon the firm foundation of dualism, and this necessarily leads towards the almost invisible, ontological abyss, which the reader cannot avoid being shocked by. The dualistic split in the literature of the world seems to have reached a climax with the works of Henry James.

Iwano's writings took French naturalism as their point of departure, and developed in the trace of French symbolism. Iwano himself thought that his own work and not least his literary theory would be valid all through the world. In his own imagination he was one of the greatest names in world literature. But thanks to his typically Japanese nature and his Japanese cultural background, he escaped the European *fin de siècle* malady — the dualistic split. He was and remained just as healthy and vivid as the gods of ancient Japanese history that he had believed in ever since reading the oldest Japanese history book *Kojiki* (AD 712).

2.2. Point of View Theories through Time and Iwano Hōmei's Theory

> The one *who speaks* (in the narrative) is not the one *who writes*
> (in real life) and the one *who writes* is not the one *who is*.
> Roland Barthes

Through time, point of view theories have been developed from different theoretical positions. In the following, we will look at Iwano Hōmei's theory of monistic narration and compare it with some of the most representative point of view theories. This comparison should help us estimate the relevance of the theory in a broader perspective.

2.2.1. Norman Friedman

Norman Friedman's article 'Point of View in Fiction: The Development of a Critical Concept' (1955) is without doubt one of the first and most comprehensive studies of point of view.[20]

First, Friedman provides a thorough analysis of the theories of his predecessors, from Plato to his contemporaries. Still in the first section, he goes

---

20. Printed in PMLA (Publications of the Modern Language Association), vol. 70, no. 5, Wis., 1160-84.

on to classify the narrator's relation to his work depending upon his attitude
to the following four questions:

1. Who speaks to the reader?
2. From what position does he speak?
3. What is his medium?
4. Where does he place the reader in relation to the narrative?

The result is eight categories:[21]

1. *Editorial Omniscience*
   The author's voice dominates the work because he often speaks as 'I' or
   'we'.
   For example: Henry Fielding and Leo Tolstoy.
2. *Neutral Omniscience*
   The same as the above, but the author is not directly involved in the
   narrative.
   For example: Thomas Hardy, *Tess of the D'Urbervilles.*
3. *'I' as Witness*
   The narrator takes part in the narrative and addresses the reader in the
   first person. For example: Joseph Conrad and Scott Fitzgerald.
4. *'I' as Protagonist*
   The narrator 'I' is the protagonist of the narrative. For example: Charles
   Dickens, *Great Expectations.*
5. *Multiple Selective Omniscience*
   With this type of narration the narrator of 1. and 2. and the narrating 'I'
   of 3. and 4. disappear. The narrative is developed directly from the inner
   worlds of the characters. For example: Virginia Woolf, *To the Lighthouse.*
6. *Selective Omniscience*
   The same as 5. except this type only allows the reader access to the inner
   world of one of the characters. For example: James Joyce, *A Portrait of the
   Artist as a Young Man.*
7. *The Dramatic Mode*
   The reader can only follow the plot of the narrative by observing what the
   characters do and say. There is no revelation of their inner worlds. For
   example: Ernest Hemingway, 'Hills Like White Elephants', Henry James,
   The Awkward Age.

21. Ibid., 1168-69.

8. *The Camera*

Only the things which pass before the author's eye are registered and written down. For example: Christopher Isherwood, *Goodbye to Berlin*.

It seems almost superfluous to say that Iwano's theory belongs to the sixth category, that of 'selective omniscience'. Norman Friedman goes on to divide this category into three groups which are separated according to the extent of the author's exploration of the protagonist's inner world. Henry James is thus said to remain at the first level of the protagonist's inner world and Virginia Woolf in the middle. Finally James Joyce reaches into the depths of his protagonist's mind. Generally speaking, Iwano seems to place himself at the same level as Henry James.

2.2.2. Wayne C. Booth

The next work which we will look at is Wayne C. Booth's by now legendary and classic *The Rhetoric of Fiction* (1961). He does not approach the problem of point of view directly, but chapter 6 discusses various 'Types of Narration'.[22] Here he cites the following as factors which determine the nature of the narrative:

PERSON: Who is telling the story? He classifies these into three groups:

The Implied Author
Undramatised Narrator
Dramatised Narrator

Among the *dramatised narrators* he includes *observers* and *narrator agents* who do not function as protagonists in the narrative.

SCENE AND SUMMARY: Does the narrator provide the reader with a description of the plot or an explanation of it? In short, does he 'show' it or 'explain' it?[23]

COMMENTARY: Does the narrator comment on the narrative?

SELF-CONSCIOUS NARRATORS: Does the narrator express an awareness of his being the author?

---

22. W.C. Booth, The Rhetoric of Fiction, 149-65.
23. Cf. Percy Lubbock's theory of 'show the story' versus 'tell the story'. Op. cit., 62.

VARIATIONS OF DISTANCE: Is there a distance (moral, physical, intellectual or emotional) between:

1. the narrator and the implicit author
2. the narrator and the characters in the narrative
3. the narrator and the reader (or rather the reader's standards)
4. the implicit author and the reader
5. the implicit author and the characters in the narrative

VARIATIONS IN SUPPORT OR CORRECTION: Is the narrator reliable or not? Is the narrator's account confirmed or corrected by other narrators of the same narrative?

PRIVILEGE: Is the narrator privileged in his knowledge of the narrated events?

INSIDE VIEWS: How far does the author go in his exploration of the characters' inner world?

Wayne C. Booth simply lists these different elements without actually providing concrete examples of typical narrator/work relations as Norman Friedman did. It is not possible to place Iwano Hōmei's narrative theory in any of the specified groups, but we can, however, examine Iwano's theory on the basis of and in relation to the different elements that Booth emphasises. If we do not base our analysis on each of Iwano's works, we run the risk of generalising because exceptions undoubtedly do exist. But if we approach Iwano's *oeuvre* as a whole, keeping in mind his theory of narration, it is possible to make the following analysis:

With regard to PERSON, the narrator in Iwano's autobiographical work is undoubtedly the implied author.

The narrator always 'shows' the plot (SCENE) and he does not comment on it (COMMENTARY). (Cf. Iwano's discussion of *byōsha* (description) versus *setsumei* (explanation).)

The narrator is aware of his position as author (SELF-CONSCIOUS NARRATOR).

There is nearly always a moral as well as an intellectual and emotional DISTANCE between the implied author and the reader, and the author and the characters in the narrative. (Cf. Iwano's 'semi-animalism' (*hanjū-shugi*) which was misunderstood by his contemporaries, as well as his highly inaccessible philosophy of 'momentariness' (*setsuna-shugi*).)

Just as Iwano was a loner who always insisted on being right, likewise his narrators required no SUPPORT or CORRECTION from other characters or narrators.

Since Iwano did not write romantic or supernatural stories, it is not possible to speak of PRIVILEGE in his work.

INSIDE VIEW was something which Iwano focused a great deal on in his work. He placed this problem at the centre of his theory and experimented with 'inner realism' (*naibuteki shajitsushugi*) right until his death in 1920.

2.2.3. Bertil Romberg

In 1962, Bertil Romberg published his academic thesis at the University of Lund, with the title *Studies in the Narrative Techniques of the First-Person Novel*. As the title indicates, the book limits itself to the 'I-novel', but some parts of the book deal with point of view issues in general (particularly the second section in chapter 1). As it turns out, Romberg's theory is largely based on Norman Friedman's system of classification with regard to types of point of view.[24] Bertil Romberg uses the following four groups as his point of departure for his own modified classification:

A. The author is omniscient, visible and omnipresent.
B. The author as a role renounces his Olympian views and omniscience, and confines himself to the mind(s) of one or more of the characters.
C. The author registers and records as a behaviourist observer, a film camera with (apparently) entirely objective reproduction and with no insight into that which is not perceptible to the senses.
D. The author is hidden behind the narrator = first-person novel.[25]

The connection between Bertil Romberg's and Norman Friedman's systems of classification is apparent. Romberg's A corresponds to Norman Friedman's 1 and 2; B corresponds to 5 and 6; C to 7 and 8; and D to 3 and 4.

Iwano's theory coincides with Bertil Romberg's category B, in which the author limits himself to describing the inner world of one character.

Because Bertil Romberg has chosen to focus on the first-person novel, he develops his theory exclusively on the basis of category D. But in the third section of chapter 3, he approaches the problems related to interior monologue and the stream of consciousness. This is of particular interest to us, but he does not explore these techniques closely because they potentially exceed the limits of the 'I-novel' (interior monologue and/or the stream of consciousness usually require an 'invisible narrator' who is not the 'I').

24. Bertil Romberg, *Studies in the Narrative Technique of the First-Person Novel*, 24-30.
25. Ibid., 27.

2.2.4. Scholes and Kellogg

Robert Scholes and Robert Kellogg approach the problem quite differently in 'Point of View in Narrative', chapter 7 of their book *The Nature of Narrative* (1966).[26] Their point of departure is a concept called 'narrative irony' which they describe as follows:

Irony is always the result of a disparity of understanding. In any situation in which one person knows or perceives more — or less — than another, irony must be either actually or potentially present. In any example of narrative art there are, broadly speaking, three points of view — those of the characters, the narrator, and the audience. As narrative becomes more sophisticated, a fourth point of view is added by the development of a clear distinction between the narrator and the author. Narrative irony is a function of disparity among these three or four viewpoints. And narrative artists have always been ready to employ this disparity to make effects of various kinds.[27]

They work their way through the world's literary history and analyse various types of narrative using the notion of an 'ironic gap' between the three or four points of view in a work, as their tool. Finally they create a rather peculiar division of the different types of narrators:

     1. The 'eye-witness'
     2. The 'histor'
     3. Other narrative postures

In the 'eye-witness' account, the eye of the witness is either turned 'inward' in such a way that his own figure is placed at the centre, or turned 'outward' — and his interest is consequently in other people or the surrounding world. In this type of narrative, the narrator's relation to the characters is the most important aspect of the issue of point of view. If the narrator is one of the characters, then this person dominates the narrative. He/she goes ahead of the event (the plot) that is to be recounted. This is true no matter whether the narrator is a real or a fictive person. On the other hand, if the narrator is clearly removed from the author, then this creates an ironic distance between the two. When the narrator is then furthermore differentiated from his self, which takes an active part in the narrative, another ironic gap is created. (Cf. Norman Friedman's types 3 and 4)

---

26. Robert Scholes and Robert Kellogg, *The Nature of Narrative*, 240-82.
27. Ibid., 240.

Furthermore, three variations of the 'eye-witness' form are mentioned:

1. The witness speaks of the protagonist while trying to understand him by re-creating his experiences in his imagination.
2. The use of multiple narrators. For example William Faulkner, *Absalom, Absalom!*
3. The use of an unreliable witness. For example Jonathan Swift, *Gulliver's Travels*.[28]

Most of Iwano's narrative art belongs to this 'eye-witness' group. The witness is the author himself with his eyes turned inwards. But at this stage it is impossible to distinguish Iwano's art from that of *watakushi shōsetsu* in which the author is identical to the narrator and the protagonist. (Cf. VI.1, page 169ff)

The other group is called the 'histor' and it is described in the following:

The 'histor' is the narrator as inquirer, constructing a narrative on the basis of such evidence as he has been able to accumulate. The 'histor' is not a character in narrative, but he is not exactly the author himself, either. He is a person, a projection of the author's empirical virtues.[29]

In the narrative, the 'histor' is usually intrusive with his commentary. (Cf. Norman Friedman's 1 and 2.) Works which are representative of this narrative mode include Henry Fielding, *Tom Jones* and Leo Tolstoy's *Vojna i mir* (*War and Peace*).

The group 'other narrative postures' includes the 'bard' who can reveal the unspoken thoughts of others; the 'maker' who shows the reader the technical problems he has in constructing the narrative (Cf. Henry Fielding, *Tom Jones*); the 'self-effacing narrator' who is equal to the sort of narrator employed by Henry James; and finally the 'recorder', an impersonal and invisible narrator as in, for example, Ernest Hemingway's 'Hills Like White Elephants'. (Cf. Norman Friedman's classification 7.)

Robert Scholes and Robert Kellogg go on to analyse and broaden Henry James' attack on omniscience. Iwano was also known for his sharp criticism of narrator omniscience.

As can be seen from the above, the narrators in Iwano's works turn their gaze inwards and can thus be seen as belonging to the 'eye-witness-group'.

28. Ibid., 261-63.
29. Ibid., 265-66.

However, the book still lacks the precision of Norman Friedman's article — especially with regard to 5 and 6. Scholes and Kellogg do not distinguish between the 'I' as narrator and the third person (not-'I') as narrator. Variation 2 in the 'eye-witness'-group which involves the use of multiple narrators is admittedly very similar to Norman Friedman's 5 'multiple selective omniscience'. But the point of view, which allows precisely for the kind of author/narrator/character/reader relation that Iwano presented in his theory of narration, is missing.

2.2.5. Mikhail Bakhtin

We go back in time to study Mikhail M. Bakthin's work 'Avtor i geroj v éstetícheskoj dejatel'nosti' (The author and the protagonist in the aesthetic work) from the middle of the twenties.[30]

The article has a section with the heading 'Problema otnoshenija avtora k geroju' (The problem of the author's relationship to the protagonist), which catches our attention.[31] It is interesting both in relation to Iwano's theory and to the other theories, which we will discuss in more detail later.

The section is written as an introduction to the whole article and it is here that Bakhtin presents the issue which he will confront. He introduces a variety of perceptions of the author/protagonist relationship, among these Theodor Lipps' philosophy of aesthetics — the theory of *Einfühlung*. Then Mikhail Bakhtin presents his general definition of the relationship between the author and the protagonist as 'correlative elements of the whole work of art', and afterwards he 'provides a formula for the mutual growth of author and protagonist'.[32]

Bakhtin defines the author as 'the carrier of the intense and active unit of the final totality, the whole protagonist and the whole work'.[33] He then gives an outline of the three main types of author/protagonist relationships:

1. *The protagonist rules over the author* — The protagonist is independent both in emotional and ethical matters to such a degree that the author can only view the world through his eyes. The protagonist moves the plot onward.

---

30. Printed in *Éstetika slovesnogo tvorchestvo* (The aesthetic of literary works), Moscow 1979, 7-180. We do not know for sure when this article was written. See the note in the book, 384.
31. Ibid., 7-22.
32. Ibid., 13-14.
33. Ibid.

Mikhail Bakhtin adds that this type of work usually has several characters and that the relationship which has been described only exists between one character and the author. Examples of such ruling protagonists can be found in nearly all of Dostoyevsky's work, in some of Leo Tolstoy's work and likewise in the work of Søren Kierkegaard and Stendahl.

2. *The author rules over the protagonist.* This category can be divided into two groups:

A. The protagonist is not autobiographical, but he is the voice of the author's reflections.

B. The protagonist is an autobiographical character.

Mikhail Bakhtin calls the protagonists of group A quasi-classical and the protagonists of group B romantic.

3. *The protagonist is the author.* He reflects on his own life aesthetically as if he had a role to play. He often appears complacent.

This division shows how Mikhail Bakthin's classification of the relationship between author and protagonist derives from aesthetic-philosophical principles. Iwano's centripetal monistic theory of narration builds on 2, but the first relationship should also be noted. While Iwano repeatedly criticised the relationship described in 3, he did not consider the possibility which is developed in 1, at least not in the way that Mikhail Bakhtin has formulated it.

Iwano regarded Dostoyevsky as a trite author. Like so many of his contemporaries, Iwano did not recognise Dostoyevsky's innovative narrative technique, polyphonic narration.

2.2.6. Franz Stanzel

Franz K. Stanzel investigates three typical narrator positions in his book *Typische Formen des Romans* (1964). They are:

1. *Die auktoriale Erzählsituation*
2. *Die Ich-Erzählsituation*
3. *Die personale Erzählsituation*

In 1 the narrator occupies an authorial position which is omniscient and omnipresent. This narrator is placed between the fictional world of the narrative and the real world of the author and reader.

However, in 2, the narrator holds the position of the 'I' and as such he belongs wholly to the fictive world. He experiences and observes all events described in the work.

The personal narrator of 3 is positioned behind the characters of the novel.

That the narrator is hidden in this way, gives the reader the illusion of entering into the fictive world because he sees the events of the novel through the eyes of one of the characters. In this way the character becomes a 'persona' — a mask.[34]

F.K. Stanzel's classification resembles Bakthin's system significantly, but the bibliography shows no indication that he was familiar with Bakthin's ideas.

It is difficult to place Iwano's theory, or rather the typical narrator in Iwano's work, in F.K. Stanzel's model. His categories are simply too broad. Iwano's narrators seem to place themselves somewhere between 2 and 3 or, more precisely, on the way from 2 to 3. The subject matter of a representative selection of Iwano's work is autobiographical, but the form is *'personale'*. This means that an event or act in the fictive world is *described* from the point of view of the protagonist, as opposed to the 'I'-narrative in which the event or act is *told* as something that has already happened or been experienced by the protagonist 'I'.

2.2.7. Tzvetan Todorov

With minor modifications, Tzvetan Todorov bases his classification of the relationship between the narrator and the protagonist in his book *Littérature et signification* (1967) on Jean Pouillon's *Temps et roman* (1946).[35]

There are three models for the relationship:

1. *Narrateur > Personnage (la vision 'par dernière')*
   The narrator knows more about an event than the protagonist or any of the other characters do. The narrator does not tell the reader where he has his information from. The protagonist and the other characters have no secrets from the narrator. This model is often used in classical works.
2. *Narrateur = Personnage (la vision 'avec')*
   The narrator knows as much as the protagonist and the other characters. This means that the narrator cannot explain a given event before the protagonist or another character has found an explanation for it. A story based on this model can be narrated both in the first and in the third person. Tzvetan Todorov cites Franz Kafka's novel *The Castle* as an

---

34. F.K. Stanzel, *Typische Formen des Romans*, 16-17.
35. Cf. Tzvetan Todorov, *Littérature et signification*, the third section *'Le récit comme procès d'énonciation'*, 79-89. The similarities between this theory and Bakhtin's theory are actually striking.

example of a novel that was first written in the first person and later rewritten in the third person without changing the '*avec*' relationship
between the narrator and the protagonist.[36]

3. *Narrateur < Personnage (la vision 'du dehors')*

The narrator knows less about an event than the protagonist or other
characters. He can only write about that which he has seen or heard.
Tzvetan Todorov calls this model an expression of pure 'sensualism'. He
adds that this model first appeared in the 20th century and that it is very
rare in the history of literature.[37]

Iwano's theory of monistic narration quite obviously builds on the second relationship ('*avec*') with a third-person narrative. However, the interesting
thing about Tzvetan Todorov's theory is that in 2, he points towards the possibility of a narrator who can shift his point of view (systematically or hapha-
zardly) from one character to another. In continuation of this, he discusses the
particular cases where different characters all tell about (or are witnesses to)
the same event. He calls this particular use of point of view '*vision stéréo-
scopique*'. He names Choderlos de Laclos' epistolary novel *Les Liaisons
Dangereuses* as an example where the same story is told several times from
different points of view.[38]

This reminds us of the method Iwano employed in the short-story couple
'*Jisshi no hōchiku*' (Expelling children from home) and '*Konashi no Tsutsumi*'
(Tsutsumi, the childless). They were meant to complement one another and
create a whole. A similar experiment is attempted in William Faulkner's *The
Sound and Fury* (1929). It consists of four sections. Each section gives an
account of the same event in the Compson family, but they are narrated from
four different points of view. The same is the case in Philip Toynbee's *Tea
with Mrs Goodman* from 1947, and in Robert Pinget's *Autour de Mortin* (1965)
which is the story of Mortin's life and death, recounted by a set of characters
with strongly opposing interpretations of his person. Another example is a
Danish novelist Svend Åge Madsen's (1939-) *Jakkels Vandring* (Jakkel's
wandering) from 1974 where Jakkel, who is a Jesus-like figure, and his
wanderings are described by his seven disciples. Another work to be
mentioned in this connection is Akutagawa Ryūnosuke's brilliant short story

36. Ibid., 80.
37. Ibid.
38. Ibid., 81

'*Yabu no naka*' (In a grove) from 1922. It describes and reconstructs the same murder from the viewpoints of the different witnesses.[39]

Tzvetan Todorov furthermore writes:

The value of the viewpoints in a narrative has rapidly changed since the epoch of Laclos. The tecnique of presenting a story through its projections in the consciousness of one of the characters has been used more and more during the 19th century, and, after having been systematized by Henry James, it has become an obligatory rule in the 20th century.[40]

Iwano's theory of narration resembles Henry James' point of view theory in several essential points. However, whether Akutagawa Ryūnosuke, who was an expert on Western literature, was inspired by Iwano or by Henry James or perhaps by some third person, remains unknown.

2.2.8. Lubomír Dolezel

In the article 'The Typology of the Narrator: Point of View in Fiction' (1967), Lubomír Dolezel divides narrative types into six categories using thorough (Czech) structuralist methodology.

1. *Objective narration*
   All 'facts', both material and psychological, are revealed to the reader as if he were 'seeing' them directly. In what is naturally only an illusion, the narrator functions as the objective camera or as the scientific apparatus that records with exactness. (J. Mukarovský: *Kapitoly z ceské poetiky II*, Prague 1948)[41]
2. a) *Rhetorical narration*
   This type is characterised by the narrator's involvement in the story and consequently by his/her judgments and his/her power over the reader's viewpoints.
2. b) *Subjective third person*
   Its form consists of 'signals' from the speech of the characters permeating through the narrative. Thus the objectivity of the narrative becomes

---

39. In the same year (1922), Akutagawa Ryūnosuke published 'Hōonki' (A story of reciprocated compassion), another short story with a similar construction. It develops three different accounts that overlap each other and create a whole.
40. Tzvetan Todorov, op. cit., 82. My translation.
41. Cf. '*Fortællerens typologi*' in *Tjekkisk strukturalisme*, Copenhagen 1971, 217. Cf. Norman Friedman's classification 8. *The Camera*.

falsified and when this falsification becomes the norm, then the narrative becomes subjective.

This characterisation is very abstract. We will cite Lubomír Dolezel's own example from his article. The piece is taken from Karel Čapek's novel *Krakatit*. The scene is consistently told from the subjective point of view of the protagonist Prokop:

Shortly after ten o'clock the princess came out. She was escorted by the crown prince and they were heading towards the Japanese pavilion. Prokop suddenly felt dizzy. It seemed as if he were falling down head first, he clung convulsively to the branches while his whole body trembled.

Nobody followed them, on the contrary, those remaining in the park, left quickly and gathered in front of the castle. This was presumably the decisive conversation or something of the like. Prokop bit his lips to prevent himself from screaming. He seemed to take an eternity, perhaps an hour or rather five hours. Then the crown prince ran back alone, red in the face and with his fists clenched ...[42]

We are naturally looking closer at 2b) because Iwano's theory can be classified within this group. Lubomír Dolezel describes the attributes of the subjective narrative more precisely in the following:

Generally speaking, the subjective narrative does not simply give a description of the 'told events', it also expresses the inner reactions of a character. This simultaneity of 'extraspection' and 'introspection' can be regarded as the main characteristic of the subjective narrative. It is also the main source of the great effectiveness of the modern psychological novel.[43]

The above is so well expressed that we can almost use it as a resumé of what Iwano meant when he said that his inner realism, a kind of subjective narrative, was 'objective'.

In continuation of this, Dolezel describes the extreme version of the subjective narrative in which the narrator is entirely hidden — we can *feel* his presence, but we cannot *see* him. Lubomír Dolezel cites Alain Robbe-Grillet's

42. Ibid., 219.
43. Ibid., 220.

method as an example of this sophisticated narrative technique. It is used consistently in Robbe-Grillet's novel *Jalousie*.

3. *Different types of first-person narrative*
   For the sake of clarity we will also briefly present this group.
3. a) *The authorial first-person narrative*
   This narrative type is common in prose writing from the Middle Ages. It is very rarely used in modern literature. The narrator of such works simply observes the exterior world, but he also adds his rhetorical comments and judgments. A good example of use of this type in Japanese literary history, is Yoshida Kenkō's *Tsurezuregusa* from the beginning of the 14th century.
3. b) *The observer's first-person narrative*
   This group is typified by having a passive narrator. In this regard it is a first-person variation of the objective narrative 1).[44] The narrator does not express judgments or comments. This narrator typically perceives himself as a witness.
3. c) *Personal first-person narrative*
   In works with this type of narration, the narrator participates actively. He functions as an active character in the work and participates fully in the plot. But he is also active at the level of narration. The story is told as his experience, often in an idiosyncratic style which expresses the essential experience, the attitudes and the 'story' of the narrator's personality. The Japanese school of confessional writing, *watakushi shōsetsu*, belongs to this group.

2.2.9. Jurij Lotman

The Russian semiotician Jurij M. Lotman devotes a section in his book *Struktura khudozhestvennogo teksta* (The structure of fictional texts, 1970) to a discussion of point of view. He expresses his basic concept of 'the literary system' in the following:

A literary system is composed of a hierarchy of relationships. The very notion of 'having meaning' presupposes a certain relationship, the presence of a defined sense of direction. But since the literary model at its most general recreates an image of the world as seen by a particular consciousness, that is, provides a model for the relationship between a personality and the world (frequently, a perceiving

---

44. Ibid., 221

personality and a perceived world), this sense of direction will be both subjective and objective.[45]

Jurij Lotman does not examine or classify the different points of view. Instead he concentrates on an analysis of (1) the 'unification of point of view' which he regards as 'a synonym for Romantic subjectivism',[46] and (2) 'multiple renarration of a single content from various points of view'.[47]

Jurij Lotman's analysis of (1) is of interest for our investigation. Just before the above cited passage, we can read the following in his book: 'In Romantic narrative the points of view of the micro- and macrotexts are combined in a single fixed center of narration — the author-figure'. In other words, a unified point of view *can* be an expression of Romanticism or at least a tendency towards the same. Such a tendency is certainly detectable in some parts of Iwano's autobiographical works which were written in accordance with the principles of monistic narration.

In relation to (2), Jurij Lotman goes through Pushkin's *Eugene Onegin*. This is actually a repetition of what Tzvetan Todorov attempted to clarify in his analysis of Choderlos de Laclos's *Les Liaisons Dangereuses*. For the same reason we will not discuss the analysis here.

Meanwhile, another interesting claim in Jurij Lotman's article is that, 'the concept of "point of view" is analogue to that of perspective in painting and film'.[48]

2.2.10. Boris Uspensky

In a footnote to his book, Lotman mentions Boris A. Uspensky, a fellow countryman who also worked and published on this subject in his book *Poétika kompozicii* (*A Poetics of Composition*, 1970).[49] Even though the book is concerned with points of view in art in general, he primarily analyses the use of point of view in literary works. He emphasises the difference between 'internal' and 'external' points of view with respect to the work. The purpose of his in-depth analysis is to describe and classify the structure of 'artistic

45. Cf. Jurij Lotman, 'Point of View in a Text', in New Literary History, vol. 6, Winter 1975, no. 2, 339-40.
46. Ibid., 343.
47. Ibid., 351
48. Ibid., 339.
49. The translation, *A Poetics of Composition*, is published by University of California Press, 1973.

texts' by an investigation of point of view. 'Artistic' (*khudozhestvennyi*) should here be understood 'in the same sense as the English word "artistic"', and text is defined as 'any semantically organised sequence of signs'. He writes:

> It is assumed that the structure of the artistic text may be described by investigating various points of view (different authorial positions from which the narration or description is conducted) and by investigating the relations between these points of view (their concurrence and nonconcurrence and the possible shifts from one point of view to another, which in turn are connected with the study of the *function* of the different points of view in the text).[50]

Uspensky does not use point of view as a simple tool with which to analyse an artistic text. For Uspensky, point of view is as essential an aspect of the text, as it was for Iwano. But Uspensky's analysis is more general, more comprehensive, more exhaustive and more systematic than Iwano's. He formulates his intention with the book in the following way: 'to consider the typology of compositional options in literature as they pertain to point of view'.[51] Even though his analyses of the different types of point of view are developed 'independently of any one particular author', he mainly draws his examples from Tolstoy's and Dostoyevsky's works, particularly from Tolstoy's *War and Peace*.[52]

   Uspensky's study of 'point of view on the phraseological plan' is not really of interest in relation to Iwano's theory of narration. Uspensky assumes:

> ... that an event to be described takes place before a number of witnesses, among whom may be the author, the characters (the immediate participants in the event), and some other, detached spectators. Each of the observers may offer his own description of the events; presumably these versions would be presented in the form of direct discourse (in the first person). We would then expect these monologues to be distinct in their particular speech characteristics; however, the facts described by the various people — who may be in different relations to each other and may describe each other — would coincide, intersect, and complement each other in specific ways.
>
>   Theoretically, the author, constructing his narrative, may use first one and then another of these various narrations. These narrations, originally assumed to be in direct discourse, may merge and be transposed into authorial speech. Within the

---

50. Ibid., 5.
51. Ibid.
52. Ibid., 6-7.

authorial speech the shifting from one point of view to another is expressed in different uses of forms of someone else's speech.[53]

As a simple example of the possible positions, Uspensky suggests:

... a narration has begun. A character has been described (apparently from the point of view of an observer); he is in a room, and the author wants to say that the character's wife Natasha, is now entering the room. The author may say: (a) *'Voshla Natasha, ego zhena'* (Entered Natasha, his wife), (b) *'Voshla Natasha'* (Entered Natasha), (c) *'Natasha voshla'* (Natasha entered).[54]

Actually there are no other possibilities. By using these examples we can rewrite Iwano's theory in the following manner: an author must avoid the 'flat' description of (a) and choose either (b) or (c); the author's (narrator's) point of view must be identical to/that of one of the characters. The character that represents the author's (narrator's) point of view can be the main character or a minor one. In other words, the story can be narrated either in the first or in the third person. But as already mentioned, the distinction between first and third-person narration is sometimes blurred in Japanese and in certain cases, the first and third person may even be interchangeable.

Uspensky distinguishes sharply between (b) and (c) because he operates with notions of what is 'given' and 'new' in the functional sentence perspective.[55] In (b) of the above, 'entered' is the 'given' and 'Natasha' is the 'new' information while the opposite goes for (c).

In Japanese (b) and (c) would read as follows:

(b) *Natasha 'ga' haittekita.*

(c) *Natasha 'wa' haittekita.*

Indeed, in Japanese these sentences serve as deductive examples of Uspensky's own models, but not necessarily as inductive examples. The function of the particles *'ga'* and *'wa'* in the Japanese sentences is not entirely unambiguous and as such these sentences are not precisely the equivalent of the original models. Moreover the sentence (c) in Japanese is impossible if it is expressed from Natasha's point of view. The *'-tekita'* form (*tekuru* in the

53. Ibid., 17-18.
54. Ibid., 18.
55. The English translators of Uspensky's text point out that 'what is "given"' and 'what is "new"' correspond to the theme and rhema of a sentence. Ibid.

present tense) can only be used by the person whom the subject (Natasha) of the plot (*haitte*) is approaching. The sentence (c) is impossible not only in Japanese, but also in Russian *if* Natasha is describing her own action. If this is the case then the sentence would read as follows in Japanese: '*Watashi wa haitteitta*' (I enter) and in Russian: '*Ia voshla*'. The subject of both sentences is 'I' and they are thus examples of first-person narration.

The Japanese sentence ending with the '*-teitta*'-form ('*-teiku*' in the present tense) is used to describe the grammatical subject's movement towards something or someone. In sentences with this construction, point of view is not determined by the subject's being in the first or third person (theme/rhema, *wa* or *ga*). Instead the auxiliary verbs '*-tekita*' and '*-teiku*' are the sole indicators of point of view.

Uspensky is not very interested in those incidents where only 'one character functions as the vehicle for the author's point of view in the whole work'.[56] In his endeavour to provide us with a complete description of the various types of point of view, Uspensky is naturally most interested in 'those narratives in which several points of view are present — that is, where a distinct shift in the authorial position can be treated'.[57]

Uspensky writes the following on the topic of narrated monologue:

... narrated monologue, where the speech of the character interlocks with the authorial speech ... narrated monologue is typically detached from the *specifica* of the expression. We may consider this case an instance of the internal point of view.

The less differentiation there is between the phraseology of the described (the character) and the describing (author or narrator), the closer are their phraseological points of view. The two opposite poles are: the faithful representation of the *specifica* of the character's speech (the case of maximum differentiation), and the narrated monologue (the case of minimal differentiation).[58]

Furthermore, Uspensky is right when he observes: 'The naturalistic representation of distinctive features of speech is often used by the author to convey to the reader a general sense of the style which is characteristic of the person described'.[59] But, as we have already discussed, it is not always possible to distinguish between direct and indirect speech in Japanese. Thus

56. Ibid., 19-20.
57. Ibid.
58. Ibid., 52.
59. Ibid.

in Japanese, the possibility arises for narrated monologue to represent the *specifica* of a character precisely. Consequently it becomes pointless to distinguish between maximum and minimal differentiation in Japanese.

In his analysis of the psychological aspects of a description, Uspensky discerns between perceptions and facts, subjective and objective. In principle, he advances two ways in which to describe a person's actions:

First, it may be described from the point of view of an outside observer ... who describes only the behaviour which is visible to an outlooker. Second, behaviour may be described from the point of view of the person himself or from the point of view of an omniscient observer who is permitted to penetrate the consciousness of that person. In this kind of description we find revealed the internal processes ... which are not normally accessible to an external observer ... The point of view is internal to the person who is being described ... Accordingly, it is possible to speak about external and internal points of view (in relation to the object of description).[60]

He then goes on to discuss the formal aspects of the two types of description. He characterises one as the '"transpersonal" ... form of a court recording' and the other as a type which frequently uses *verba sentiendi* (verbs of feelings) and 'special modal expressions' ('apparently, evidently, as if, it seemed' and so forth).[61]

On the basis of the techniques for external and internal descriptive techniques, Uspensky poses the following classification:[62]

I. *Consistently external* — Cf. epic works.
II. *Consistently internal* — Either *Icherzählung* (narrated in the first person) or a narrative presented from the point of view of a particular character (in this case narrated in the third person).

Uspensky regards this type of narration as 'one of the transformations of *Icherzählung* — the first person pronoun is replaced by a personal name or by a descriptive designation'.[63] It is precisely this narrative variant — consistently internal in the third person, which is a variation of *Icherzählung* — that Iwano was such an eager spokesperson for. Uspensky

---

60. Ibid., 83. In relation to Uspensky's internal and external points of view, cf. my discussion of the use of the '-tai' and '-tagaru' forms in V.2.3., page 163-64.
61. Ibid., 84-5.
62. Ibid., 87 ff.
63. Ibid., 88.

names *The Eternal Husband* by Dostoyevsky as a typical example of this kind of narration.

III. Change of the authorial position in sequence — Each scene is described from a particular point of view. Thus different scenes in a work are told from different points of view. Iwano's attempt to describe the same scene from different points of view may be taken as a fusion of II and III.

IV. *Changing authorial positions; the simultaneous use of different positions* — We encountered this sort of description in our discussion of *heimen-byōsha* (flat narration). Uspensky's system of classification is particularly interesting because he concludes that the last three types (I, II and III — those connected with internal points of view) 'may be obtained by combining more and more complex transformations of *Icherzählung*'.[64]

Furthermore, he writes about type II that 'the consistently internal description of one particular person (while all the others are given through his perception) may be a straightforward case of *Icherzählung*, or it may be easily transformed into *Icherzählung* narration by the substitution of a first-person pronoun, of a personal name, or of a descriptive designation'.[65]

Uspensky considers *Icherzählung* to be at the heart of the psychological description in a narrative. That a narrative of type II may be reduced to a first person narration although it is usually told in the third person, is not a new idea. However, it is of interest in relation to Iwano's theory of monistic narration and in relation to *watakushi shōsetsu*. Iwano attempted to base his works on his own experience (not necessarily with himself as the protagonist) and to describe his experience of them objectively, while by definition a *watakushi shōsetsu* writer is always the narrator *and* the protagonist of the work, which is written either in the first person or a simulated third person. The *watakushi shōsetsu* narrative is characterised by a necessary exclusion of the narrative types I, III and IV.

Uspensky writes about the significance of the external point of view:

The external point of view, as a compositional device, draws its significance from its affiliation with the phenomenon of *ostranenie*, or estrangement. The essence of this phenomenon resides primarily in the use of a new or estranged viewpoint on a familiar thing, when the artist 'does not refer to a thing by its name, but describes it as if it had been seen for the first time — and in the case of an event,

---

64. Ibid., 97.
65. Ibid.

as if it were happening for the first time'. In the context of our approach, the device of estrangement may be understood as the adoption of a point of view of an outside observer, a position basically external to the things described.[66]

On this issue Iwano's theory was not articulate enough. But of course he did not have the theoretical tools which the Russian formalists developed and used. But his experiments with other points of view which he hoped would throw new light on the experience of his own life, can be regarded as a sort of estrangement. This was Iwano's notion of 'conscious objectification', a narrative trait which is absent in the work of *watakushi shōsetsu* writers.

It is possible to tell a story exclusively in the first person without the use of points of view of other characters by employing *Icherzählung*. In other instances, the author can choose other characters to represent his point of view in situations where he uses an internal point of view. Uspensky describes the relationship between the author and the chosen character in the following way:

... the author may assume the point of view of one of his characters in all the possible aspects. In this case the author would consistently describe the internal state of the viewpoint character, while all of the other characters would be described from the outside, as they are perceived by the viewpoint character. Thus authorial position would fully concur with the position of the viewpoint character on the psychological plane. Also, the author would move through time and space together with this character, adopting his horizons — accordingly, the position of the author would concur with that of the character on the spatial-temporal plane. In describing what the character has seen and observed, the author would use the character's language — in the form of quasi-direct discourse, internal monologue, or in some other form; thus the author's position would also concur with the position of that particular character on the phraseological plane. Finally, the position of the author and that of the character can concur on the plane of ideology.[67]

These are not Iwano's words, but the similarity in Uspensky's and Iwano's formulation is striking.

Furthermore, in his 'concluding remarks' Uspensky draws attention to the idea that an author's 'description ... may be said to be subjective — that is,

66. Ibid., 131 According to Uspenksy, the quote is from V. Shklovskii '*Iskusstvo kak priem*' (Art as device), *Poetika. Sbornik po teorii poeticheskogo iazyka*, Petrograd 1919, 106.
67. Ibid., 101-2.

it makes reference to one or another subjective point of view held by the author, a point of view which is inevitably accidental'; that an author's 'knowledge is limited'; and that there are 'some things he does not know'.[68] Furthermore Uspensky is aware of 'the conscious limitation which the author imposes on his own knowledge, and by means of which he hopes to ensure a greater degree of verisimilitude'; and that an artist (including a writer) 'represents the object as it is and not as it appears to him.'[69]

An author always has to choose how he is going to tell his story: 'whether to reproduce his perceptions of the events sequentially, or to present them in some rearranged form'. This reorganisation is thought 'to produce a stronger effect, a principle which is used in the detective story', or 'to produce an *objective* account of the facts' [the emphasis is mine].[70] It is as if Uspensky were speaking on behalf of Iwano.

2.2.11. Gérard Genette

When we come from a reading of Uspensky's theory, Gérard Genette's long article *'Discours de récit, essai de méthode'* from *Figures III* (1972), deals with familiar material.[71] Genette does indeed refer to Uspensky's work in his bibliography. He names both the original Russian version from 1970 and the French *'Poétique de la composition'* which was printed in *Poétique* 9 (1972). But Genette's study of point of view includes a more comprehensive historical rendering of point of view theories, as well as a more thorough theoretical analysis.

For a comparison with Iwano's theory, however, 'Perspective', 'Focalizations', and 'Person' are the relevant sections to study.

The greatest merit of Genette's theory is the sharp differentiation between 'the question *who sees*?' and 'the question *who speaks*?' in a work of fiction. Likewise he distinguishes between 'the question *who is the character whose point of view orients the narrative perspective*?' and 'the very different question *who is the narrator*?'[72] Genette made this discovery by making a critical analysis of existing point of view theories. He starts his critique with Cleanth

---

68. Ibid., 168.
69. Ibid., 168-69.
70. Ibid., 172.
71. This article is indispensable for any study of narrative. It has been translated into English and published as a book with the title *Narrative Discourse*, Cornell University Press, 1980.
72. Ibid., 186.

Brook's and Robert Penn Warren's theory and the use of their term 'focus of narration' (1943). He then continues his analysis of the theories or systems of classification that we have already looked at: F.K. Stanzel's, N. Friedman's, Bertil Romberg's and finally Tzvetan Todorov's theories. Genette differs from his predecessors by his use of the abstract term 'focalization' which is actually the same as Brook's and Warren's 'focus of narration'. His intention is to avoid 'the too specifically visual connotations' of the expression 'point of view'. The term focalisation is used to stress the fact that the focus is on 'the question *who sees*?' and thus has nothing whatsoever to do with 'the question *who speaks*?'.[73] Genette uses the term 'focalisation' to re-classify the different types of narrative 'perspective' in the following manner:

1. zero focalisation
2. internal focalisation
   a) *fixed* — canonical example, *The Ambassadors*
   b) *variable* — as in *Madame Bovary*
   c) *multiple* — as in the film *Rashōmon*
3. external focalisation – Hemingway's short stories

There is little difficulty in recognising that the three types of internal focalisation 2. (a), (b) and (c) respectively correspond to Uspensky's classification of I, II and III. Likewise we recognise that Iwano's theory of monistic narration belongs to Genette's 2. a) fixed internal focalisation. The only difference is that in Iwano's work the one who speaks and the one who sees are not only inseparable, but actually fused.

With regard to internal focalisation, Genette makes the following interesting observations (which we are already familiar with at this stage): '... the very principle of this narrative mode implies in all its strictness that the focal character never be described or even referred to from the outside, and that his thoughts or perceptions never be analyzed objectively by the narrator'.[74] And furthermore, 'Internal focalisation is fully realised only in the narrative of "interior monologue".'[75] Genette draws on Roland Barthes' definition of 'the *personal* mode of narrative' when he goes on to cite 'the minimal criterion' for 'internal focalisation: '... this criterion is the possibility of rewriting the narrative section under consideration into the first person (if it is not in that person already) without the need for "any alteration of the

73. Ibid., 189.
74. Ibid., 192.
75. Ibid., 193.

discourse other than the change of grammatical pronouns".'[76] In continuation
of this, he puts forth two sentences as examples. The first — '[James Bond]
saw a man in his fifties, still young-looking ...' — is an example of internal
focalisation because it can be rewritten in the first person. The second — '...
the tinkling of the ice cubes against the glass *seemed* to awaken in Bond a
sudden inspiration' — belongs to the category of external focalisation because
it cannot be rewritten in the first person 'because of the narrator's marked
ignorance with respect to the hero's real thoughts'.[77]

After having mentioned what seems an altogether too simple 'purely
practical criterion', Genette once again emphasises the danger in confusing
'focalization' and 'narrating'. He continues: 'The narrator almost always
"knows" more than the hero, even if he himself is the hero, and therefore for
the narrator focalisation through the hero is a restriction of field just as
artificial in the first person as in the third.'[78] Genette is obviously right, but
his observation holds no news for those already familiar with Iwano's theory.

In the section entitled 'Person', Genette classifies stories according to two
narrative postures. The writer may either (1) choose a character in the story
to narrate or (2) choose a narrator who does not actually partake in the
story/plot. Genette calls the first type 'homodiegetic' narration and the other
'heterodiegetic' narration.[79] The first type can be divided into two more
categories. In the first of these the narrator is also the protagonist of his own
story and in the other, he has a secondary role in the story. Genette calls the
first variation 'autodiegetic' — a term he finds unavoidable.[80]

Genette's book takes its point of departure in an analysis of Marcel
Proust's *À la recherche du temps perdu* (1913-27). In his analysis, Genette
naturally takes particular interest in this text as an example of autodiegetic
narration and its version of the relationship between the protagonist and the
narrator Marcel and the author Marcel Proust. The novel is written as a
'direct autobiography' with Marcel as the protagonist, narrator and author.
Genette makes an interesting comment in this connection:

... as if Proust first had had to conquer a certain adhesion to himself, had to
detach himself from himself, in order to say 'I,' or more precisely the right to have

---

76. Ibid.
77. Such a relationship has already been described in connection with the discussion of
    'narrated monologue' and Iwano's theory in section V.2.3., page 160 ff.
78. Op. cit., 194
79. Ibid., 245.
80. Ibid.

this hero who is neither completely himself nor completely someone else say 'I.' So the conquest of the *I* here is not a return to and attendance on himself , not a settling into the comfort of 'subjectivity,' but perhaps exactly the opposite: the difficult experience of relating to oneself with (slight) distance and off-centering ...[81]

There are clear similarities between Proust's narrative technique and Iwano's theory of monistic narration, especially with regard to the *fusokufuri* (neither-identification-nor-differentiation) relation between the author and protagonist (mediator). Genette's reading of Proust's intention with regard to the objective and subjective aspects in the novel's narrative construction, is similar to what Iwano attempted in his novel-series. However, Proust was not satisfied with 'the too-remote "objectivity" of heterodiegetic narrative', because this sort of objectivity 'kept the narrator's discourse set apart from the "action" (and thus form the hero's experience)'. On the other hand, he was not satisfied with the subjectivity in autodiegetic narration because it seemed too personal and 'seemingly too confined to encompass without improbability a narrative content widely overflowing that experience'.[82]

Iwano would probably have agreed with Proust on the first point (cf. his fight against 'flat narration'), but not on the second point, because this had to do with the *protagonist's* fictional experience.[83]

In Proust's novel, the protagonist's experience is limited in accordance with the author's limitations — nothing happens which surpasses Proust's own experience. Meanwhile the protagonist's knowledge of the other characters in the novel is greater than the author's own knowledge of them. The autobiographical material has deliberately been dispersed throughout the novel.[84] Genette points out that this results in certain problems with the narrative because the novel is dependent on a paradoxical narrative situation — the first-person narrator is sometimes expected to be omniscient.

This is not in accordance with Iwano's theory of narration. Proust actually destroyed objectivity in narration by making the subjectivity of his narration illusory and thus untrustworthy.

Iwano's life conviction was narrow, but intensely true — and so was the core of his theory of narration.

81. Ibid., 249.
82. Ibid., 251.
83. Ibid.
84. Ibid.

Eleven years after the publication of *Discours du récit* in *Figure III*, Genette published *Nouveau discours du récit* (1983). In this book he clarifies the problems which the first book was criticised for. For example, Dorrit Cohn criticised Genette for having left out a discussion of interior monologue and free indirect style.[85] First Genette points out that free indirect style '... corresponds very clearly to the era of the psycho-realistic "modern" novel, from Jane Austen to Thomas Mann, and more precisely to the narrative mode I call "internal focalization", one of whose favorite instruments is definitely free indirect style.'[86] In response to Dorrit Cohn's criticism he then goes on to analyse three types of 'presentation of consciousness': *psycho-narration*, *quoted monologue*, and *narrated monologue*. In Genette's terminology, these become 'narratised speech', 'reported speech' and 'transposed speech', respectively.[87] He notes that 'thought' is treated as 'speech' in both Cohn's and his own terminology. He compares the two types of monologue — quoted and narrated — with Dolezel's *Erzählertext* and *Personentext*. He then finds himself tempted to classify the four types of narrative in a table.[88] After this manoeuvre, he finally begins to work his way through a (self-) critical analysis of his earlier theories.

In 'Perspective', he recognises the need to replace the old question '*who sees?*' with '*who perceives?*' (Cf. Iwano's formulation). He realises that '... my study of focalization ... was never anything, but a reformulation, whose main advantage was to draw together and systematise ... standard ideas'.[89] On the subject of 'Focalization', he points out that:

... by focalization I certainly mean a restriction of 'field' — actually, that is, a selection of narrative information with respect to what was traditionally called *omniscience* ... In internal focalization, the focus coincides with a character, who then becomes the fictive 'subject' of all the perceptions, including those that concern himself as object. The narrative in that case *can* tell us everything this character perceives and everything he thinks (it never does, either because it refuses to give irrelevant information or because it deliberately withholds some bit of relevant information [paralipsis]).[90]

85. Cf. the English translation, *Narrative discourse revisited*, translated by Jane E. Lewin, Cornell University Press, 1988, 51.
86. Ibid., 54.
87. Ibid., 58-9.
88. Ibid., 62.
89. Ibid., 64-5.
90. Ibid., 74.

It is interesting to note that, in an explanation of the rather unfortunate expression 'focalization through the narrator', Genette adds the following:

... which I assert is 'logically implied by the "first-person" narrative'. What we are obviously dealing with is the restricting of narrative information to the 'knowledge' of the narrator *as such* — that is, to the information the hero has at the moment in the story as *completed by his subsequent information*, the whole remaining at the disposal of the hero-become-narrator. Only the hero at that moment in the story deserves *stricto sensu* the term 'focalization'; for the hero-become narrator, we are dealing with extradiegetic information, which only the identity of person between hero and narrator justifies us, *by extension*, in calling 'focalization'.[91]

This last point may rightly be regarded as a brief description of the narrative situation in *watakushi shōsetsu*.[92]

In continuation of this, Genette analyses the question surrounding 'the narrator's relation (presence or absence) to the story he tells' in the chapter entitled 'Person'.[93] Genette emphasises that 'in my view every narrative is, explicitly or not, "in the first person" since at any moment its narrator may use that pronoun to designate himself'. Genette then goes on to define the function of the first and third-person perspective in a narrative: '"first person" indicates his presence as a character of whom mention is made, "third person" his absence as such a character'.[94] In other words, by choosing the 'I' as the subject, we establish that a character in the narrative is the narrator of the same narrative. By choosing he/she, we indicate that the narrator is not a character in the narrative.

Subsequently Genette comments on Philippe Lejeune's theory of 'third-person autobiography'. He names two narrative situations. The one implies that '[the reader perceives that] the author, speaking manifestly about himself, pretends to be speaking about someone else', and the other that 'the author, still speaking manifestly about himself, pretends that someone else is speaking about him'. In the first case, 'the author is indistinguishable from the narrator, and the character is fictively dissociated', while in the second case

---

91. Ibid., 77.
92. More about this in the conclusion, p. 216 below.
93. Ibid., 97.
94. Ibid.

'the author (the person whose name goes on the text) is indistinguishable from the character ..., and the narrator ... is fictively dissociated'.[95]

It requires little discussion to conclude that Iwano's theory of monistic narration belongs to the first type of 'third-person autobiography'. The (main) characters in Iwano's work are clearly separated from the narrator. They are described by a narrator (author) who is placed at a distance which ensures that the description becomes and is perceived as 'objective'. In this connection, it is important to note that in both narrative situations the narrator and character are entirely independent of each other. Where this is not the case, the work is either decidedly autobiographical or a fictional equivalent, for example *watakushi shōsetsu*.

Genette restates his earlier classification of 'Narrative Situations' in *Nouveau discours du récit*. The 'narrative situations' were based on two types of narrating relations (heterodiegetic and homodiegetic) and three types of focalization — authorial (zero focalization), actorial (internal focalization), and neutral (external focalization) — a total of six possible narrative types.[96] He incorporates a third classification based on the 'narrating relations' and the 'narrating level' (intradiegetic or extradiegetic), to distinguish whether the narrator plays a role in the plot or not. Thus he advances twelve narrative types altogether, but three of them remain empty because they are only possible in theory, at least at present.[97] It appears that Genette, who once started his analysis of narrative types by criticising his predecessors' complicated systems of classification, has reached the end of the road or perhaps the dead end of the labyrinth.

Iwano's theory of monistic narration is simply one of Genette's nine narrative types, namely a hetero-extradiegetic narrative with internal focalization. It is a narrative type in which the narrator tells the story of another person from the narrator's point of view, without the narrator having a role in the story. Thus the story is obviously narrated in the third person. As representative works in this category, Genette mentions Henry James' *Ambassadors* and James Joyce's *A Portrait of the Artist as a Young Man*.[98]

---

95. Ibid., 106-7. Genette refers to Lejeune's book *Je est un autre*, Paris 1980, Chapter 2.
96. Ibid., 120-21.
97. On the subject of these 'empty' possibilities, Genette writes the following: '...it would be an unnecessary affront to the future to exclude that form from the "real possibilities of narrative types". Cézanne, Debussy, Joyce are full of features that Ingres, Berlioz, and Flaubert would undoubtedly have declared "unacceptable" — and so on. No one knows where the "possibilites", real or theoretical, end, with respect to anything.' Ibid., 126-27.
98. Ibid., 121, 128.

Our exposition of the many different theories of point of view clearly reveals where Iwano's theory fits in. Even upon the publication of his article, Iwano knew that his theory was profound, but narrow (cf. the title of the section 'Part 4. Narrow, but Profound'). It *was* revolutionary in its originality, but it was *not* of universal validity as he thought. The theory was effective as long as it was used for his own literary production. But it had a limited legitimacy. Iwano's theory of narration was born as a child of naturalism, but it had an ephemeral life. Only the spirit of the man who wrote it survives. And Iwano's method of narration is no longer required as a theory. As a method it is now used widely both in and outside of Japan.

Iwano's theory was written for himself and in truth it never became anybody else's.

VII. Conclusion

> ... it is the conviction that counts and, with the conviction,
> the energy of creation that springs from it.
> Anthony Burgess

Iwano Hōmei's theory of monistic narration is not a universal theory of narration, but rather a method of narrative technique which is valid only for Iwano's own 'inner naturalism', in which the greatest importance is attached to the description of the protagonist's *inner* world. Iwano explains the relation between the theory and inner naturalism in the following way:

A novelist must cut off a piece of the life that he himself is familiar with, and on that foundation he shall then construct another (fictitious) life in its entirety. In a work of fiction, the nature that we may observe from the interior of life, is made up by the protagonist's *inner* world. Even if the inner world of that protagonist can only be fully comprehended by himself, there is nevertheless a chance that a writer may place himself in his situation, even in his mood, by the means of observations and experiences from the writer's own life.[1]

Iwano calls this the 'introduction of the author's subjective viewpoint in the protagonist', and the protagonist who expresses the subjective point of view of the author, is called a 'mediator'.

Iwano's theory of narration is thus based mainly upon the relationship between the author and this 'mediator'. The authorial point of view is always expressed by the mediator, and consequently only the things that the mediator is able to see, hear or feel, are described in the work, no matter whether the author may know more about him or about something else. Even when the author makes his mediator use the third person, he still makes him speak as if in the first person. This is the reason why narrated monologues are found so often in Iwano's short stories. The story 'Ietsuki nyōbō' (The

---

1. Cf. 'Ichigen-byōsha no jissai shōmei', June 1919. Cf. HZ vol. 10, 575-76.

woman with a house, November 1918),[2] which is almost entirely built upon the inner monologue of a jealous wife, is a typical example of this.

The introduction of the concept 'mediator' is thought to be a means to relativise and thereby objectify the authorial 'I'. This is, by the way, one of the principle demands of naturalism. But there has always been a risk that this objective narration would be replaced by a subjective confession. There is no problem if the content of the objective narration is autobiographical, but when the distance between the 'mediator' and the author disappears in an attempt to create an increased verisimilitude in the narrative, then the work is no longer 'naturalistic' but one of *watakushi shōsetsu*, in which the author, the narrator and the protagonist are identical, though disguised.

Contrary to Iwano's expectations, his theory came to be part of the foundation for the bloom of *watakushi shōsetsu* in the twenties' and thirties' Japan, as far as both narrative techniques and ideas are concerned.

The influence of Iwano's theory on the theoretical ideas behind *watakushi shōsetsu* requires further clarification. Iwano's 'naturalistic symbolism' or his 'new naturalism', which is the more advanced version of his 'mystic semi-animalism', has two poles; the one is its content, i.e. the philosophy of the heart-rending reality *'hitsū no tetsuri'* (the metaphysics of sufferance), and the other is its method, i.e. the suggestion or the use of symbolic description rather than concepts and explanations. In other words, Iwano's work is concerned with suggesting the naked, heart-rending reality of the surrounding world in a work of fiction. The choice of subject material is naturalistic, while the method is symbolic. The designation 'the naturalistic symbolism' comes from this combination.[3] Iwano's high-flown philosophy of the heart-rending reality is a tool with which he confronts the surrounding world in an objective way.

But the objective aspect of the philosophy was gradually misunderstood and distorted, and in the end the emphasis was moved to the 'heart-rending', personal situation of the *individual* in society. This happened parallel to the development of *watakushi shōsetsu*. And in the end, the authors themselves

2. Cf. *HZ* vol. 6, 382-426.

3. It almost goes without saying that Iwano's comprehension of symbolism was too simple and naive. He considered symbolism a method in which 'suggestion' is used instead of 'realistic description', 'metaphor' instead of 'comparison', and 'symbol' instead of 'epithet'. Cf. *'Shōsetsu-hyōgen no yon kaidan'* (The four ways of expression in fiction, June 1912), in *HZ* vol. 10, 519 ff.

began to stage their own miserable, self-destructive lives in order to provide material for their writings.

With monistic narration, Iwano makes the 'mediator' function as the mouthpiece for his own almost excentric subjective points of view. Nevertheless Iwano paradoxically succeeds in maintaining objectivity in his narration, and this thanks to the independent status of the mediator in a work of fiction; he is independent of the author and self-contained, even though he is basically identical to the author.[4] In *watakushi shōsetsu*, on the other hand, narration is ambigious; the narrator 'interferes' with the thoughts and senses of the protagonist either by explaining and clarifying them and/or by giving an 'objective' (probable) interpretation of them. In this way there is a spontaneous 'subjectivisation' of the narration, and consequently the authorial 'I' surfaces and is revealed as a manipulator of what has been narrated. At the same time he/she is revealed as the protagonist in disguise. Who is able to act and at the same time comment on the action in a narrative which is told by the first person 'I'? Only one person, the writer, may do this.

While in his writings Iwano attempted a thorough objectificatition of his 'I' and in this way created another fictitious 'I', the *watakushi shōsetsu* writers described their own 'I' in disguise; in this way their real faces were introduced as if they were unreal, fictitious, but artistic. Iwano created an independent character in his novels — a fusion of the author and the protagonist. But the narrator in his works tells the story of the protagonist seen only from his/her point of view; the story is thus always told in the third person. Contrary to this, in *watakushi shōsetsu* the narrator plays an ambigious double role: he/she relates the author's veiled confession in the form of the protagonist's story; the protagonist is described both from the inside and from the outside ('objectively'). This is either an 'I' narrative in disguise, or a third-person narrative, which is really an 'I' narration, and in which pronouns denoting the protagonist with a 'he' or 'she' may be substituted by 'I' without further ado. To this we may add the fact that the description of the protagonist is often incomplete, since it is generally based upon extra-literary information. In this way it becomes a prerequisite that the reader is already familiar with the protagonist (the author in reality).

As far as an author's autobiographical narrative is concerned, and to this group we may see Iwano's work as belonging, Iwano's monistic narration *may* be classified within the group of *watakushi shōsetsu*. Here his literature may

---

4. On the 'paradox' in the objectivity of Iwano's narration of his own subjective points of view, cf. Noguchi Takehiko, '*Shajitsuteki-shukan no gengo genri — Iwano Hōmei*' in *Nihongo no sekai 13, Shōsetsu no nihongo*, 197-210.

be placed in a special genre in which there is no description of the protagonist as he/she is seen from the outside. This is presumably the reason why still today Iwano is spoken of in connection with *watakushi shōsetsu*, and the reason why the definition of *watakushi shōsetsu* is still cloaked in much confusion. But Iwano was different.

Iwano had always thought that he was the first writer in the world who had conceived of monistic narration. As far as the relationship between the author and 'the mediator' is concerned, even Japanese literary history had known of works written in accordance with the same principle: Izumi Kyōka (1873-1939)'s *Kōya hijiri* (The monk on the mountain Kōya, 1900), Natsume Sōseki's *Botchan* (Young man, 1906), and *Sokkyō shijin* (1892-1901), Mori Ōgai's translation of Hans Christian Andersen's novel *The improvisator* (1835), to mention some. But these works were so-called *Ich-Romane* and different from Iwano's works, which were narrated in the third person and only from the point of view of the protagonist.

Contrary to the use in the *Ich-Roman*, in which the narrator's point of view is placed *inside* one of the characters, in Iwano's novels the narrator's point of view is found *outside* the protagonist, while what is described is the protagonist's personal observations and thoughts. The relationship between the narrator (the author) and the protagonist ('the mediator') is thus monistic, but it has a double structure. This is precisely where we find the originality of Iwano's theory — the originality which for a time made him overestimate his own talent and the validity of his theory.

It is true that he was the first in modern Japan to be aware of this original kind of narration, and to succeed in formulating it in theoretical terms. A similar narration had, however, already been employed in numerous novels several centuries earlier. For instance we find a similar narrative technique in *Genji monogatari*. In Japanese works of fiction, the narrative technique 'narrated monologue' has always been a widely used means to achieve access to the inner world of the characters; a linguistic characteristic of Japanese has made the so-called 'monistic' relation between the narrator and the protagonist possible. Iwano did indeed rediscover the 'monistic' relationship, but he did not notice the linguistic side of the issue. He was not at all aware of the significance that the Japanese language had upon his work and his theory. This strange circumstance and ignorance can only be explained by the fact that Iwano was one of the Japanese writers who typically found inspiration in the literature of the West. Iwano was thus closer to French naturalism and French symbolism than to classical Japanese literature.

If we disregard the fact that Iwano's theory has both a naturalistic and a symbolist background, then the attitude that the narrator holds to the work (or especially to the protagonist) in Iwano's work, is of the kind that Norman Friedman classifies as 'selective omniscience'. Friedman mentions James Joyce's *A Portrait of the Artist as a Young Man* as a representative example of this attitude. Iwano was familiar with the French symbolists as well as with Henrik Ibsen and August Strindberg, but he knew neither James Joyce nor Henry James, whose literary theory is in many ways amazingly similar to his own theory of monistic narration.

Iwano's method, however, and Henry James' as well, does not diverge from the general tendency which is particular for a work of fiction; in a modern fictitious work there is always one character at the centre and all other characters in the work play their roles as 'objects', seen from the point of view of that character.

But Iwano's theory is very narrow and very restrictive. In his theory Iwano stressed the importance of an inner realism, which differs significantly from Western realism and from the romanticist, subjective confessional writings. We may say that the originality of Iwano's theory as well as of his work lies in his ability to reduce the possibilities. He chose only the elements that he needed himself, and considered this the only right thing to do.

This was closely connected to Iwano's other *extra*-literary work, which was characterised throughout by his 'monistic' thinking: his philosophy of momentariness was centripetal, truth-seeking and directed towards the centre of nature, the 'I'. Iwano was a pantheist, but he accepted only the Japanese gods of the universe of *Kojiki*. This belief later crystallised in his fanatical, irrational 'Nipponism'. Iwano propagandised the introduction of 'liberal marriage' and took an active part in the debate that surrounded the women's emancipation movement, which flared up in Japan after the Russo-Japanese war. However this opinion merely expressed a male chauvinist wish for 'liberty' in the dissolution of marriage, even though Iwano claimed that it was to be based on a mutual understanding. In reality he was an adherent of the 'serial *monogamy*' that we know today. Iwano put his principles into practice and married thrice.

When Iwano generalised his theory and believed in its universality without realising the limitations of its validity, he stepped close to the abyss of arrogance. But at least he was convinced of one thing: His theory was *not* a copy of anybody else's. It was his own. It was the product of his attempt to find that 'Japanese' expression for naturalism, of which he had been dreaming since 1907. The aim was not an Europeanisation of the Japanese tradition, but a Japanisation of Western literature.[5]

Iwano's egoism, his male chauvinism and his monistic narration led to his nationalism — 'Nipponism'. But the foundation for his tendency to monism was already found in his rejection of Christianity and the associated Western culture; in his younger days he turned his back on the Church and swallowed Emerson, *Kojiki* and Wang Yang-ming (1472-1528).[6]

The return to 'the origins' in the form of monism, which was basically a modification of dualism (no matter whether this is Chinese or Western), is a specifically Japanese trait. In that respect Iwano's writings and especially his literary theory, were typically Japanese.

5. Cf. Iwano's article '*Shizenshugi zōgon*' (Various points on naturalism, September 1907), in *HZ* vol. 15, 248-51.

6. Cf. Ban Etsu, *Iwano Homei ron*, 40-3, as well as Iwano's essay '*Ō Yōmei to Emason*' (Wang Yang-ming and Emerson, not dated), in *HZ* vol. 18, 112-20. Wang Yang-ming is mentioned together with one of his Japanese followers Ōshio Chūsai (1793-1837) in Iwano's short story '*Gimeisha*' (The man with the false name, November 1911), in which Western civilisation is criticised and Nipponism praised.

Appendix:
Iwano Hōmei's Major Works

1894   (The Sino-Japanese War breaks out)
The tragedy *Katsura Gorō: Tama wa mayou getchū no yaiba* (Katsura Goro: The soul wanders and the dagger flashes in the moonlight), December 1901.
The first collection of poetry *Tsuyujimo* (Dew and frost), August.

1904   (The Russo-Japanese War breaks out)
The second collection of poetry *Yūjio* (The wash of waves at night), December.

1905   (The Russo-Japanese War ends)
The third collection of poetry *Hiren hika* (Unhappy love, unhappy poem), June.
Play in verse *Kaiho gishi* (The dike technician), November.

1906   *Shinpiteki hanjū-shugi* (The mystic semi-animalism), collection of essays, June.
Hōmei shishū (The collected poems of Hōmei), November.

1907   *Shintaishi no sakuhō* (The method of the new style of poetry), December.

1908   The fourth collection of poetry *Yami no haiban* (The cup of darkness), April.
Shin-shizenshugi (The new naturalism), collection of essays, October.

1909   *Tandeki* (Dissolute living), novel, published in *Shinshōsetsu*, February.

1910   (Japan annexes Korea)
'Hitsū no tetsuri' (The metaphysics of sufferance), article, published in *Bunshō sekai*, January.
Hōrō (Wandering), novel, July.

1911   *Dankyō* (The broken bridge), novel, published in *Mainichi denpō* in January-February and in *Tokyo nichinichi shinbun* in March.
        '*Gendai shōsetsu no byōshahō*' (Narrative techniques in the modern novel), article, published in *Bunshō sekai*, February.
        Hatten (Development), novel, published in *Osaka shinpō*, December 1911 - March 1912.

1912   (Emperor Meiji dies)
        The novel *Hatten* is published as a book, July. (Banned in August)

1913   *Bonchi* (The young master), collection of short stories, June.
        Gonin no onna (The five women), collection of short stories, September.
        '*Hyōshōha no bungaku-undō*' (Arthur Symons' *The Symbolist Movement in Literature*), translation.
        Kindai shisō to jisseikatsu (Modern thinking and real life), collection of essays, December.
        Sumiya no fune (The coal-dealer's boat), collection of short stories, December.

1914   (World War I breaks out)
        Dokuyaku o nomu onna (The woman who takes poison), novel, published in *Chūōkōron*, June.
        Dokuyaku o nomu onna, 1st volume of the novel, December.

1915   *Kakei hakushi no Koshintō taigi* (On Dr Kakei's 'The essence of old shintoism'), critical essays, January.
        Kindai seikatsu no kaibō (An analysis of modern life), critical essays, January.
        Akumashugi no shisō to bungei (Ideas and literature of 'diabolism'), literary criticism, February.
        Dokuyaku o nomu onna, 2nd volume of the novel, February.
        The fifth collection of poetry *Koi no sharekōbe* (The skeleton of love), March.
        Danjo to teisō-mondai (Man and woman and the question of fidelity), collection of essays, October.
        The novel *Tandeki* is published as a book, May.

1916   *Shin-nihonshugi* (The new Nipponism), journal, January. (The title was changed to *Nipponshugi* (Nipponism) in October.)

1917 (The October Revolution in Russia)
'*Naibuteki shajitsushugi kara*' (From the perspective of inner realism),
published in *Shinchō*, August.

1918 (World War I ends)
Tsukimono (The possessed one), novel, published in *Shinchō*, May.
'*Gendai shōrai no shōsetsuteki hassō o isshinsubeki boku no byōsharon*' (My
theory of narration which will renew the idea of the novel today and
in the future) article, published in *Shinchō*, October.

1919 '*Seifuku hiseifuku*' (The conqueror and the conquered), short story pub-
lished in *Chūōkōron*, February.
Nekohachi (Nekohachi), collection of short stories, May.
Hibonjin (The talented man), collection of short stories, May.
Seifuku hiseifuku, collection of short stories, June.
Hōrō, revised edition of the novel, July.
Dankyō, revised edition of the novel, September.

1920 '*O-sei*' (O-sei), short story published in *Kaizō*, February.
Ietsuki nyōbō (The woman with a house), collection of short stories,
February.
Moeru juban (The lingerie on fire), collection of short stories, February.
'*Jō ka mujō ka*' (Mercifully or mercilessly), short story, April. (This
edition also includes two plays.)
Iwano Hōmei died on May 9, 1920.
Tsukimono, revised edition of the novel, May.
Hitsū no tetsuri, collection of essays, June. (Published together with
Shin-shizenshugi and *Hanjū-shugi*.)
Kōshaku no kimagure (The whims of the duke), collection of short
stories, June.
Hatten, revised edition of the novel, July.
Onna no shūchaku (A woman's stubbornness), collection of short
stories, September.
Setsuna-tetsugaku no kensetsu (The construction of the philosophy of
momentariness), collection of essays, October.
Honoo no shita (The flame's tongue), collection of plays, November.

1921 *Hōmei zenshū* (The collected works of [Iwano] Hōmei), 18 volumes
altogether, January 1921-July 1922.

1995 *Iwano Hōmei zenshū*, a revised edition, 16 volumes altogether, in the
process of publication at Rinsen-shoten, Kyoto.

Bibliography

The following bibliography consists of 3 parts:
1. Works by Iwano Hōmei (in chronological order)
2. Works on Iwano Hōmei (in alphabetical order)
3. Secondary literature (in alphabetical order)

1. Works by Iwano Hōmei

1953   Gendai shōsetsu no byōshahō. In *GBT* 2.
1954   Iwano Hōmei Chikamatsu Shūkō shū. In *GNBZ* 13.
1954   Gendai shōrai no shōsetsuteki hassō o isshinsubeki boku no byōsharon. In *GBT* 13.
1964   Iwano Hōmei Chikamatsu Shūkō shu. In *NBZ* 13.
1966   Tokutomi Roka Kinoshita Naoe Iwano Hōmei shu. In *GBT* 5.
1969   Honoo no shita. In *MBZ* 86.
1969   Iwano Hōmei shū. In *NBZ* 13.
1970   Tayama Katai Iwano Hōmei Chikamatsu Shūkō shū. In *NB* 8.
1970   Iwano Hōmei Kamitsukasa Shōken Mayama Seika Chikamatsu Shūkō shū. In *GNBT* 21.
1971   Hōmei zenshū; 2nd edition (Photographic reprint of 1st edition of 1921-22), 18 vols.
1971   Ibyō shosan no geijutsu — Masamune Hakuchō ron. In *KBHT* 4.
1971   Nakazawa Rinsen ron. In *KBHT* 4.
1972   Nakajima-shi no 'Shizenshugi no rironteki konkyo'. In *KBHT* 3.
1972   Gendai shōsetsu no byōshahō. In *KBHT* 3.
1972   Gendai shōrai no shōsetsuteki hassō o isshinsubeki boku no byōsharon. In *KBHT* 5.
1973   Shizenshugiteki hyōshōshi ron. In *NKBT* 59.
1974   Iwano Hōmei Chikamatsu Shūkō Masamune Hakuchō. In *NKBT* 22.
1975   Shizenshugiteki hyōshōshi ron. In *Meiji shijin shū* 2.

Translation
1969   Zena, kterā si vzala jed (Dokuyaku o nomu onna). Prel. Miroslav Novāk. In *5 japonsk'ych novel*. 37-147. Praha: Odeon.

2. Works on Iwano Hōmei

Akiba Tarō 1969. Meiji kindai gikyoku no ayumi — 11. In *MBZ* 86.

Araki Tōru 1977a. Nihonshi no shigaku 1. *Bungaku* 45(11), 68-84.

Araki Tōru 1977b. Nihonshi no shigaku 2. *Bungaku* 45(12), 30-43.

Asai Kiyoshi 1978. Iwano Hōmei — buntairon no shomondai. *KKKK* 23(15), 48-49.

Ban Etsu 1972. Senwa — Iwano Hōmei. *KKK* 37(10), 142-43.

Ban Etsu 1977a. *Iwano Hōmei ron.* Tokyo.

Ban Etsu 1977b. Iwano Hōmei. *Kindai Bungaku* 3, 71-80.

Ban Etsu 1978. Ishikawa Takuboku to Iwano Hōmei. *Takuboku Kenkyū* 4, 107-16.

Ban Etsu 1980. Iwano Hōmei bungaku no ichi. *KKK* 45(11), 102-7.

Benl, Oscar 1953. Naturalism in Japanese Literature. *MN* 9, 1-33.

Bonneau, George 1940. *Histoire de la littérature japonaise contemporaine 1868-1938.* Paris. 136-38.

Chirō (pseudonym of Abe Jirō) 1910. Byōsha no daizai to byōsha no taido. In *KBHT* 3, 357-60.

Ebe Ōson 1979. Hōmei-shi no rinjū (1920). In *Iwano Hōmei shomoku.* 130-39.

Enomoto Takashi 1976. Hōmei yuigonshū nado. In *Nihon kindai bungakukan* 33, 9.

Funabashi Seiichi 1971. *Iwano Hōmei den.* Tokyo.

Haruhara Chiaki and Kajitani Tetsuo 1971. Iwano Hōmei. In *Gendai bungakusha no byōseki*, 233-41.

Hashimoto Kei 1965. Gobusaku no shūhen. *Jinbun gakuhō* 45, 37-57.

Hinatsu Kōnosuke 1968. *Meiji roman bungakushi.* Tokyo. 134-38, 157-62.

Hirano Ken 1964. Kaisetsu. In *NBZ* 13, 520-24.

Hiratsuka Raichō 1949a. Seitō jidai no hitotachi — Endō Kiyoko no maki 1. *Tō* 1949(6), 78-81.

Hiratsuka Raichō 1949b. Seitō jidai no hitotachi — Endō Kiyoko no maki 2. *Tō* 1949(7), 78-82.

Hiratsuka Raichō 1971. 'Ai no sōtō' ni arawaretaru ryōsei mondai. In *KBHT* 4, 222-31.

Hisamatsu Sen'ichi 1936. Shizenshugi bungaku no hatten. In *Nihon bungaku hyōron shi, kinsei-saikinsei hen.* 1467-76.

Hisamatsu Sen'ichi 1975. *Zō-shin Nihon bungakushi* 6 and 7. Tokyo. 136-42, 253-54, 335, 374, and 790-91.

Horie Nobuo 1974. Kindai sakka to shūkyō — Iwano Hōmei. *KKK* 39(8), 81.

Ibuse Masuji 1974a. Moshō no tsuiteiru shinne (1934). In *Ibuse Masuji Zenshū* 1, 273-88.

Ibuse Masuji 1974b. Hajimete atta bunshi (1935). In *Ibuse Masuji Zenshū* 9, 146-51.

Ibuse Masuji and Miura Tetsuo 1979. Taidan — Kaku no wa tanoshi. *Nami* 10, 6-11.

Ikuta Chōkō 1918. Iwano Hōmei-shi no byōsha ron. In *NKBT* 5, 97-100.

Inagaki Tatsuo 1957. Iwano Hōmei. In *Kindai bungaku no fūbō*, 145-55.

Ino Kenji 1958. Iwano Hōmei no 'Shin-shizenshugi'. In *Shizenshugi no bungaku 2, Iwanami kindai nihon bungakushi* 11, 76-96.

Ishikawa Jun 1976. Iwano Hōmei. In *Bungaku taigai*, 225-52.

Itō Noe 1916. Iwano Hōmei-shi. *Chūōkōron* 4, 85-86.

Itō Sei 1971-2 *Nihon bundanshi* 13, 14, and 15.

Iwanaga Yutaka 1956. Iwano Hōmei no rirekisho. In *Shizenshugi no seiritsu to tenkai*, 329-33.

Iwano Kiyoko 1913. Fujin no mitaru Iwano Hōmei-shi. *Shinshōsetsu* 6, 99-102.

Kamakura Yoshinobu 1976. 'Tandeki' no kōsō. *Nihon bungaku* 25(4), 35-46.

Kamakura Yoshinobu 1978a. Shohyō; Ban Etsu 'Iwano Hōmei ron'. *Nihon bungaku* 27(8), 105-10.

Kamakura Yoshinobu 1978b. Iwano Hōmei no shisō. *Nihon bungaku* 27(12), 14-23.

Kamakura Yoshinobu 1980. Iwano Hōmei — shōsetsu seiritsu e no ichi-kōsatsu. *Nihon bungaku* 29(8) 90-99.

Kamakura Yoshinobu 1994. *Iwano Hōmei Kenkyū*. Tokyo.

Kamei Shunsuke 1968. Iwano Hōmei no sanbunshi to Hoittoman. In *Taishō bungaku no hikakubungakuteki kenkyū*, 87-121.

Kamei Shunsuke 1973. Itan shijin Iwano Hōmei. In *Kōza hikaku bungaku* 2, 143-88.

Kamitsukasa Shoken et al. 1915. Iwano Hōmei-shi fusai no bekkyo ni taisuru bundan shoka no konponteki hihan. *Shinchō* 10, 41-56.

Kanbara Ariake 1973. 'Hyōshōha no bungaku-undō' ni tsuite. In *KBHT* 8, 81-91.

Kawakami Tetsutarō 1965a. Iwano Hōmei, 1934. In *MBZ* 71, 401-6.

Kawakami Tetsutarō 1965b. Iwano Hōmei. In *Nihon no autosaidā*. 86-103.

Kawamura Jirō 1973. Ginga to jigoku. *Gunzō* 7, 224-37.

Kawazoe Kunimoto 1972. Iwano Hōmei no ren'ai to hōrō. *KKK* 37(9), 31-32.

Keene, Donald 1977. Iwano Hōmei. In *Nihon bungaku o yomu*, 68-71.

Keene, Donald 1979. Iwano Hōmei. *Umi* 8, 343-48.

Keene, Donald 1984. Iwano Hōmei. In *Dawn to the West* vol. 1. New York. 288-95.

Kitagoe Tarō et al. 1915. Iwano Hōmei-shi no teisōkan ni taisuru wakaki hito no hanbaku. *Shinchō* 12, 102-8.

Kokusai bunka shinkōkai (ed.) 1939. *Introduction to Contemporary Japanese Literature*, Part I, 1902-35. Tokyo. 32-35.

Kōno Toshirō 1974. Iwano Hōmei-shū kaisetsu. In *NKBT* 22, 8-21.

Kōno Toshirō 1978. Iwano Hōmei no henshūbon — 'Yamamoto Roteki ikō'. *KKKK* 23(1), 164-65.

Kōno Toshirō and Yoshida Kimiko (eds.) 1979. *Iwano Hōmei shomoku*. Tokyo.

Masamune Hakuchō 1965a. Hōmei-shi no 'Hōrō'. In *Masamune Hakuchō Zenshū* 6, 40-41.

Masamune Hakuchō 1965b. Iwano Hōmei (1928). In *MBZ* 71, 388-401.

Masamune Hakuchō 1965c. Bungei jihyō 'Hōrō'. In *Masamune Hakuchō Zenshū* 8, 319-20.

Masamune Hakuchō 1965d. Hōmei o tsuiokusu (1947). In *Masamune Hakuchō Zenshū* 12, 251-58.

Masamune Hakuchō 1974. Shizenshugi seisui-shi shō (1948). In *NKBT* 22. 385-432.

Matsubara Shin'ichi 1974. Iwano Hōmei ron. In *Gusha no bungaku*. 117-39.

Mita Hideakira 1970. Iwano Hōmei shōron — sono yukeiteki jigyō to mukeiteki jigyō (bungaku) to no kankei. In *Nihon bungaku ronkō*, 380-410.

Miyajima Shinzaburo 1919. Iwano Hōmei-shi ichimen-kan. *Chūōkōron* 2, 35-44.

Nagashima Yōichi 1984. 'Ichigen-byōsharon' to 'Kankaku-ron'. *KKK* 49 (12), 89-98.

Nagashima Yōichi 1996. Iwano Hōmei, Akutagawa, and Strindberg. In *Florilegium Japonicum — Studies Presented to Olof G. Lidin on the Occasion of His 70th Birthday*. Copenhagen. 197-203.

Niimi Mitsuo 1975. Shinpiteki hanjū-shugi e no katei. *Nihon bungaku* 23(5), 48-57.

Noguchi Takehiko 1980. Shajitsuteki-shukan no gengo genri — Iwano Hōmei. In *Nihongo no sekai 13, Shōsetsu no nihongo*, 197-210.

Nojima Hidekatsu 1973. Kakyō to dankyō, Iwano Hōmei ron. In *Seijitsu no gyakusetsu*, 76-107.

Ogata Akiko 1971. Iwano Hōmei 'Tandeki'. *KKK* 9, 128-29.

Oka Yasuo 1973. Shohyō — Ōkubo Tsuneo cho 'Iwano Hōmei no jidai'. *KKK* 38(6), 214-15.

Okazaki Yoshie (comp. & ed.) 1955. *Japanese Literature in the Meiji Era*. Tokyo.

Ōkubo Tsuneo 1962. Shizenshugi zengo. In *Gendai nihon bungaku kōza, shōsetsu* 2, 261-73.

Ōkubo Tsuneo 1963. *Iwano Hōmei*. Tokyo.

Ōkubo Tsuneo 1973a. *Iwano Hōmei no jidai*. Tokyo.

Ōkubo Tsuneo 1973b Shizenshugi to sensō. *KKK* 38(11), 38-42.

Ōkubo Tsuneo 1974. Iwano Hōmei, sakka to sakuhin. In *NBZ* 13, 420-52.

Ōkubo Tsuneo 1975. Iwano Hōmei — Hōrō Dankyō no Yoshio. *KKKK* 20(15), 106-7.

Ōkubo Tsuneo 1976. Iwano Hōmei ni okeru shi to geki. In *Gendai bungaku kōza* 6, 140-68.

Ōkubo Tsuneo 1977. 'Moeru juban' no onna. In *Chikuma gendai bungaku taikei*, geppō 55, 4-5.

Ōkubo Tsuneo 1980. Iwano Hōmei 'Dokuyaku o nomu onn' no O-tori. *KKKK* 25(4), 64-65.

Ōnishi Akio 1960. Hōmei to James. *Eigo eibungaku ronshū* 2, 67-97.

Ōsugi Sakae 1965. Iwano Hōmei-shi o ronzu (1915). In *MBZ* 71, 387.

Ōtsuka Takayori (Kōyō) 1921. Kaisetsu. In *HZ* 1, 1-9.

Ōtsuka Takayori (Kōyō) 1948. Omoide. In *Iwano Hōmei senshū* 1, 311-18.

Ōtsuka Takayori (Kōyō) 1949. Kaisetsuteki ni. In *Iwano Hōmei senshū* 2, 315-21.

Sekii Mitsuo 1995. Seiai to seimei no ekurichuuru. In *Taishō seimei shugi to gendai*. 86-95.

Senuma Shigeki 1959. Taishō demokurashii to sono shisō. In *Iwanami kindai nihon bungaku-shi* 15, 3-10.

Senuma Shigeki 1979. *Nihon bundan-shi* 1, 20, 22, and 24. Tokyo.

Seragaki Hiroaki 1971. Iwano Hōmei no shoki no hyōron. *Nihon kindai bungaku* 14, 129-38.

Shōwa joshidaigaku kindai bungaku kenkyūshitsu (ed.) 1962. Iwano Hōmei. In *Kindai bungaku Kenkyū sōsho* 19, 217-362.

Sibley, William F. 1968. Naturalism in Japanese Literature. *HJAS* 28, 157-69.

Sōma Tsuneo 1980. Shinpiteki hanjū-shugi' shichū. *Bungaku* 48(1), 17-32.

Sugimoto Kuniko 1965. Sankō bunken. In *MBZ* 71, 438-43.

Sugiyama Yasuhiko 1976. Heimen-byōsha to ichigen-byōsha. In *Kotoba no geijutsu*, 234-41.

Suzuki Sadami 1995. Taishō seimei shugi, sono zentei, zenshi, zen'ya. In *Taishō seimei shugi to gendai*.

Tanaka Yasutaka 1961. Ichigen-byōsha ronsō. *KKK* 7, 39-41.

Tanaka Yasutaka 1970. Hōmei to Shūkō. In *GNBT* 21, Geppō 38, 1-3.

Tanizawa Eiichi 1962. Ichigen-byōsha ron. In *Taishō-ki no bungei hyōron*, 310-16.

Tanizawa Eiichi 1971. Iwano Hōmei no bungaku shikō. In *Meiji-ki no bungei hyōron*, 139-63.

Tayama Katai 1972. Byōsharon (1911). In *KBHT* 3, 369-84.

Terada Tōru 1965. Iwano Hōmei (1948). In *MBZ* 71, 407-19.

Tsuchida Kyōson 1972. Iwayuru ichigenteki byōsha o ronzu (1918). In *NKBT* 5, 101-6.

Uchimura Gosuke 1973. Parodii toshite no Hōmei. *Bungei* 12(10), 264-73.

Yamada Seizaburō 1976. *Kindai nihon nōmin bungaku-shi* 1.

Yamamoto Kenkichi 1954. Kaisetsu. In *Iwano Hōmei Chikamatsu Shūkō shū*, 402-5.

Yanagida Tomotsune 1969. *Iwano Hōmei ronkō*. Tokyo.

Yanagida Tomotsune 1973. Iwano Hōmei 'Asama no rei'(warai). *KKK* (477), 114-15.

Yano Mineto 1975. Kaisetsu. In *MBZ* 61, 411-27.

Yokota Shun'ichi 1935. Jidentai shōsetsuka toshite no Iwano Hōmei. *Kokugo kokubun*, 82-92.

Yoshida Seiichi 1949. Heimen-byōsha ron to ichigen-byōsha ron. *KKK* 3, 7-13.

Yoshida Seiichi 1958. Romanshugi no seiritsu to tenkai. In *Iwanami kindai nihon bungaku-shi* 11, 17-26.

Yoshida Seiichi 1965. Kaidai. In *MBZ* 71, 420-428.

Yoshida Seiichi 1955-5. *Shizenshugi no Kenkyū* 1 and 2. Tokyo.

Yoshida Seiichi 1977. Nipponshugi to Hōmei. In *Chikuma gendai bungaku taikei*, geppō 55, 3-4.

Yoshie Kogan et al. 1972. Hōmei-shi no Hōrō [shō] (1910). In *KBHT* 3. 438-41.

Wada Kingo 1960. Ichigen-byōsha ron no seiritsu. *Kokugo kokubun kenkyū* 1960(6), 40-65.

Wada Kingo 1975. *Byōsha no jidai*. Sapporo.

3. Secondary Literature

Akutagawa Ryūnosuke 1971a. Taishō hachi-nendo no bungeikai. In *Akutagawa Ryūnosuke zenshū* 5. Chikuma shobō, 231-43.

Akutagawa Ryūnosake 1971. Iwano Hōmei-shi. In *Akutagawa Ryūnosuke Zenshū* 6. Chikuma shobo, 161.

Alain 1931. *Système des beaux-arts*. Edition nouvelle avec notes. Paris.

Auerbach, Erich 1953. *Mimesis. Dargestellte Wirklichkeit in der abendländischen Literatur*. (1946) [English translation by Willard R. Trask. Princeton UP.]

Backtin, Michail Michailovic 1979. Avtor i geroj v écteticheskoj dejatel'nosti. In *Éstetika slovesnogo tvorchestvo*. Moskow. 7-180.

Banfield, Ann 1973. Narrative Style and the Grammar of Direct and Indirect Speech. *Foundations of Language* 10, 1-39.

Barthes, Roland 1975. An Introduction to the Structural Analysis of Narrative. *New Literary History* 6(2), 239-72.

Björck, Staffan 1970. *Romanens formvärld*. Stockholm.

Booth, Wayne C. 1961. *The Rhetoric of Fiction*. Chicago.

Burgess, Anthony 1971. *The Novel Now*. London.

Cogny, Pierre 1968. *Le Naturalisme*. Paris.

Cohn, Dorrit 1966. Narrated Monologue: Definition of a Fictional Style. *Comparative Literature* 18(2), 97-112.

Cohn, Dorrtit 1978. *Transparent Minds, Narrative Modes for Presenting Consciousness in Fiction*. Princeton.

Dolezel, Lubomír 1967. The Typology of the Narrator: Point of View in Fiction. *In* To honor Roman Jacobson I. The Hague. 541-52.

Dolozel, Lubomír 1971. Fortællerens typologi. In *Tjekkisk strukturalisme*. Copenhagen. 208-22.

Ebisaka Takeshi 1980. Bunka to keiken. *Misuzu* 240, 13-28.

Emerson, R.W. 1863-65. *R.W. Emerson's Writings*. Vol. 1-7. Boston.

Etō Jun 1973. *Kobayashi Hideo*. Tokyo.

Fowler, Edward 1988. *The Rhetoric of Confession, Shishōsetsu in Early Twentieth-Century Japanese Fiction*. Berkeley.

Friedemann, Käte 1910. *Die Rolle des Erzählers in der Epik*. Leipzig.

Friedman, Norman 1955. Point of view in fiction: The developement of a critical concept. *PMLA* 70(5), 1160-84.

Furst, Lilian and Skrine, Peter N. 1971. *Naturalism*. London.

Genette, Gérard 1972. Discours de récit. In *Figures* III. Paris.

Genette, Gérard 1980. *Narrative discourse*. [Tr. by Jane E. Lewin]. Ithaca, N.Y.

Genette, Gérard 1983. *Nouveau discours du récit*.

Genette, Gérard 1988. *Narrative Discourse Revisited*. [Tr. by Jane E. Lewin]. Ithaca, N.Y.

Hibbett, Howard S. 1955. The portrait of the artist in Japanese fiction. *The Far Eastern Quarterly* 14, 347-54.

Hijiya-Kirschnereit, Irmela 1981. *Selbstentblössungsrituale, Zur Theorie und Geshichte der autobiographischen 'Shishōsetsu' in der modernen japanischen Literatur*. Wiesbaden.

Hijiya-Kirschnereit, Irmela 1992. *Shishōsetsu, jikobakuro no gishiki*. Tokyo.

Hijiya-Kirschereit, Irmela 1996. *Rituals of Self-Revelation, Shishōsetsu as Literary Genre and Socio-Cultural Phenomenon*. Harvard East Asian Monographs 164. Cambridge, Mass.

Hirano Ken 1960. *Shimazaki Tōson*. Tokyo.

Hirano Ken 1964. *Geijutsu to jisseikatsu*. Tokyo.

Ikushima Ryōichi 1980. Ōgai nichinichi. *Tosho* 1980(7), 22-29.

Ino Kenji 1976. Nihon shizenshugi to sono tairitsushatachi. In *Iwanami kōza bungaku* 7, 99-123.

Inoue, Ken 1996. Translated Literature in Japan. In *The Japan Foundation Newsletter* 24(1), 1-7.

The International House of Japan Library (comp.) 1979. *Modern Japanese Literature in Translation, a bibliography*. Tokyo.

Ishikawa Takuboku 1966. Jidai heisoku no genjō. In *Nihon tetsugaku shisō zenshū* 13, 259-72.

Jespersen, Otto 1924. *The Philosophy of Grammar*. London.

Kai Mutsuo 1977. Genji monogatari no bunshō hyōgen no shikumi. *Heian bungaku kenkyū* 58, 89-101.

Kamei Hideo 1978. Kindai bungaku ni okeru katari no mondai. *Nihon bungaku* 27(305), 1-8.

Katagami Tengen 1910. Shizenshugi no shukanteki yōso. In *NKBT* 57, 347-58.

Katō Shūichi 1990. *A History of Japanese Literature 3, The Modern Years (1979)*. Tokyo.

Keene, Donald 1976. *World Within Walls, Japanese Literature of the Pre-modern Era, 1600-1867*. London.

Keene, Donald 1984. *Dawn to the West*. 2 vols. New York.

Kimura Ki (comp. & ed.) 1957. *Japanese Literature; Manners and Customs in the Meiji-Taisho Era*. Tokyo [Translated and adapted by Philip Yampolsky].

Kuroda, S.Y. 1973. Where epistemology, style and grammar meet, a case study from Japanese. In *A Festschrift for Morris Halle*. New York. 377-91.

Lotman, J.M. 1971. Tochka zrenija teksta. In *Struktura Khudozestvennogo teksta*. Providence. 320-35.

Lotman, J.M. 1975. Point of View in a Text. *New Literary History* 6(2), 339-52.

Lubbock, Percy 1921. *The Craft of Fiction*. London.

Mishima Yukio 1975. Shōsetsuka no kyūka. In *Mishima Yukio zenshū* 27.

Mitani Kuniaki 1978. Genji Monogatari ni okeru katari no kōzō. *Nihon bungaku* 27(305), 37-52.

Miyoshi Masao 1974. *Accomplices of Silence: The Modern Japanese Novel*. Berkeley.

Miyoshi Masao 1991. *Off Center*. Cambridge, Mass.

Morita Shiken(koji) 1887. Shōsetsu no jijotai kijutsutai. *Kokumin no tomo*, 38-40.

Novák, Miroslav 1962. Watakushi shōsetsu: The Appeal of Authenticity. *Acta Universitatis Carolinae, Philologica* 2 (Orientalia Pragensia II): 27-43.

Ōkura Hiroshi 1977. Nikki bungaku ni okeru 'idōshiki shiten' no igi. *Heian bungaku kenkyū* 58, 128-35.

Ortega y Gasset, José 1956. Point of view in the Arts. In *The dehumanization of art*. 97-120.

Romberg, Bertil 1962. *Studies in the Narrative Technique of the First-Person Novel*. Lund.

Ryan, Marleigh 1976. Modern Japanese Fiction: Accommodated Truth. *JJS* 2(2), 249-66.

Scholes, Robert and Kellogg, Robert 1968. *The Nature of Narrative*. Oxford

Shimamura Hōgetsu 1972. Jo ni kaete jinseijō no shizenshugi o ronzu (1909). In *KBHT* 3. 253-58.

Shimamura Hōgetsu 1906. 'Hakai' — hyō. In *NKBT* 57, 258-60.

Shimamura Hōgetsu 1907. 'Futon' — hyō. In *NKBT* 57, 261-64.

Shimamura Hōgetsu 1908. Shizenshugi no kachi. In *NKBT* 57, 291-313.

Shimizu Takazumi 1971. Shōsetsu riron no hatten to ryūha no tenkai. In *Nihon kindai shōsetsu. Hikaku bungaku kōza* III, 1-31.

Stanzel, Franz K. 1964. *Typische Formen des Romans*. Göttingen.

Stinchecum, Amanda Mayer 1980. Who tells the Tale? 'Ukifune': A Study in Narrative Voice. *MN* 35(4), 379-403.

Surmelian, Leon 1968. *Technique of Fiction Writing*. New York.

Suzuki Kazuo 1978. Genji Monogatari no hōhō, buntai; shinnaigo no mondai. In *Genji Monogatari II (Kōza nihon bungaku)*. KKK bessatsu 1978(5), 163-84.

Suzuki Sadami 1994. *Nihon no 'bungaku' o kangaeru*. Tokyo.

Suzuki Sadami 1996. *'Seimei' de yomu nihon kindai*. Tokyo.

Suzuki Tomi 1996. *Narrating the Self, Fictions of Japanese Modernity*. Stanford.

Swan, Michael 1963. Introduction. In *Henry James: Selected Short Stories*. Harmondsworth. 7-11.

Symons, Arthur 1899. *The Symbolist Movement in Literature*. London.

Tayama Katai 1966. Rokotsunaru byōsha (1904). In *GBT* 10, 435-38.

Tayama Katai 1972. 'Sei' ni okeru kokoromi (1908). In *KBHT* 3, 448-51.

Tayama Katai 1917. Tokyo no sanjūnen. In *NKBT* 60, 97-125.

Thibaudet, Albert 1923. *Le Bergsonisme*, deuxiéme édition. Paris.

Todorov, Tzvetan 1967. *Littérature et signification*. Paris.

Tokieda Motoki 1977. Gengo bunshō no byōsha kinō to shikō no hyōgen. In *Nihon bungaku kenkyū no hōhō, koten-hen*, 84-92.

Tokuda Shūsei 1967. Hōmei-shi no hito oyobi geijutsu. In *Genten ni yoru nihon bungaku-shi, kindai*, 109-11.

Uspensky, Boris 1973. *Poetics of Composition. The structure of the artistic text and typology of a compositional form*. [Tr. by Valentina Zavarin and Susan Wittig]. Berkeley.

Usui Yoshimi 1975. *Kindai bungaku ronsō*. Tokyo.

Wada Kingo 1966. Watakushi shōsetsu ni okeru watakushi no ichi. *Bungaku* 1977(9), 67-77.

Wellek, René and Warren, Austin 1949. *Theory of Literature*. New York.

Wilson, Colin 1956. *The Outsider*. London.

Zabel, Morten Dauwen 1968. Introduction. In *The Portable Henry James*. New York. 1-29.

Index to the Writings of Iwano Hōmei

Aa yo no kanraku 31
Akumashugi no Shisō to bungei 46
Arishima Takeo-shi no ai to geijutsu ron 111, 120
Baka to onna 119
Bijin 137
Boku no sōsakuteki taido o akirakanisuru 84
Boku no izumu-kan o nobete shoka no izumu-kan o hyōsu 104
Boku no jūdai no me ni eijita shojinbutsu 23
Boku no yōgorei 80
Boku no jūdai no me ni eijita shojinbutsu 22
Bonchi 44
Bunkai Shigi 2 71
Bunkai Shigi 4 71
Buraku no musume 137
Busshitsuteki byōsharon o nanzu 88-89
Byōsha sairon 92
Byōsharon hoi 124
Dai-shijin to bundan 25
Danjo to teisō-mondai 45, 53, 98
Dankyō 36, 39-40, 92, 122, 168
Danpengo 88
Dokutan to futari no onna 123
Dokutan kengisha to futari no onna 123
Dokuyaku o nomu onna 12, 28, 38-40, 53, 99, 102, 129, 166
Doryoku 38
Empukuka toshite no Ōsugi Sakae-shi 51
Enma no medama 44
Fujioka hakushi no shintaishiron 72
Fumikiriban 87

Futabatei to Doppo 37
Geisha Kotake 34, 79, 137
Geisha ni natta onna 119
Gendai shōrai no shōsetsuteki hassō o isshinsubeki boku no byōsharon 42, 74-75, 90, 104
Gendai shōsetsu kontei no gokai; futatabi Nakamura Seiko-shi ni 96
Gendai shōsetsu no byōshahō 41, 52, 74, 85, 88, 94, 117
Genei to jijitsu 99, 117
Gimeisha 174
Gisei 47
Gokai-sareta hanjūshugi 59
Gonin no onna 119
Hata no saikun 22
Hatten 32-33, 38-40, 44, 58, 91-93, 97, 100, 102, 167-168, 172
Hinode mae 34, 79
Hiren Hika 31, 34
Hiren no uta 31
Hirotsu, Harada no ryōshi ni kotau 133
Hito no shugi 104
Hitsū no tetsuri 43, 59, 167
Hōmei gobusaku 16
Hōmei shishū 34
Hōmei Zenshū 16
Honoo no shita 34
Hōrō 18, 36, 38-41, 82-85, 90, 94, 97, 122, 129, 168, 172
Ibusen-ron shiken 71
Ibyō shosan no geijutsu 111
Ichigen-byōsha no jissai shōmei 41, 129, 216
Ietsuki nyōbō 47, 137, 216
Jijitsu to gen'ei 53, 99

Jikkō-bungei to dekadanron 82
Jisshi no hōchiku 48, 49, 125, 138, 140-61, 164-66, 176, 197
Jō ka mujō ka 138
Junrei-go no O-sei 48, 138, 140-41
Kagurazaka-shita 34
Kaiho-gishi 34
Kakei hakushi no Ko-shintō taigi 46
Kanojo no junrei 48, 138, 140
Karafuto tsūshin 36
Kare no kyū-nikki yori 137
Katai-ron no ittan 111
Katsura Gorō 27
Kekkon 34
Kindai Shisō to jisseikatsu 46, 117
Kindai seikatsu no kaibō 46, 117
Kioku jussō 19, 21
Kodama-shū 27
Kohan no ichinen 29
Koi-inja 34
Kōmoto-shi 38-39
Konashi no Tsutsumi 48-49, 125, 138, 141, 146-61, 164-66, 176, 197
Kūkijū 47, 124-26, 128, 137
Kyōdo geijutsu to byōsha mondai 105
Kyōshi no ie 21
Ma no yume 89
Mitsubachi no ie 47, 137
Motto bungei o rikaiseyo 53
Naibuteki shajitsushugi no rikkyakuchi 102
Naibuteki shajitsushugi kara 103, 112
Naimenteki, gaimenteki 103
Nakamura Seiko-shi e 124
Narutohime 30
Nekohachi 47
Neyuki 39
Nikurei gatchi = jiga dokuzon 71
Nippon onritsu no kenkyū 98
Nipponshugi (Journal) 46
O-masu no shinjin 137
O-sei no heizei 48, 138-39

O-sei no junrei 48, 138
O-sei no shippai 48, 133, 138-39
O-sei 48, 132-33
O-shima to teishu 119
O-take bāsan 47, 137
O-tori no kurushimi 39, 168
O-yasu no teishu 129
Ō Yōmei to Emason 221
Onna no shūchaku 48
Ono no Fukumatsu 34
Osei no shippai 16
Rikon made 47, 138
Rōba 34, 79
Sando tsuma o kaeta hanashi 43
Sangai dokuhaku 31, 78
Seifuku hiseifuku 47, 137
Segai no dokuhaku 31
'Sei' no hyō 80
Senwa 34, 79
Setsuna-tetsugaku no kensetsu 89, 98
Setsunashugi to seiyoku 71
Shiku kakuchō kanken 29, 30
Shin-nihonshugi (Journal) 46, 98
Shin-shizenshugi 32, 58-59, 71, 79, 135
Shin yori Tamae e 22
Shinpiteki hanjū-shugi 30-33, 35, 57-73, 79, 112, 135
Shinri no jinbutsu 25
Shintaishi no sakuhō 29
Shirayuri (Journal) 31
Shizenshugi zōgon 71
Sho-hyōka no shizenshugi o hyōsu 71, 80
Shoku no yuragi 31
Shōsetsu-hyōgen no yon kaidan 94-95, 217
Shōsetsuka toshite no Shimazaki Tōson-shi 91, 111
Shūhen Neyuki 39
Shūkyō yori bungei ni 21, 30
Sōsaku to shugi no kankei 101, 114
Soshō yori rikon made 138

Sumiya no fune 44
Tandeki 11, 14, 33-35, 38, 40-41, 57,
    79-82, 85, 136, 175
Tayama-shi no 'Ippeisotsu' ni okeru
    byōsha-jō no ketten 118
Tentō 119
Tetsuko 47
Tetsurijō no yobiteki chishiki 130
Tokiwa no izumi 31
Tsuchida-shi ni kotau 126, 128
Tsukimono 36, 39, 40, 168

Tsumetai tsuki 102
Tsuneko 87, 119
Tsuyujimo 27, 29
Ware wa ikanishite shijin to narishika
    24
Yama no Sōbei 47
Yami no haiban 35
Yami no yokogi 31
Yūjio 31, 34
Zokuhen Neyuki 39

Index of Persons

Abe, Jirō 83, 110, 113

Akutagawa, Ryūnosuke 51-52, 104, 129, 197, 198

Andersen, Hans Christian 219

Andrejev, Leonid N. 82

Araki, Ikuko 48

Arishima, Takeo 111, 120

Artsybaschev, Michail Petrovisch 123

Austen, Jane 212

Avatamsaka Sutra 130

Awaji, Narutozaemon (pseudonym for Iwano Hōmei) 27

Baba, Tatsui 23

Bakhtin, Mikhail 194-96

Ban, Etsu 37, 59, 169-70, 221

Banfield, Ann 163

Barthes, Roland 187, 209

Baudelaire, C. 46, 53, 75, 123, 180

Beckett, Samuel 69

Benl, Oscar 11

Berlioz, Hector 214

Bonneau, George 11

Booth, Wayne C. 174, 189-90

Brentano, Franz 130

Brook, Cleanth 208

Brøgger, Suzanne 64

Burgess, Anthony 216

Cervantes Saavedra, Miguel de 171

Cézanne, Paul 180, 214

Čapek, Karel 199

Chardin, Pierre Teilhard de 11

Chekhov, Anton 180

Chikamatsu, Shūkō (pseudonym for Tokuda Shūkō) 91

Chikamatsu, Monzaemon 110

Chirō (pseudonym for Abe Jirō) 83-84

Cohn, Dorrit 76, 162, 182, 212

Coleridge, Samuel Taylor 110

Conrad, Joseph 188

Davidson, J.C. 27

Dazai, Osamu 172

Debussy, Claude 214

Dickens, Charles 188

Dolezel, Lubomír 198-200, 212

Dostoyevski, F.M. 174, 180, 195, 202, 206

D'Annunzio, Gabriele 180

Ebe, Ōson 48-49

Eguchi, Kiyoshi 133-35

Ema, Nakashi 104

Emerson, Ralph W. 24-25, 31-32, 57, 59-62, 64, 124, 221

Endō (Iwano), Kiyoko 43-47, 98-99, 137-38

Faulkner, William 197

Fielding, Henry 188, 193

Fitzgerald, J. Scott 188

Flaubert, Gustave 180, 214

Fowler, Edward 15-17, 171

Friedman, Norman 187-89, 191-94, 198, 209, 220

Friedmann, Käte 78

Fukuchi, Ōchi 26

Fukuzawa, Yukichi 23

Funabashi, Seiichi 25, 178

Futabatei, Shimei 18, 36-37, 5

Genette, Gérard 17, 208-14

Goethe, J. W. von 24, 119

Gorkij, Maxim 119, 122, 180

Gresham, Sir Thomas 24
Hagesawa, Tenkei 71-73, 81
Hara, Takashi 44
Harada, Minoru 133-34
Hardy, Thomas 188
Hachisuka family 19-20
Hemingway, Ernest 189, 193, 209
Hijiya-Kirschnereit, Irmela 13-17, 171
Hirano, Ken 81
Hiratsuka, Raichō 43
Hirotsu, Kazuo 100-101, 104, 113-14,
     132-34
Holz, Arno 71
Hōmeishi (pseudonym for Iwano
     Hōmei) 27
Husserl, Edmund 130
Ibsen, Henrik 71, 82, 119, 220
Ibuse, Masuji 179-80
Ikuta, Chōkō 117, 125-26
Inada family 19-20
Ingres, J.-A.-D. 214
Inoue, Tetsujirō 60
Isherwood, Christopher 189
Ishikawa, Jun 31, 57, 173
Ishikawa, Takuboku 37
Ishimaru, Gohei 47
Iwamoto, Yoshiharu 26-27
Iwanaga, Yutaka 21
Iwano, Iwao 35
Izumi, Kyōka 219
James, Henry 17, 50, 136, 179-87, 189,
     198, 214
Jespersen, Otto 163
Jesus 62
Joyce, James 76, 174, 188, 214, 220
Kafka, Franz 196
Kajii, Motojirō 172
Kamei, Hideo 17
Kamei, Shunsuke 79
Kamitsukasa, Shōken 45, 47, 122
Kanbara (Iwano), Fusae 45-46, 48, 98,
     142, 146

Kanbara, Ariake 34
Kaneko, Chikusui 27
Kaneko, Yōbun 102
Kasai, Zenzō 172
Katagami, Tengen 83
Katō, Hiroyuki 60
Kawakami, Tetsutarō 44
Keene, Donald 13
Kellogg, Robert 77, 192-94
Kierkegaard, Søren 195
Kikuchi, Kan 123, 129
Kitagoe, Tarō 45
Kitamura, Tōkoku 26
Kobayashi, Hideo 44
Kobayashi, Saisaku 35
Kūkai 140
Kumagai, Matsu 27-28
Kunitane, *see* Inada family
Kuroda, S.Y. 165
Laclos, Choderlos de 197-98, 201
Lagercrantz, Olof 18
Lejeune, Philippe 213
Lipps, Theodor 113, 124, 194
Lotman, Jurij M. 200-201
Lubbock, Percy 181-83, 185, 189
Madsen, Svend Åge 197
Maeda, Akira 48, 87-90, 119-20,
     126-27
Maeda, Ringai 30
Maeterlinck, Maurice 31, 59, 60, 64,
     71
Mann, Thomas 212
Man'yōshū 25
Masamune, Hakuchō 18, 34, 43, 47,
     70, 83, 86, 94, 99, 110-11, 122
Masuda, Shimoe 33, 42, 51, 137
Maupassant, Guy de 180
Milton, John 25
Mishima, Yukio 171
Mitani, Kuniaki 163
Miyagawa, Nobuteru 21-23
Miyake, Yūjirō 60

Miyoshi, Masao 15
Montaigne, Michel de 24
Mori, Ōgai 18, 219
Morita, Shiken 17
Morita, Sōhei 99, 100, 104
Mukarovský, J. 198
Mushanokōji, Saneatsu 101
Nagayo, Yoshio 104
Nakae, Chōmin 23, 60
Nakagawa, Kojūrō 36
Nakahara, Chūya 44
Nakamura, Seiko 48, 94-96, 112, 124-25
Nakatani, Tokutarō 117
Nakawa, Kamesuke 118
Nakazawa, Shizuo 46
Napoleon I 24, 67-68
Natsume, Sōseki 18, 71, 219
Nietzsche, Friedrich Wilhelm 62
Niijima, Jō 22-23
Nogami, Yae(ko) 122
Noguchi, Takehikō 14, 16, 218
Noguchi, Yonejiro 11, 48
Novák, Miroslav 12, 171
Ogata, Ryūsui 72
Oguri, Fūyō 35
Okamoto, Kanoko 48
Okazaki, Yoshie 12
Ōkubo, Tsuneo 14, 29, 48
Osanai, Kaoru 34
Oshikawa, Masayoshi 25
Ōshio, Chūsai 221
Ōsugi, Sakae 51
Ōtsuki, Takayori 46
Pinget, Robert 197
Plato 24, 187
Plutarch 45-46, 98
Poe, Edgar Allan 46
Pouillon, Jean 196
Proust, Marcel 210-11
Pushkin, Alexander 201
Robbe-Grillet, Alain 199, 200

Romberg, Bertil 191, 209
Rousseau, Jean-Jacques 23, 60
Ryan, Marleigh 78
Saijō, Yaso 48
Saionji, Kinmochi 44
Scholes, Robert 77, 192-94
Schopenhauer, Arthur 31, 62, 67, 69
Shakespeare, William 24-26, 110-11, 119
Shakyamuni 62
Shiga, Naoya 126, 172, 178
Shih-ching 25
Shimamura, Hōgetsu 71-73, 80-81
Shimazaki, Tōson 18, 26, 34, 53, 57, 70, 86, 91-94, 102, 111, 121, 177
Sibley, William F. 12
Sodō (pseudonym for Ogata Ryūsui) 72
Sōma, Gyofū 30-31, 83
Sōma, Tsuneo 57
Stanzel, Franz 195-96, 209
Stinchcum, Amanda Meyer 163
Strindberg, August 18, 69, 119, 220
Sugimoto, Kuniko 11
Suzuki, Kazuo 163
Suzuki, Tomi 16
Swedenborg, Emanuel 24, 31, 59, 61-62, 64
Symons, Arthur 44, 53, 57, 64
Takekoshi, Kō 27-28, 42, 44-45, 48, 98, 132, 138
Takizawa, Bakin 25
Tanabe, Renshū 26
Tanimoto, Tomi 68
Tanizaki, Jun'ichirō 121
Tanizawa, Eiichi 65
Tayama, Katai 18, 34-35, 57, 70,77, 79-82, 84, 86-87, 90, 92-95, 97, 102, 106, 109-12, 117-18, 129, 172, 177-78
Thibaudet, Albert 68
Todorov, Tzvetan 196-98, 201, 209

Togawa, Shūkotsu 26
Tokuda, Shūkō 91
Tokuda, Shūsei 18, 47, 92, 94, 99-100,
    114, 122
Tokutomi, Sohō 23
Tolstoy, Leo 71, 122, 180, 188, 193,
    195, 202
Toynbee, Philip 197
Toyoshima, Yoshio 48, 104
Toyotomi, Hideyoshi 51, 67-68
Tsuchida, Kyōson 128, 130
Turgenev, Ivan 122
Ueda, Bin 71
Ukita, Kazutami 45
Uspensky, Boris 17, 201-9
Verlaine, Paul 53, 64
Wada, Kingo 14-15, 124

Wang, Yang-ming 221
Warren, Robert Penn 208
Whitman, Walt 79
Wilde, Oscar 46, 71
Wilson, Colin 74, 171, 179
Woolf, Virginia 76, 188-89
Yamamoto, Roteki 46
Yanagita, Kunio 34
Yano, Ryūkei 25
Yoda, Gakkai 17
Yosano, Akiko 30
Yosano, Hiroshi 30
Yoshida, Kenkō 200
Yoshida, Seiichi 16, 168
Yoshie, Kogan 83
Yoshino, Gajō 25
Zola, Émile 82